1,000,000 Books

are available to read at

www.ForgottenBooks.com

Read online
Download PDF
Purchase in print

ISBN 978-1-331-24730-2
PIBN 10163939

1 MONTH OF
FREE
READING

at
www.ForgottenBooks.com

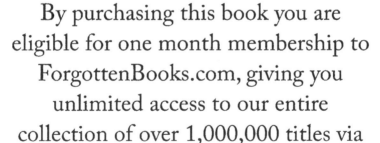

By purchasing this book you are eligible for one month membership to ForgottenBooks.com, giving you unlimited access to our entire collection of over 1,000,000 titles via our web site and mobile apps.

To claim your free month visit:
www.forgottenbooks.com/free163939

English
Français
Deutsche
Italiano
Español
Português

www.forgottenbooks.com

Mythology Photography **Fiction**
Fishing Christianity **Art** Cooking
Essays Buddhism Freemasonry
Medicine **Biology** Music **Ancient
Egypt** Evolution Carpentry Physics
Dance Geology **Mathematics** Fitness
Shakespeare **Folklore** Yoga Marketing
Confidence Immortality Biographies
Poetry **Psychology** Witchcraft
Electronics Chemistry History **Law**
Accounting **Philosophy** Anthropology
Alchemy Drama Quantum Mechanics
Atheism Sexual Health **Ancient History**
Entrepreneurship Languages Sport
Paleontology Needlework Islam
Metaphysics Investment Archaeology
Parenting Statistics Criminology
Motivational

REMAINS

HISTORICAL & LITERARY

CONNECTED WITH THE PALATINE COUNTIES OF

ANCASTER AND CHESTER

PUBLISHED BY

(THE) CHETHAM SOCIETY.

VOL. I.

1843/44

PRINTED FOR THE CHETHAM SOCIETY.

M.DCCC.XLIV.

DA
670
L19C5
V.1

Richards, Printer,
100, St Martin's Lane.

Council.

TRAVELS

IN

HOLLAND THE UNITED PROVINCES

ENGLAND SCOTLAND

AND IRELAND

M.DC.XXXIV.—M.DC.XXXV.

BY

SIR WILLIAM BRERETON, BART.

EDITED BY

EDWARD HAWKINS, ESQ.

F.R.S. F.S.A. F.L.S.

PRINTED FOR THE CHETHAM SOCIETY.

M.DCCC.XLIV.

INTRODUCTION.

THE travels here presented to the reader are contained in a thin folio volume, which consists of sixty rather closely written leaves, bound together in a parchment cover. Its history cannot be traced higher than the time of Percy, Bishop of Dromore, in whose possession it once was, and who inserted the following note on the inside of the cover: " The writer of these travels seems to have been a gentleman of the Egerton family in Cheshire. He lived at Handford, which I conceive to be in that county." By Bishop Percy the volume was presented to Mr. Joseph Cooper Walker, a gentleman of some literary eminence, and Secretary to the Royal Irish Academy, who died about the year 1813. After his death, it passed into the hands of his sister, who for some years entrusted it to the care of Sir William Betham, Ulster King-at-Arms. While in this gentleman's possession, it was seen by Mr. Monck Mason, who, in his " History of St. Patrick's Cathedral, Dublin," p. 7, makes mention of it as " The Travels of a Person of the Egerton family, who dwelt at Handford in Cheshire, and visited Ireland in 1635," deriving his opinion evidently from the autograph note of Bishop Percy.

From Miss Walker it was afterwards purchased by Mr. Christopher Bentham, a member of the Society of Friends, and at that time a printer in Liverpool, but who has now retired to a residence at Birkenhead in Cheshire. During a temporary sojourn in Ireland, he shewed it to several gentlemen with whom he had the pleasure of being acquainted, and amongst others to the Rev. Sir Francis Lynch Blosse, who published, in the " Church of Ireland Magazine" for the year 1826, copious extracts of those parts which referred to Ireland; but, unfortunately, without adding any illustrative notes which, from local knowledge, might have much enhanced the interest of the work.

It was afterwards " placed in the hands of Sir Walter Scott, who was much interested with it, and strongly urged its publication, tendering his own services as editor, and offering to supply all the necessary explanatory notes." The reader cannot lament more than the editor, that, from some disinclination towards Sir Walter Scott's publisher, this most valuable offer should have been declined. Had the editor been aware of this fact at an earlier period, it is probable that he would have shrunk from an undertaking, in which, at every page, will be forced upon the reader the deteriorating comparison between what is, and what might have been.

It is a somewhat singular illustration of the different estimate which may be formed by different people of the same performance, that this work, which so much interested Sir Walter Scott, should have been rejected by the Camden Society as unworthy to take a place amongst their more interesting publications. By Mr. Bentham it was afterwards presented to Sir Philip de Malpas Grey Egerton, Bart. of Oulton Park, Cheshire, who has kindly granted the use of it to the Chetham Society, that it may be printed for the gratification of its members.

This volume contains the journal of two excursions made by the writer: one in the year 1634 through the United Provinces ; the other in 1635 through parts of England, Scotland, and Ireland.   There cannot be any doubt that the traveller, though connected with the Egertons by intermarriages, was not himself of that family, as supposed by Bishop Percy, but Sir William Brereton of Handford in the county of Chester, the great Parliamentary general, whose exploits in that distracted period are inseparably interwoven with the history of his native county.   He was born in 1604, created a baronet in 1627, and died in 1661.

In the course of the work, he mentions several persons as relatives, and some with the indefinite title of cousin, the exact connexion with whom we have been unable to trace; but enough of evidence remains to identify the writer with the Parliamentary General ; his frequent reference to Handford as his home would be sufficient, without the mention of " my Brother Booth," that is, the brother of his wife, Susan, who was daughter of Sir Geo. Booth, of Dunham; or of " my sister Egerton, at Allerstone in the county of York," who was his only sister, Margaret, married to Richard Egerton of Ridley, by whom the Ridley estate was sold and the property squandered, and whose brother, Thomas Egerton, was of Allerstone, Co. York, and ultimately inherited the unsold estates of his father.   " My brother Urian at Westminster" was his youngest brother ; and this Christian name occurs frequently in the pedigree of his family.

He may be also identified by the character of his handwriting, comparing it with what appears in three volumes of MSS. in the Brit. Mus. (Additional MSS. 11331, 2, 3) which consist of transcripts of letters to and from Sir William Brereton, about the year 1645, and some few in 1642. Some of the notes are signed by himself, " W. B." and there are some drafts and observations in his own handwriting, which corresponds exactly with that of these travels.

This volume, it may be safely concluded, was not the companion of his travels, neither was this journal exactly what he wrote down from day to day. It was, however, probably made up, and in a great degree transcribed, from notes actually made at the time; for there are abrupt changes of construction which give the appearance to a passage of having been put together from two separate memoranda; there are in the same sentence repetitions of the same fact or the same observation, which may be attributed to the same cause. There are also references to another book, which may have been the original journal, or possibly a different work altogether; and there are also allusions to circumstances which had not occurred at the time when he was actually on his travels. But although not written at the time, it is chiefly transcribed from what was so written, and it has consequently all the freshness of originality.

It is a plain, unimpassioned statement of what he saw and observed. The beauties of nature never warm him into admiration; nor do the feelings, habits, or phenomena of the people, or the countries which he visited, seduce him into any philosophical investigation. Perhaps the most remarkable circumstance in these journals is the almost entire absence of any remarks upon the political

and religious subjects of excitement which at the time
agitated these kingdoms, in which he was himself, within a
very short period, so deeply involved, and in the settlement
of which he acted so prominent a part. It seems probable,
indeed, that these distractions of his country had not at
this time excited his feelings, or much engaged his attention. The principal subject of his observation in Holland
was the management of their decoys, of which he seems
to have had one at Handford, and in which he took great
interest; while in Ireland, the following year, his remarks upon the value, product, and cultivation of land,
as well as his mention of some ineffectual negociations,
shew that he was engaged in looking out for some profit-
able investment of money in that country, with which he
appears to have already had some tie of the kind, as he
mentions Ralph Brian as his tenant at Dublin.* He seems
to have been deeply impressed with religious feelings, but,
though a professed member of the Church of England,
he seems not to have understood her nature or her privileges, and his attachment to her could not have been great,
nor exclusive, for we find him as ready to attend the
ministry and listen to the discourses of a Brownist, or an
Anabaptist, as to any the most eminent of the priests of
his own invaluable Church.

The editor has attempted little more than by a few notes
to explain some of the provincial or obsolete words, and
to identify the persons and places mentioned in the text.
He laments that his endeavours at illustration have not
been more successful; and that he has found it necessary

* See Summary of his Journey, p. 190.

to leave not a few points to the more successful researches of the reader. In Scotland, and more particularly in Ireland, the orthography is so unsettled, names of places have been so changed, and all works of reference treating upon those countries are so imperfect, especially in an almost systematic omission of an index, that places which furnish long articles in the topographical dictionaries cannot be discovered in any map; and again, names conspicuous in the maps have no place in the dictionaries.

In a work written at so late a period as 1635, it has not been deemed adviseable to retain the peculiar orthography of the writer, except in the proper names of persons and places. In such cases, as an invariable mode of spelling is even at this time scarcely attained, and as that adopted by the author appears to have been acquired by the ear, it is here preserved; the rather, as it not unfrequently affords an interesting indication of the pronunciation then in common use.

EDWARD HAWKINS.

MY TRAVELS

HOLLAND AND THE SEVENTEEN PROVINCES,

1634.

May 17, 1634.—WE departed from LONDON by water; we came to GRAVESEND about eight of the clock in the evening; we came in a light-horseman;[1] took water about three clock in afternoon. A dainty cherry orchard of Captain Lord's, planted three years ago, near unto Thames, not forty roods distant. The stocks one yard and a half high; prosper well; but I conceive the top will in a short time be disproportionable to the stock. Very many of the trees bear. It is three acres of ground; planted four hundred and forty-odd trees. An old cherry orchard near adjoining nothing well set: this year the cherries sold for £20: it is but an acre of ground: the grass reserved and excepted. A proper ship came from Middleborough on Saturday at noon, 17 May. Stiff N.W. wind all Sunday; turned E. on 19 Monday morn. Passed by Gravesend on Monday about four. Captain Boare went from Gravesend on 15 May; went to Rotterdam; returned thither 20. Another ship came in twenty-four hours from Brill to Gravesend.

A delicate kiln to burn chalk lime; it is the Duke of Lenox,

---

[1] Light-horseman, a small boat, term now obsolete. "In this storm, one night, haling up our boats to free the water out of them, one of our younkers, that went into them for that purpose, had not that regard (which reason required) unto our light-horseman; for with haling her up, to step into her, out of the boat, he split her asunder, and so we were forced to cut her off."—*Observations of Sir R. Hawkins, &c.* 1622, p. 100.

B

near Gravesend,[1] upon the river side; it is made of brick, narrow at bottom, round, and wider at top; it is emptied always at the bottom; they hook out so much as is cold, until they pull out fire, and then cease. It is supplied with fire and chalk at top; one basket of sea-coals proportioned to eight of chalk; the fire extinguisheth not from one end of the year to the other. When it is kindled, fire is put to the bottom: it is sold for a groat, one hoop burnt. The pit is in the side of an hill, which is thirty yards high; one of the workmen fell (with whom I conferred) from top to bottom, not slain, but bruised and still sore. An horse stuck by the fore-legs, and held and cried out like a child, and stuck until he was helped up by men.

Thursday, 22 *May.*—About 7 clock we went aboard Mr. John Tompson's Pink (Mr. Jacob, his mate), which is about fifty ton burthen; all under decks full of merchants' goods as can be thrust. Passengers 67, two women, four children. We came to Leigh about 10 of clock; it is on Essex shore, twelve miles from Gravesend. We were some six hours becalmed; we came between the Noore[2] and Nests,[3] where on both sides appeared bones of ships, which had been swallowed in those devouring sands. We were constrained upon the turning of tide to return back, by the shore to QUINDBORROW,[4] where we lodged all night; it is but a village, and yet a mayor-town, seated in the isle of Sheppey. A fine little uniform castle, round built, outside walls and windows in good repair: isle seven miles long. No corn gotten by the inhabitants of this town, nor no barn; live by the sea. Here was a most ingenious copperas work erected. A square plot of ground, about an acre, the earth hath been taken all away, and a kind of stone brought from Essex shore,[5] which, falling into the sea, is

[1] At Northfleet.   [2] Nore.   [3] Sheerness.
[4] "Queenborough Castle. Once a noble pile, till it was pulled down, soon after the year 1650. It was built by Edward III, about the year 1361, under the direction of the famous William of Wykeham."—*Pennant, Journey to Isle of Wight*, p. 64.
[5] The stone brought from the Essex shore was iron pyrites, which abounds there, as it does also at Sheppey. "All the water of the island is so impregnated with the taste of the pyrites, or copperas stone, with which it abounds, that it is scarcely drinkable." —*Pennant*, p. 65.

tempered by salt water; which stone, by rain and sun, is beaten and reduced to soil; this ground is clayed in the bottom, and is made a fair bottom. Betwixt every bed is a trough made with three deane[1] boards, bored full of holes; this is digged over every summer, the bottom laid highest and the top lowest. This trough receives and conveys away all the liquor and moisture which doth flow from that soil in rainy and moist weather; old barrels, into which these troughs lead, are prepared and placed in the earth, in clay, which receive the moisture, out of which the liquor is conveyed into divers great cisterns of boards, two bayes of buildings, all which are laid and set in clay; out of which it runs into a great tub, placed in another spacious house, and near unto a mighty cistern of lead, wherein this liquor is boiled. Under this cistern are fire furnaces, a partition 'twixt them; these furnaces spend half a chaldron of coals a day, and this leaden cistern will last four years. There is half a barrel of old iron boiled in this liquor, which is consumed to dirt. When it is sufficiently boiled, it runs through a leaden pipe into cisterns of lead, six of them at least, and it cools in those cisterns; the copperas matter thickens and adheres to birch twigs, or bushes, which they hang upon overcross poles, into the cisterns. It is worth £5 a ton; one boiling will yield three or four ton. When this earth is cast with bottom upward, a fleece of this stone is laid upon it, which resolves to earth; the thicker the richer. We lodged at Ship,[2] in Quindburrow, and were well uséd; six lobsters bought for one shilling; one quick; a convenient place in the remotest part of the marsh for a coy.[3]

Upon *Friday the* 23, in the evening, after supper, we were all shipped, and hoisted up sail next morning, at spring of day. The Unicorn, the king's ship, newly built, was hauling by ropes, drawn by boats, towards Chatham. We vailed our topsail, and demanding whence we came, and whither we were bound, it being

---

[1] Deal.

[2] This house still remains, and, in external appearance at least, little changed.

[3] A decoy for taking wild fowl.

answered that we were of London and bound for Rotterdam, we
were dismissed; and having a fair, pleasant gale of wind, went
away amain; and because we endeavoured to strike over at next,
and to go as near the shore as possible, we fathomed the depth of
the water, and once found it so shallow as we were constrained to
turn the ship round upon a sudden.   The wind continuing fair
and fresh, we came in good time to pass the Flats, about eleven of
clock, where buoys are placed, 'twixt which all ships are to sail;
and we saw divers which went to the northward, down the King's
channel, which framed their course to pass through and betwixt
the said buoys, whereof we observed four.   These are placed over
against the Isle of Tennett,[1] against which we sailed two hours;
and about twelve of clock we came over against Margrett,[2] and to
the Land's End.[3]   It was then a great calm, about an hour, and
afterwards the wind wakened, and as the master of the ship conceived we ran seven leagues in a watch, in four hours; and about
such time as we lost sight of land, we first discovered three gallant
stout ships, at a great distance, which (by a perspective glass)
seemed to be the States men of war; another ship was discerned afar
off to the southward, which lay at anchor, and hoisted up sail, and
seemed a good while to follow us, but with disadvantage, seeing the
longer he pursued us the more he was cast behind.   But there was
another, which seemed towards evening to cross us, and which the
master feared had been a Dunkirker[4] (who had taken a ship lately,
wherein Mr. Thatcher, a merchant, a passenger, had some goods), but
he passed by, and made no attempt at all.   The next morning early,
being Whit Sunday, was discovered land; one of the islands belonging to the States.   We passed by Flushing and Middleburgh, and left
them at a great distance southward.   We passed by, and discerned
nearer unto us, a church, and Gaurie[5] Land, and so came to the
Brill, where the tide being something spent, we had a hazardous

---

[1] Thanet.   [2] Margate.   [3] Foreness.
[4] The inhabitants of Dunkirk subsist almost entirely by privateers, and, being not
very scrupulous as to the nation whose vessels they attacked, the place was little better
than a nest of pirates.   [5] Goree.

passage ; and fathoming the depth of the water over against Brill, we found it there where the buoys are placed to warn all seamen of the danger of that passage, that we had not above two feet more water than the ship drew, which was heavy laden with merchants' goods, and more overpressed with passengers. Mr. Thatcher, a merchant of London, who had goods therein, was so apprehensive of the danger, that he changed colours, and said he was undone, " Oh Lord !" and such like passionate expressions, which increased our fears, and the rather because the master himself was doubtful, though his mate was confident, of our safe passage : over against us also remained the bones and masts of a ship not long since swallowed by those devouring sands ; and that which most increased our danger, was the violence of the wind and the rough seas, which, had the ship struck never so little, would have rent her, and broken her in pieces. But here, as it pleased God to order, our fears were greater than our dangers ; and then passing by the Brill, and through their ships (gallant ships), we turned into the river of Maze,[1] leaving Gravesend[2] on the one side, and Blackwall,[3] and so come to SCHEDAM,[4] which stands upon the Maze. I went this 26 of May to see this town on foot ; it stands about four miles English from Rotterdam, a dainty, sweet, pleasant town, larger than Namptwitch ; a delicate, spacious market-place ; a fine church ; a great channel, walled on both sides with freestone, runs along the middle of the street, whereunto their ships come : this street, paved most evenly with brick, easy to go upon, and dry, be the weather never so moist. Hence we hired a waggon to carry us to Rotterdam for three Dutch shillings.

After we passed Scedam, we came to DELPHESHAVEN[5] (which I also saw this 26 *of May*.) It might well be accounted a fine town subsisting of itself, seeing it is so curiously built, and so dainty a harbour for shipping even in the streets : but this depends upon

---

[1] The Maas, or Meuse.   [2] Gravescende, on the S.E. corner of Delftland.
[3] Blackwall is Swarte Wael, on the opposite side of the Channel, in Voornland.
[4] Schiedam.   [5] Delfthaven.

and belongs unto Delph,[1] being only intended, as it is called,
Delphs-haven. No town in England worth such a haven.

We came then about one clock in afternoon on Whitsunday
into the stately city of ROTTERDAM; it being about twenty-five
hours since we came from England's Land's End, until with safety
we all arrived at Rotterdam. We went in the afternoon to the
English church, and heard Mr. Peters,[2] a right zealous and worthy
man. This was formerly intended for a playhouse, but now converted to a better use to a church; Mr. Peters being there entertained, who is allowed by the States one hundred pounds per
annum,—five thousand gilders. Here is little respect had to sanc-
tify the sabbath: the young children girls walked all the Sabbath
in the afternoon with cups or tuns in their hands; they were about
five or six years of age; others elder, about ten, and thirteen, and
fourteen years of age, guided these little ones, and sung, screaming,
and squeaking, and straining their voices. Such as they met gave
them money, which they put into the cups, which was intended to
buy a wassail-cup, a carouse: this they continued all Monday.
This city (which seems to be as large in circumference as any in
England, save London) is seated upon the river of Maze, a fair
navigable river, which will carry as great a ship as can sail. An
infinite number of tall and gallant ships belong unto this city; they
say there belongs to the Maze about thirty of the States men of
war; and other stout ships not to be numbered, which are disposed
of into every street (into a channel there deep and walled on both
sides with free-stone), save one or two. The channels or docks
seem to be about fifty or sixty yards broad; drawbridges in every
river pulled up by huge iron chains, and the masts thereby have
passage. Here is a spacious dock for herring-busses; all of them
now gone out to sea save one. Near unto that dock the Prince of
Orange[3] his ships lyeth, for which is prepared a dainty spacious
house to receive and cover the same. His own ship, wherein himself is disposed, is a rich curious vessel, both within and without;

---

[1] Delft.   [2] The celebrated Hugh Peters.
[3] Frederic Henry, grandfather of King William III.

a fair gilt lanthorn and curious gilded cabin on top and sides, and the middle story all chambers and rooms of state; all the walls most richly gilded, both on the sides and top; curious chimney, rich marble mantle-tree, the bottom paved with such black and white square stones of marble or touch[1] as are any in York House. In this vessel, no houses of office; all the rooms are for state. Another rich and less vessel lyeth near unto it, gilded and adorned as the former, which is to wait upon the Prince's vessel, and wherein is his kitchen and his victuals prepared. A third, a Dutch huy, is to wait upon these, and to carry their goods, luggage, &c. These never go to sea, but are for their rivers, and to carry the Prince when he goes to leaguer.[2] Another brave vessel of Count Solmes[3] lyeth in this dock, which we boarded also, more spacious than either of the other, so as when you are under hatches in any of them, it may seem unto you that you are rather in a house than a ship. This of Count Solmes hath lyen in the dock three years, and some say it cannot be brought up the rivers, but it is in danger to be seized by the enemy. Among the fair bridges which are in this town is one most observable, on the side whereof is placed the portraiture of Erasmus, of very large stature, with a book in his hand. The river over which this bridge leadeth, is not above twenty yards broad, and yet the bridge is seventy or eighty yards broad, and a fair market-place upon it. Near hereunto is the fairest church in the city, the Dutch church, a dainty, curious, and spacious thing. The French church is the second fair church. The Arminians multiply here, and greatest resort to their church, a fine neat thing; two lofts very spacious in it. The English church was a play-house. The Anabaptists and Brownists have their houses of meeting and places of assembling, but not so public,

[1] Properly, hard black smooth granite, used as a test for gold; but the term is often applied to fine black marble.

[2] Leaguer seems to be here used for the assembly of leiges, from the various states and cities of the United Provinces. Leiger, ambassador, or resident minister. "A special man of that hasty king, who was his leiger, or agent, in London."—*Leicester's Commonwealth*. See page 15.

[3] Brother-in-law to Prince Frederic Henry. See p. 6.

nor so much allowed as the other; but the Anabaptists have a dainty fine church.

As touching the government of this town.

Three Burgomaisters, which hold their places, some one, some two, some three years, they are equivalent to our bailiffs of cities or towns corporate. No charge in housekeeping extraordinary, nor no entertainment extraordinary, no more attendance nor state assumed than at any other times, only in the State-house, insomuch as not a man waits on them in the streets; sometimes you may see a woman, a maid, following them. They have an allowance from the city for the loss of their time from trading. Eight schepens, which are men most of them well versed in the laws, these joined in commission with the burgomaisters to consult and conclude all business for the town. Five of these in place, together with two burgomaisters, determine all differences, and sentence all malefactors. If any dislike the judgment of these seven judges, viz. two burgomaisters and five scepens, he may appeal to the High Court at Hage, and there bring it about before the Council of the States-General there resident. These officers only, called the States of the city. My host of St. John the Baptist's Head in a Platter, being here an English harbour, Mr. Henry Custis appealed to the Court at Hage, and prevailed. But all the officers of the city combine and join together against him that so appeals.

Twenty-four Vornscapp, or aldermen, who have been or are in commission to be burgomaisters; out of these the burgomaister is chosen by these twenty-four, and the sckepons, who sometimes continue judges, two, or three, or four years, and afterwards are in election to be burgomaisters. But no constant, certain number of these vornscapps.

Three Friend-makers, which have authority to call any man before them that hath any suit or controversy, and are chosen by the burgomaisters and sckepens, who are thought to be men of the best understanding and integrity; these are to mediate in a friendly manner, in a way of arbitration, and are to compose and conclude differences. These have no fee nor allowance, and are made choice of to ease the burgomaisters and sckepens. If any dislike their orders he may appeal to burgomaisters and schepens. If it be any matter of misdemeanour or quarrelling, they have power to punish by imprisonment or otherwise. No charge save two stivers for summons to any of those that are summoned before the friend-makers.

One baylie or scout (*id est*, high-sheriff), and his under-baylie or under-scout, his under-sheriff, which are chosen by States-General, and hold these places *durante vita :* the scout, the chief man above the burgomaister; and they are attended by officers, thief-leaders (under-bailiffs), armed to apprehend all offenders. This is equivalent to our high-sheriff in England, and hath such a like office ; the under-scout as under-sheriff.

Six weys-maisters,[1] or officers of the hospitals, who take care of and seize upon orphans' goods, and see it equally divided amongst them all, youngest as much as eldest ; and if any man die childless, they dispose it under his next of kindred ; if no kindred, to the poor. These men are to seize all men's goods that decease, and they divide the goods equally, the one half to the wife, the other to the children ; and if he have no children, the other half to his next of kindred ; except the wife and husband condition and conclude formally in writing drawn by counsel in perfect health, that the longest liver take all, and this deed to be recorded in the State-house, after it is penned by the notarius publicus, and then it is not to be revoked.

Officers of church ; elders and deacons. These govern church affairs, and provide sufficiently for all the poor of the town ; so as none of them have cause to complain, nor need not to go abroad to beg : only Lazaruses, whereof are some twenty, which are permitted to beg their victuals ; and if they eat[2] any meat not begged by themselves or by others in their name, their disease, a leprosy, encreaseth upon them, and they are much more distempered: they are clothed and lodged in the alms-houses, only suffered to beg

[1] Wees, an orphan.

[2] This I dare not confidently report, because I did not receive any confirmation of it.—*Note by author.*

victuals:[1] most of them are boys, never live to be in years; and
so soon as they have this disease, they are brought to the Lazarus
house; it is incurable. And about half a mile from this town is
this alms-house, this Lazarus house, a dainty fine house, well
accommodated with fine gardens and orchards, like a gentleman's
house; women to attend them, chamber-pots, and all other necessaries. They hold, except their victuals be begged, or money
begged to buy victuals, their disease prevails against them, and
rages exceedingly; and therefore many rich men's sons are sent
to this Lazarus house, whose friends are able to maintain and
keep them; but if they be removed out of this house, and eat not
begged victuals, their leprosy, which is only upon their heads, will
extend itself over their whole bodies.

· Six companies of burghers, which are trained soldiers, and are
about twelve hundred martial men, which are to be at command of
the States, to be disposed of for the defence of any other town,
any neighbour-town, and to strengthen the garrison.

One hundred householders to watch every night, fifty at the
State-house, and fifty at the Ports. Mr. Peters, the minister of the
English here, informed [me], a religious burgomaister, two years ago,
endeavoured to reform the profanation of the Sabbath, and imposed
and collected, by distress or otherwise, one guilder from every man
trading or working on this day: at length the brewers (whereof
are abundance in this town) made a head, came into the State-
house, and in a mutinous manner told the burgomaister that they
would not be subject unto his new laws; and hereby all quashed
formerly effected, and the hoped for reformation came to nothing.
This honest burgomaister would not admit players that came to
this city to act; but being pressed by some of the town to give

---

[1] They were not allowed to accost any one, but attracted attention by making a
noise with two pieces of wood, called Lazarus klap. In Glasgow, lepers, by an order of
the Town Council in 1610, were allowed to pass only by the side of the causeway, were
ordered to have clappers in their hands to apprise people of their approach, to keep
their mouths well muffled, and to keep as far off as possible from those who gave
them alms.

way, and alleged it would be an advantage to the poor; every third penny would derive unto the poor, and so it would be worth £50 to the poor; he went up and fetched £50, and said he would supply that loss, and dismissed the players, and gave this £50 to the poor. Mr. Forbes told Mr. Peters, travelling with him through High Germany to see the king of Sweden, that being at Basill,[1] which stands towards the head of the Rhine, there died one of the Jews' most learned rabbins, and desired upon his death-bed that his will and testament might be published and proclaimed to all the Jews his brethren in all parts, which was done accordingly, the substance whereof was this: that they long had expected a Messiah and Saviour, and if he came not within thirty-four years or thereabouts, fourteen or sixteen of which years remained only at that time to be fulfilled, that then they should not expect any longer, but rather embrace the Saviour of the Christians.

I was in the scout's house here, the chief man. He is a very gentle, courteous man; his hall adorned over mantle-tree with birds cased, seven or eight several sorts.

In copper pans they season their nets for herring fishing, and all other nets; they are there boiled with a kind of bark until the water look yellow and brown.

Windmills here in the top of houses. I went to the top of a very high house to see a windmill, which grinds malt; it is a pretty nimble stone. A poor Exchange, not worth three-pence; nothing therein to be sold but ballads and knives; it is much neglected, and goeth to decay. The town watered about the walls, and fair ditches in all their back sides. A dainty quay here is, and many yarne-crofts[2] here about, such like as are about Dort, whereof at large in the following discourse of Dort. Here is a dainty Doole-house, where the great officers meet and feast, as also consult; here are the burgo-masters' and chief officers' pictures placed in both ends, and the Roman emperors on both sides of the room. Here were two companies feasting (their flags hung out into the street); I do

---

[1] Basle. [2] Rope yards.

believe scarce one sober man to be found amongst them, nor was it safe for a sober man to trust himself amongst them; they did shout, sing, roar, skip, leap, &c. Abundance of busses not to be numbered sent out to fish for herrings; sometimes they cast out nets almost an English mile long out of one buss; in stormy weather they take down all their masts, and fish, the vessel lying at hull.

Upon Whitsun Tuesday, about eleven of clock, we took waggon for Dort, and came thither about three clock in afternoon. We paid for our waggon two gilders and a Dutch shilling, for passage over two ferries eighteen stivers; twixt Rotterdam and Dort, a stone wall, along the Wall[1] above a mile, and how far further *non constat*. We passed a great ferry over the Maze at Isermaunton, one Dutch mile from Rotterdam, and two Dutch miles from Dort; the boat is a long narrow boat which carries horses and waggons, and is sixty or seventy foot long. We observed sowed by the way good wheat, oats, much flax, some hemp and rape; a stork's nest on the top of a chimney of a low boor's house.

DORT is compassed almost round with the Maze on the north and west, and the Wall on the east. It is placed in an island about four or five English miles round, and it is in Holland. It is called the Maiden town, because never taken by the enemy. A city more populous than Rotterdam; eleven companies of burgers harged with arms, two hundred in a company, one hundred whereof watch every night. Two colonel's companies in garrison here: Count Maurice his Dutch company, consisting of two hundred Walloons; Colonel Goreing's company, consisting of two hundred English: captains of these companies, Captain Valiers of the Dutch; Captain Gerard of the English: captains pay twenty gilders a-week, gentlemen bearing arms two gilders a-week, eight days reckoned to the week, and their lodging free; ordinary soldiers three English shillings for eight days, their lodging free.

This town governed by a scout, one burgo-master, and sckepens. This scout and burgo-master attended always by their halberds

---

[1] River Waal.

and thief-leaders. This scout is equivalent to the high-sheriff, and precedes the burgo-master, because he represents the prince his person. Two very fair streets leading from the north to the west, more uniform and complete building than I saw any in Rotterdam, both of them an English mile in length, and betwixt them a. very fair spacious haven at least one hundred broad and of the same length, and full thronged with ships. Other two fair spacious havens, about half an English mile long, and about eighty yards broad. Five or six greater ports leading into this city, and some three or four less ports, four of them very fair and curious gates. The great church is more neat and curious than that of Rotterdam, not so large, but the top, sides, pillars, and all most daintily and curiously white-limed, and so very lightsome. The chancel like ours, but never used but to receive the sacrament, which is administered four times a-year. Another less church, reported unto us to be a most neat, complete thing. The burgo-maister's house, a fair and high-built house, six stories high. Here is an English church, Mr. Vincent, Predicant, a man of mean parts. The States allow him 600 gilders per annum, and 300 gilders out of the Latin school, whereof he is usher, and 100 gilders more gratuities, so as his place is thought worth unto him £100 per annum. Here is also a French church; Arminians, Brownists, and Anabaptists, and Manists,[1] do lurk here and also swarm, but not so much tolerated as at Rotterdam. Four Dutch churches in this city. Here is the Doole,[2] a spacious place for the assembling of the states of the town, wherein the synod, the famous and orthodox synod of Dort, was held about twenty years ago; over which room is a high and commanding turret, wherein we drank two cans of wine, which gives you a full view of the whole town, both the rivers and the country, which is a flat and level, and lieth lower than the water, and would doubtless be drowned, were it not preserved by high banks twenty yards high, and so thick and broad as two waggons

[1] Mennonites, Menonistes, or Mennistes, a sect prevalent in the United Provinces, and frequently considered a sect of the Anabaptists.
[2] The Doole, or Klovenier Doelen, now a public-house, of poor repute.

may conveniently meet upon the top; these banks made and maintained all along every river-side. You may hence discern Git-
ternberg,[1] Breda, Rotterdam, Delph, Girkham,[2] Willamstat,
Clenniard,[3] Sevenbergen, the four last and first garrison towns.
One almshouse for old men, two for old women, and one for
maimed soldiers, almshouses called Ghuesthouses, three for fatherless and motherless children,—all these seven maintained by the
town. All the poor provided for sufficiently by the officers of the
church, so as none wander abroad and beg; unto some of them
allowed four, unto others five, unto others six, Dutch shillings
a week. And all the poor are disposed of into the almshouses,
and maintained by voluntary contributions, and without any taxation. Near unto the Doole build herons,[4] which breed in the
middle of the city, which by proclamation are not to be molested
or destroyed. The scoute here represents the person of our high-
sheriff, and the burgo-maister of the mayor.

A coy-duck at supper at Dort, and another at dinner.

The fatherless children are maintained with meat, drink, and
apparel; are put to such trades as they are most fit and capable of;
trained up to read, and thence dismissed when able to maintain themselves. If any soldier, marine, or tradesman die, his children disposed
of into these ghuest-houses. Abundance of yarne-crofts about this
town; some containing an English acre, worth per annum £100;
others two acres, worth £200 per ann. Betwixt every twelve yards,
a narrow ditch about one yard broad, out of which water is cast upon
the yarn. The burgers have dainty garden, orchards, and summer
houses, near unto the town. A terrible flood last winter, which
put this town and all the inhabitants of the country in great fear.
It overflowed their banks, which are twelve yards high, which were
showed us this day by the waggon man in our return. It drowned
abundance of cattle in the country; it came into the streets of
Dort so deep as that boats might pass therein; it came also into

---

[1] Gertruydenberg.   [2] Gorcum.   [3] Klundert.
[4] He probably means storks, not *ardea cinerea*.

the streets of Rotterdam, and into the houses a yard deep. You might pass in boats over all that part of the country. About half a Dutch mile from this city is brick made. The clay brought by water, and there tempered and moulded, and burnt in standing kilns of brick; *id est,* brick walls on four sides; in the middle a square vacant place, wherein the moulded brick is disposed and placed and burnt. Here is in this town a mint, it being one of the principal and most ancient towns in Holland, and which sends a committee to be leiger[1] at the Hage, out of which committees the States-General are chosen, and all ambassadors sent to foreign princes. Here is copper ore smelted in a little earthen pot, and made into bars; it runs into bars about a yard and an half long, and afterward in the copper mills is beaten into thin bars four yards long. There are three of these copper mills, one water mill, whose wheel gives motion unto some six iron hammers which strike very strongly and nimbly; there are other two copper mills, horse mills, drawn by two strong horses, which stand upon a wheel which is sufficiently broad to contain two horses together. This wheel stands much aslope, on the middle whereof, I mean neither the highest part nor the lowest, these horses are placed and fastened by the neck by iron chains; their removing their feet and the weight of their bodies gives motion unto this wheel without any great strain or coaction, being placed aslope, and as it should seem upon a slender turn, no thicker than your arm. These employ six iron-hammers as nimbly and strongly as the water-mill, and I conceive that a mill framed in this manner would have served for a rape-mill, a mill half so great. Here is a fine glass-work near unto the Blue Port; and about forty roods from the town a mighty long salt house, wherein they make bay-salt. The brine is part fetched out of the sea, about Brill, and part out of Spain. I was in one of their houses wherein they work, which little less than sixty yards long; in the middle placed two mighty spacious iron pans, some six yards asunder, which are about six-

---

[1] See page 7.

teen yards square; in the one they boil the Brill brine, in the other the Spanish. The Spanish is much the stronger, and makes a whiter salt and hard, but it is a mighty great grained salt, as big and some larger than a peppercorn. The salt made is not disposed into sacks, walms,[1] or any other measures, but lieth in huge great heaps, as corn in partitions in granaries; some salt very brown and coarse. I could not well understand them, nor they my language, and therefore I could not inform myself further therein. But when I said the Spanish salt was very brave, they were so well pleased, and seemed to rejoice thereat, and a woman took an handful of salt, and threw part of it upon my foot, part in my hand, and part on my hat.

A ship, this Wednesday, May 28, coming into and within six roods of the quay, was split by another vessel going out, which had the advantage of the wind, which falling foul upon her, in all our sights, being in the parlour wherein we dined, we did sensibly perceive and discern her sinking, and in a very short time quite sunk; not many men in her, but all saved; for boats and barques, discerning them to be in distress, made out with all speed to relieve them; and as the keel was sunk under water, and the men in middle in the water ready to perish, they came in, and reaching ropes, staves, and oars unto them, they were thereby all preserved; this sunk ship speedily weighed up and drawn to the quay. They say the man that split this ship is to sustain and make good unto the owners the half of the loss.

The island wherein this fair maiden city stands, is encompassed

---

[1] *To wall* is to boil, and the word was not long ago, and perhaps may be still, in use in the Cheshire salt works. A lead-walling is the brine of twenty-four hours boiling for one house.—*Ray's Proverbs*, ed. 1742, p. 146.

For the proper regulation of the brine pits, at Nantwich, and for establishing the true price, and the time of making salt, several persons were in former times chosen from among the most wealthy of the proprietors, who were styled rulers of walling, and who were sworn to uphold the ancient customs. Their office extended to the adjusting the proportion of brine, for each wichhouse, and to inspect the pits, to see that the brine was not weakened by improper means, or received a taint from any nuisance.—*Platt's Hist. of Nantwich*, p. 17.

round by the Maze and the Wall, two great navigable rivers. This island is about six or eight English miles about, and preserved by a strong bank about twelve yards high, beyond which bank are seated many (some say a dozen or twenty) coys. We were in three coys, all well wooded; two of them adjoining close together, the one a lesser coy (which is the winter coy), hath five pipes, like unto mine; it is ten English rood long on the sides, eight rood broad; no wild fowl therein, but we were permitted to walk within the hut; the coy-ducks came boldly unto us and fed: belonging hereunto, one hundred and fifty ducks, thirteen drakes; dainty, fair, spacious, and well-proportioned pipes, higher overhead, longer and better compassed than any I ever saw in England. Twiggen nests provided for the ducks to breed in. The other coy, joining hereunto, much more spacious and larger; it hath six pipes in one end only, thirty-five rood long, and thirty broad. We were not permitted to see this larger coy. Ducks sold for sixpence a piece: two pellstarts, two smeathes,[1] two shovelars, each equivalent to a Dutch,[2] and four teals, sixpence. Another coy we saw, wherein are four pipes in one end; a great pool; the ducks fed with barley; the dog-farm, three rood from the hut or the pipes; and by the help of a little ladder, the dog is enabled to leap into the hole a yard high. The fowl in the little coy fed with barley. But we could not be admitted to take a full view of any of these coys, neither is there any spy-holes into the pond, but all their pipes are much more curious, and carry a far better proportion than ours.

This fair maiden town of Dort, the ancientest city in the land, and invested with largest privileges, sends the prime committee,

[1] Smeathes are probably smews, *mergus albellus*, a bird frequently taken in the coys of Holland. It has been suggested that pellstarts are pintail ducks. It is somewhat remarkable that no explanation of these words can be found in Yarrell, Montagu, Pennant, Ray, Willoughby, &c. &c. nor even in old Randall Holmes. Nor are these names now known in Cheshire, where they must have been familiar, from the frequent use of them by our traveller.

In Ash's Dict. the word smeath is indeed found, as the name of a sea fowl, but without stating the species.

[2] For Dutch, read duck.

who is the prime of the States General representing the cities
which send them.

Upon *Wednesday the* 29 *May,* we returned by waggon from
Dort to ROTTERDAM. We paid for our passage two gilders six
stivers, and upon our return we found my brother's coat taken
away; enquiring and searching for it, but could never hear of.
We complained to the burgomaister (who understands English),
sitting in the State-house, and had a fair hearing, Mr. Custis
having been summoned by an officer, for which we paid three
stivers. Here set the burgomaisters in one room, the scoute, or
baylue, in another, the sckepens in another, and the weismaisters
in another, and the secretary in another. Justice is here executed
six hours every day. The Friendmakers also here sit. We were
referred to be further heard at four of the clock, endeavouring to
obtain satisfaction from the host, with whom they were left in
charge, and who said whatsoever was there left should be in safety.
We were staid in Rotterdam all Thursday, and until evening on
Friday. At four hour we attended in the State-house; the burgomaisters were in *convivio quodam,* at the State Harbour, the
Cross Keys, upon Erasmus Bridge. Hither we went, desired
to speak with the burgomaister that understood English; but after
we had attended there as long as in the State-house, we were
referred until next morning at ten o'clock; but being tired out
with attendance here, discharged our inn. I writ a large letter to
the English burgo-maister, and sent away my footboy with it unto
him, who was also epicurizing at this time, as the day before at
Scedam, and because I named him not in the superscription (not
knowing his name) he did not open, but returned it. In our
reckoning was demanded one gilder four stivers for a quart of
burnt claret wine; seventeen stivers a-night for our lodging.

About seven hour at night we hired a scute for four Dutch
shillings to carry four of us and our trunk to DELPHE, where we
arrived about nine hour. This was drawn by a good strong horse
whereupon a little boy rid. He trotted altogether, a cord fastened to the top of the mast of the boat, which was also fastened

to the horse. The lazarus-house seated near unto Rotterdam upon a river cut out for boats to pass it twixt Rotterdam and Delph; this water is above the ground, and would doubtless overflow were it not kept in by the banks. This is a dainty passage, and will carry a great vessel. At this lazarus-house they reach you a box whereinto is put what you bestow, which is thrown into the water. Here are three or four tolls to be paid by the watermen. Here, by Mr. Kenerick's means, we were accommodated with a very fair spacious chamber in the English house, which is allowed for the English merchants, rent free and excise free. Here is a staple for the English cloth. In this house[1] the Princes of Orange kept their court, and I was brought into the chamber wherein the Prince was born, and here they resided until such time as this Prince's father coming ˉout of   was shot by a Frenchman, who stood behind the pillar with a pistol charged in the one hand and a partisan in the other. After the bullet went through his body it glazed and made impression in the ceiling, yet to be seen. The company of English cloth merchants live here bravely, accommodated with all necessaries, and invested with many privileges; their house rent free, victuals excise free; a stately room to dine in; a dainty bowling-alley within the court; a pair of butts; accommodated with fair, convenient lodgings.

The five ancientest cities in Holland: 1. Dort; 2. Harleim; 3. Delph; 4. Leyden; 5. Rotterdam.

Delph hath the fairest spacious market-place, as is said, in this whole land; it most complete market-place that ever I saw in England, and is four square. In the west side stands the state-house, the finest state-house said to be in all the seventeen provinces. Herein is a wooden huke,[2] a round hollow piece, so narrow as that it is of a fit size for his head to go and to hang on his shoulders. It is about one yard and half, and very heavy; the wearing whereof is enjoined as a punishment throughout all the town upon whores, petty

---

[1] This house was called Prinssenhof; in aftertimes it became a barrack, and still continues such.   [2] Yoke.

larceners, shippers that exact. It is a great shame and disgrace to
them; their faces are open and to be known, their hands held close
by their sides and cannot stir; it is very heavy, and they moving, it
knocks and breaks their chins. On the east side of the market-
place stands the new church — a delicate, high, straight steeple.
Herein is a curious monument of Prince William,[1] one in brass as
he was in arms, the other in marble; boys crying curiously, and
much to the life, made in brass; two boys holding lamps on either
side overhead, and two on either end; four curious pictures
in brass at every corner of this tomb. This by some thought
nothing inferior to any monument in Westminster. In the other,
old church,[2] as fair as this other church, there is a monument
intended (and the picture of Peter Hinde[3]) who was admiral of
Holland, and slain by the Dunkirks about two years ago. Here
over his monument hang the ragged staff, the colours of the Dunkirks taken from them. He took the Plate fleet, and was as terrible to Dunkirks, as Drake to Spaniards. Here also is a monu-

[1] William I, whose murder is mentioned above. This monument still remains.
The prince here mentioned was William of Nassau, Prince of Orange, founder of the
republic of the United States. He was murdered by a popish fanatic, Baltazar de
Guerard, a gentleman of Franche-Comté, who assumed the name of Guion, pretended
to be a Huguenot, and contrived to obtain the confidence of his victim, and shot him
with a pistol loaded with three bullets, as he was about to ascend the stairs from the
dining-room, July 10, 1584. The marks of the balls, which entered into a stone of
the gate after they had gone through the body of the prince, are shown to strangers at
this day in Delft in Holland, and I myself saw them when I was young.—*Maurier's
Lives of Princes of Orange*, 1693, p. 115.
   The superstitious Catholics and Spaniards celebrate this Balthazar de Guerard, and
have ranked him in the number of their martyrs —p. 122.
   An inscription on a stone, let into the wall, still records the event.
[2] St. Hippolytus.
[3] Peter Hein, in 1628, commanded a fleet belonging to the West India Company of
Holland, and falling in with the Spanish galleons, captured them; his own share of
the prize-money amounted to about seven hundred thousand livres, and he was promoted to the dignity of Lieut.-Admiral of Holland. In the following year he commanded a small squadron of frigates to blockade the port of Dunkirk; three privateers
attempted to force their passage, but were encountered and captured. A cannon shot,
however, at the commencement of the action, struck the admiral on the shoulder, and
instantly deprived him of life.

ment over Colonel Morgan's[1] wife. Here is a most curious port,[2] called the water sclott port, which is said to be as curious a port as any in the land. Herein dwells the Digrave, who hath the same authority and command over the country, which the scoute hath over the city, and herein he keeps his office. Of this port he hath such an absolute command that at his pleasure he can have access into the town.

This city was built about seven hundred years ago. The officers of Delph, one scoute and underscoute; who sits upon life and death, and is to punish misdemeanours and capital offences. Here are also four burgo-maisters, who are to hear and determine suits in law, matters of difference twixt party and party; seven sckepens, who are to give their verdict, as are our jurors. Vornscapps forty-four, who are the common council of the city, by whose consent all taxes are to be imposed and levied. Here are likewise freind-makers, or good men, who are to arbitrate and compose differences by consent. Here is a large and spacious ghuesthouse, capable of four hundred persons, though now very empty; one fair chamber, wherein those that are therein disposed are lodged, is built four square, and resembles our own Exchange; one rank of lodgings now void above, even upon the head and tester of those below, and another rank of lodgings below, wherein are placed those poor thereinto admitted; neatly accommodated with convenient lodging, linen, victuals, close-stool and cupboard to every of them. Hereunto belong houses of office, mighty great brewing vessels, and a fine kitchen. Hereunto belongs a church, wherein are four sermons every Lord's-day. A dainty ox-house belongs hereunto, wherein are kept their stall-fed oxen, which never go out of doors during the whole winter after they once are taken into the house. This is a most neat ox-house. Behind the groopes a gutter one foot deep to take away all their stale and dung, and before them a gutter, whereinto the water they

---

[1] Col. Morgan was governor of Bergen-op-Zoom and its English garrison when it successfully resisted the attacks of the Spanish force in 1588.
[2] Gate.

drink is pumped. They stand on both sides, and in the middle a spacious place neatly laid with smooth tile. Here is also in this ghuest-house a chamber intended and reserved to entertain poor soldiers, that have no money to pay for their lodging and their victuals. Here they have bread and cheese, and a bed, though without sheets, free cost for one night. This ghuest-house is for sick and diseased persons, but none admitted that have any infectious disease. Here is a house in this city invested with a strange privilege. It has a tapp-house, wherein they use much to buy and sell and make bargains. If any difference in this house, three men (who are yearly chosen for that end) are to call the parties before them into a room in that house, wherein is a fire in the middle, and about one yard and an half high is a tunnel to convey away the smoke. No block, back, mantel-tree, nor jaumes here needful. At the higher end, in seats prepared for this purpose, sit these three judges, and round about the fire the parties and witnesses, where they all drink liberally, and the judges make an order which binds the seller; and if before next day at ten of clock the buyer refuse to stand to that order, he is to defray the charge of what was spent by all the company at that time.

In this town tame storks and shovelars kept tame, birds with long legs, less bodies than our storks,[1] and broader bills, like our shovelars.

After dinner, Mr. Morgan and Mr. Bayneham and myself went to see Gabriel Direckson's coy, a rich boor in the country, an acquaintance of Mr. Morgan's who dwells beyond Shippley.[2] He hath £500 sterling a-year, and received £6000 portion with his wife. He is a merchant, and is interested in the East and West India company. He hath a daintier house for a boor; a neat chimney in it, the back, save where the hob is, adorned with such stones a yard and dim[3] high, as are our best hearthstones in England. He milks thirty kine; his men milk the kine, which give twenty-seven great trease-full[4] of milk; every cow about four gallons a day; they make account that every cow yields a Dutch

---

[1] Our storks are herons, *ardea cinerea*.   [2] A few miles S. W. of Delft.
[3] A yard and a half.   [4] Tray is a milk-pail; in Sussex called, now or formerly, a trug.

shilling a day; this milk is kept in a cool cellar, and in brass great vessels so soon as it is milked: it is placed in a trough of cold water to cool the more suddenly; it will keep the longer before it sour. Here is a dainty fine shippen,[1] contrived as the other, and hay overhead, and a cistern full of grains covered with sand to make his kine pottage in winter. Here is a fine barn or hay-house, the roof whereof is made light, and to be lifted higher with a screw, or lower, as you see cause; hollow your mough[2] at the bottom, that so no mouses may enter, and place water-pots at every post to drown the rats and mice. Yet this boor is a very drudge himself, and goes like a clown or sloven, yet gave he us free and generous entertainment. He is coy-man himself. His coy is seated near his own and divers other houses and the highways and navigable rivers on both sides, nearer by much than Doddleston Bridge or Findloes House is to my coy. His coy hath five pipes as mine, but better compassed, and two of them almost meet. Much wood, reed, grass and thicket within the hut, so as the fowl on one end cannot discern the dog showing elsewhere. Abundance of quince trees herein planted, which prosper very well. He hath about two hundred ducks, twenty drakes. He hath fowl bred twixt pellstarts and ducks about twenty. I saw some of them. Many gray ducks which are best; coy-dogs best that are either white or red, and the more hairy the better. These ducks as tame and familiar about his house as any tame ones can be. Smeathes he keeps in a hut near his house covered with a net. A dainty little windmill I saw to drain or drown land, whereof I will procure a model.

I met a boat twixt Shipley and Delft laden with bees. We paid for our scute five Dutch shillings. Mr. Bayneham invited us to sup upon Saturday night to the Company's ordinary, where we were kindly entertained in the great chamber. Here lives three of the daughters of the Prince of Portugals,[3] who by

---

[1] Cowhouse.   [2] Corn mow.
[3] Don Emanuel, son of Anthony, proclaimed by the people king of Portugal, but dispossessed by King Philip II of Spain, married Emilia de Nassau, daughter of

their mother, a Protestant, were trained up in that religion. Their
father still remains in a house at Brussels, maintained by the king
of Spain. One other of these sisters (whereof are five) lives with
the princess, and the five with the Grave of Cunenberg's[1] lady.
The prince of Portugal, their brother, is lately converted, hath left
his father at Brussels in a religious house; he is much at Hage,
but his lodging here. Mr. Peters told me that there was already
committed to press the causes and grounds of his changing his
opinions.

This *Sunday morning, June* 1.—About nine of clock I sent for
this demoniac, who was brought unto me by an English maid. I
conversed with her two hours at least. She is conceived by all
here to be possessed, and as herself this day related unto me, it was
in this manner. About fifty years ago (she is now sixty-five, and,
at her first coming unto us, in a sensible condition), lamenting the
death of her uncle, there presented himself one like unto her uncle
(she then being about fifteen years of age), who told her he was
her uncle. She embraced him at first, and afterwards doubted and
said her uncle was dead; whereupon she attempting to go away,
he gave her a blow on the face which drew blood; and coming into
the house wherein she dwelt, she told those there that she had seen
her uncle, and would bring them unto him, but they could then
find no uncle; but after a few days he appeared unto her again,
and then he told her he was not her uncle (though he appeared in
the same likeness as before) but he would bring her to her uncle,
and then he gave her three figs to eat, which at first she refused,
whereupon he threw her into the water, and being helped out by
others that saw her thrown in, but discerned not him. And after
she was recovered out of the water, he attempted again, and constrained her to eat them all three, whereupon she fell suddenly into
an extremity, and hath had continually such an extraordinary
unnatural hardness even under her short ribs twixt her paps and

William the Great, Prince of Orange, by his second wife, Anne of Saxony. They had
two sons, and six (not five) daughters, who are said to have made unsuitable matches.
    [1] Cullenburg.

her navel; she did unlace herself, and I felt her bare skin. When the devil troubleth her, this hardness riseth and swells and danceth within her, riseth up into her throat; her tongue is pulled down, they say, when she is violently possessed; her head and feet and shoulder-blades are turned, and she is in violent torment. The devil will not suffer her to go to the church, but if she be in church, she is constrained (or rather the devil within her) to disturb the whole congregation, and therefore she is prohibited to come to church. If she have thoughts to receive the sacrament, she is then violently possessed. When she came to Mr. Forbs his house, she could come to the door, but had no power to go in, except she were carried. In one of her fits wherein this day she seemed to be (whereof I was a witness), she seemed to swell, looked ghost-like, with most fixed eyes, and we reading that text of Christ dispossessing the man possessed with legions of devils, she seemed much troubled and violently possessed; and when I read that text of some devils to be cast out by fasting and prayer, she seemed to understand me speaking in English, and answered: " You may fast seven years if you will; must I fast, and not you? fast you if you will, not I." Mr. Bayneham reading the first of Luke, and coming to the song of Simeon, she was very unruly, so as John Ward and I could not without some difficulty hold her, but she would needs have thrown herself down, and said, "it was a lie, it was not true;" before that, her hands, knees, and all parts seemed to tremble and quake when we began to read on the Bible; but then seemed she most violent when Christ was mentioned, his office and nativity, and then offered to make a strange noise (in no language) to drown or interrupt his reading; her body seemed to swell, and to be contracted, and to be drawn strangely. And when I did read (to try whether she did counterfeit or no) in the Bible that which was no part thereof, and thereupon she seemed to begin to be troubled; but afterwards reading a psalm, she was much more violently handled. In this fit, I offered her money, a rix-dollar; but she did not accept. She saith the devil hath formerly lyen in bed with her, and appeared unto her in the shape of her

E

sweetheart, whose death increased her grief for her uncle; so as now he appears unto her in her sweetheart's shape, and presents himself every night standing at her bed's feet, and hath not lyen in bed with her since Mr. Forbyes prayed with her, and prevailed so far; she seeth him nevertheless every night at her bed's feet, and when she is to give thanks for any meat she eats, the devil will not suffer her, but she is forced to eat her meat like a swine, without giving thanks. He speaks often unto her, and once she told him she defied him; he had only power over her body. He answereth: "What! I have taken all this pains in vain? I will have thy soul in the end." When she is possessed violently, they say she will speak all manner of languages to those who come to visit her in those extremities, or rather indeed it is the devil within her who will speak in their own languages to those who come to her. He makes use of her organs, and speaks out of the hollowest and lowest parts of her body. He will tell them of their faults, and what they have done. If they be profane persons, he will disgrace them; if godly, he will call them blockhead (as he did Mr. Forbs), but speaks no evil of them. The Company's barber (of Delph merchants) came to her in this condition, and the devil spake to him in English, and called him Giggs: "Giggs, art thou come? ho! Giggs, thou art mine;" since which time always he hath been called by that name. Mr. Forbs being once sent for unto her in one of her extremities, the devil said before the messenger returned, "the logger-head cannot come;" and he did not come. This woman is a poor woman, and lives upon the alms of the town, and is provided for by the overseers of the poor. She was married, but her husband lived not above one year and an half, and then died; and as the English maid who hath been most conversant with her, told me, the devil meeting him in the streets, squeezed and bruised his body so as his death was thereby occasioned. After I left her, and that she was perfectly recovered, she was much discontented and wept, because I offered her money in her extremity, as though she did counterfeit; and being stayed to dine with the master of the house, wherein we left her being perfectly well; and when they gave thanks, she began to tremble and shake and to be troubled. Herself told us that the devil endeavours to persuade her to believe that he is God, which name he cannot pronounce when he confers with her, but pronounceth it: and as the English maid told me, one Mr. Russell coming to her in her extremity, and reading touching Christ's power over unclean spirits, the devil in her answered in English: "It was a lie; it was writ by man; and give me pen, ink, and paper, and I can write better matter than that was." The English maid also told me, coming into my chamber, that she being sent for Mr. Forbes to come to her, Mr. Forbes said (as she conceived) that he would come; the devil within her replies, "he will not come": she averred it he said he would come; whereas indeed she did mistake, for he said he could not come, and did not come. The English maid affirmed that she did sweat so extremely yesterday, when I was with her, by reason of the torment she was then in, that she soiled a clean smock put on that morning; and that coming to her this 2 Junii, the devil told her, when he appeared unto her last night, that I was a witch, and that I dealt with the devil, and that was the reason I came to see her, and that I would have her go to the devil; but he would bring her to God; —cannot pronounce God, but saith he is Jod; and Christ Jesus he will not acknowledge, but saith he is Christ and God. She was in this manner first taken at Leyden, where, as the English maid (a modest, civil woman) reported, the devil, in the proportion of a man, came into a shop and desired to buy some poison, which so soon as he had received, vanished away and paid not for it: immediately this poison was brought unto her by him, and she was persuaded to take it, but refused. But since her coming to Delph, he hath tempted her to hang herself; and once or twice she was so much overcome by the strength of the temptation, as that she did (in the house wherein now she dwells) hang up her, and had not God's providence ordered that some coming in cut the rope suddenly, she had perished.

About the 9 *of June* was Delph fair, which they call their keirmes: it holds about a week: it is equivalent to a fair with us and wakes. Upon Thursday, the women that want and desire husbands present themselves, make choice of their seats in Delph church, where the boors that want wives come to make their choice; and when they affect any woman, after some few questions: "Who are your parents and friends?" and "Who are yours?" if the woman like the man and affect him, they go out and drink, and then in their cups they treat of portions, &c.; and if all things concur, suddenly married.

Upon *Sunday*, 1 *Junii*, after dinner we went to Hage by scute, which is about three English mile; it cost one stiver et dim every person. Here is the courts of the States-General, and of the Prince of Orange, and of the Queen of Bohemia.[1] It is but a *Dorpe*,[2] but the finest in all the land. It is more populous and something larger than Delph. Here we went to the English church, where we heard a very honest, neat sermon. Hither came the Queen of Bohemia (who mourns, and it is thought will continue in that habit *durante vita*), her second son[3] (the eldest, Prince Palatine,[4] having an ague), and the Lady Elizabeth,[5] her daughter. In this little church sermon never begins until the queen come. After sermon we went to Colonel Harbert, who brought us into the Prince of Orange his garden, the fairest and most spacious platt that ever I saw in my life, and the vastest covered walks: the plot seems to be four square; walks covered go round about it, and in middle of the plot here is a fair round moat, about sixteen or twenty yards' wide, and in the middle thereof a little island round, wherein is a round covered walk and a kitchen-garden within that walk. In the middle of this garden a poor young cyprus tree.

---

[1] Elizabeth, daughter of King James I, married Frederick, Elector Palatine, who rashly accepted the kingdom of Bohemia, which he was unable to retain. He died in 1632.

[2] Dorpe, a village without a corporation.

[3] The afterwards celebrated Prince Rupert, the rash and chivalrous general of his uncle Charles I.

[4] Charles Lewis, who, more prudently than generously, adhered to the Parliament, and sat in the Assembly of Divines, in England.

[5] One of the most extraordinary women of Europe, the correspondent of Descartes and William Penn, and the envy of Christina, Queen of Sweden.

Sr. Hen. Harbert told me that the States maintained one hundred and thirty thousand soldiers by land; one hundred men-of-war for the narrow seas, and one hundred to guard the inland rivers, less vessels, every of them being in annual charge equalized to a company of foot. The States-General are possessed of eight of the Seventeen Provinces entirely: Holland, Gilderland, Zeland, Friseland, Utrecht, Over-isell, Zutphen, Grunning,[1] great part. of Brabant, three of the principal cities, Bergen-upp- Zoon, Buss,[2] and Mastricht, the chief city of Limburge; in Flanders they have only Scluse,[3] with some forts, as Isen-Dike,[4] Oldenburge,. Axel, and some others, forts and sconces.[5]

In Holland; towns that send committees, who have the places and voices of States-General during three years, who take place according to the antiquity of the towns: 1. Dort; 2. Harlem; 3. Delph; 4. Leyden; 5. Amsterdam; 6. Dergond;[6] 7. Rotterdam; 8. Brill; 9. Scedam; 10. Girkam:[7] these for South Holland. For North Holland: Anchusan,[8] Horne, and Alkmaare.

For this presents Nobles that are States-General: Baron of Brethro;[9] Count of Culenberg, Lord of Buckhurst,[10] Lord Dufenford, Lord of Asper, Lord of Summerdike,[11] Astendelfe,[12] Van Aspern, Van Schagen, Van Matheness, Poelgeest, Warmont, Revenburg, Noortwyck.

Only this to be observed: that though these nobles be always States-General, yet only three of these sit now in council: Count Culenberg, Lord of Buckhurst, Lord of Dufenford: these resident at Hage; the rest called upon great and important occasions. To be observed also, that only three of these committees always resident at Hage, so as though they be always States-General, yet only three of them constantly sit in the council of state; the rest are called when some great matter is to be resolved upon and is in consultation.

---

[1] Groningen.   [2] Bois-le-duc.   [3] Sluys.   [4] Ysendyck, Ardenburg, and Axel.
[5] Sconce, a small fort, built for defence of some pass, river, &c.—*Bailey's Dict.*
[6] Gouda, or Turgow.   [7] Gorcum.   [8] Enckhuysen.   [9] Brederode.
[10] Bronchornst.   [11] Sommelsdyk.   [12] Assendelft.

The chief towns of Gilderland which send committees, are these:
1. Arnheim; 2. Nimweigen;[1] 3. Bummell;[2] 4. Teile;[3] 5. Harder-
wigg;[4] and now of late they have taken in Venlow; 7. Rooremond; and 8. Strawleing. And they have all this land, save
Gilders, which is in the enemy's hand. So as Gilderland sends
eight committees, out of which three chosen to be resident at Hage,
and sit in council of state, the rest, though States-General, yet not
called to council but upon extraordinary important occasions.

The chief towns of Zeland which send committees: 1. Middle-
burg; 2. Flushing; 3. Terviers;[5] 4. Armue; 5. Zierick-Sea;[6]
6. Bruers-haven;[7] and 7. Dergous.[8] These also send three committees always resident at the Hage, who sit in council of state;
the rest called upon extraordinary occasions.

They have garrisons in Duke of Cleve's country. The Duke of
Cleve[9] was buried by the Duke of Newburg, who possesseth part
of his country. They have garrisons Scotch in Wesell, Reez, Limbreck, and another town in that dukedom.

Friseland maintains her claim to her ancient privileges, and will
not acknowledge Prince of Orangen or any other, but assumes to be
a free state, and sends one who sits here in council with the States-
General; and as an intelligent gentleman informed me this day
at the Prince of Orange his court, there are two degrees of States
sit here in council, the one superior and principal, who are selected
out of the committees, out of every province one, who join with the
nobles chosen as aforesaid. These resolve upon what is concluded
upon, and the other the committees consult how monies may be
raised, and how that may be effected which is resolved upon.
Friseland elects and sends committees for these towns: 1. Leu-

[1] Nimeguen.   [2] Bommell.   [3] Thid.   [4] Hardwicke.
[5] Terveer.   [6] Zurichsee.   [7] Brewershaven.   [8] Tergoes.

[9] This duke of Cleves was John William, who was born 1562, and died in March,
1609, having been twice married, but not leaving any children. A bitter war ensued
so immediately after his death between his presumptive heirs, that funereal rites were
not performed over his body till the year 1628, when his nephew, Wolfgang William,
Count Palatine of the Rhine, and of Neubourg, undertook to have this ceremony performed.— *Vanloon*, vol. ii. p. 59.

werden; 2. Dockam;[1] 3. Franaker; 4. Boleswert;[2] 5. Sneake; 6. Harling; 7. Workim; 8. Hinclopen;[3] 9. Staverne.[4] These have voices, and are as the former provinces.

Utrecht sends for itself one committee, but hath four cities within it: 1. Amordsfoarde;[5] 2. Wickdourstadt; 3. Mumford;[6] which all are called to council about any extraordinary occasion. Rhine in Utrecht forgotten. Groningen likewise a province, having within its precincts two cities, who send committees: 1. Dame, and 2. Delp-seile. Friseland now up in arms, because they will not yield to pay some taxes, contributions, and excise, imposed by the States; offered some violence to the magistrates. This Dorpe[7] of Den Hage is governed by a baylue (which is the same that is a scoute), two burgo-maisters, two under-scoutes or under-baylues, assistants to the baylue. The burgo-maisters chosen out of the aldermen, and execute that place three months, then others out of the aldermen or scepons elected. Here, in this town, and in this whole country, they are most guided by the civil law. Here are eight scepens and goodmen or friendmakers. Here are ghuest-houses, one for impovered and impotent persons, another for fatherless children.

Returning to Hage after dinner, upon *Monday, 2 Junii,* we left the scute a mile short of Hage, and went to see the Prince of Orange stable of horses, wherein were none but some thirty young horses three and four year-old: the stables capable of about sixty. Beyond the stable we saw a furious leopard of the prince, as also a young little elephant about three years old, who wanted of his growth (as he said that kept him) sixteen handful; he said they came not to their growth until they be a hundred years old, and live until they be three hundred years old. Hence I went to a dainty new house[8] of the Prince of Orange, erecting and almost

[1] Dokkum.   [2] Bolsward.   [3] Hindelopen.   [4] Slavoren.
[5] Ameersfoort.   [6] Montfoort.   [7] Village.
[8] T'Huis in't Bosch, or the House in the Wood, a palace decorated with a profusion of paintings; one room is absolutely lined with family portraits, and the great hall is painted with subjects in honour of Frederick Henry, Prince of Orange, by Jordaens and others, who, according to Reynolds' too severe criticism, have only produced a variety of wretchedness.

finished: it is about an English mile from the place where we left the scute, and as far from the Hage. This house was intended a story higher, but that the foundation would not admit it. It is most proportioned in length; the floors of all the lower rooms laid with one white, another black square stone; all the chimneys in the lower rooms almost of different works, but all stand upon marble pillars about a yard into the room. No jaumes at all, but so as the fire lieth, as it were, in the side of the room, and doth extend itself to give as much heat to either side as forward, being hollow on either side. In the second story the beauty of the rooms is the gilding on the roof, which seems to be very rich, and all marble chimneys; here is a dainty stair-case, there being two pair of stairs which come out of the hall, and land both at one stair-head, and lead into the best rooms. Some of the seats of the windows gilded in the riggott[1] that is planed. Here are mighty spacious garden plots here, sowed with herbs and roots; one or two English acres. Here is also leading from the highway to the court (leading to the house, which court is curiously paved with even narrow brick) a spacious piece of ground containing about four English acres, wherein are planted sycamore-trees curiously and in such order, as which way soever you look, they stand in order and rank. The name of the prince's chief house Hunslow Dike. Colonel Pagnall told me that the prince was possessed of a very fair estate and large possessions, insomuch as when they have travelled over the prince his own land hath been a day's journey.

This day I saw four of the daintiest, most curious mares that I did ever behold; they were the Prince of Orange's coach-mares, bred but of his own straine[2]; they are (as I conceive) twixt Barbaries and jenets,[3] brown bays, full of metal and flesh.

The prince hath a curious little garden half as long as one pile of

---

[1] In Cheshire, a gutter to a house is called a riggot; the word may here mean a channelled moulding.

[2] Strain, derived from Saxon, a breed of horses.—*Bailey's Dict.*

[3] Jenncts are Spanish or Barbary mares; how differing in breed from what he calls Barbaries, we have not discovered.

his house, close hedges, carrying round compasses as thick as though you were in an house. The ladies and gentlemen here all Frenchified in French fashion. This afternoon, about seven hour, came into this dorpe the Landgrave of Hessen's brother (a young gentleman about eighteen years of age), well mounted, and attended with some ten horses. We likewise saw the prince's little garden, wherein was a dainty fountain; in this garden, ripe oranges and lemons; a most brave, curious rock here is, and of a very large extent, and a place, in nature of a cage, wherein disposed all manner of dainty fowl.

June 3.—I dined with Colonel Goreing;[1] my lady with importunity prevailed with me to stay. Here we had royal entertainment; a brave boiled piece of beef, and two curious dainty bag-puddings, the one of suet, flower and almonds, the other with raisins and ordinary spices—an excellent good one; and at latter end of dinner a gammon of Westphalia bacon sliced in great pieces; green leaves here strewed upon the table when covered: here dainty strawberries and cream. About four hour we went to Queen of Bohemia's court, whither my lady Goreing went along with me, and presented me to the lady Elizabeth,[2] with whom I had a good deal of discourse; afterwards my lady Goreing presented me to the queen, and I kissed her hand, as I had done the princess's before. Here Mr. Stones, one of her majesty's principal gentlemen, invited me twice solemnly to stay and sup with him, and afterwards came to fetch me to see the queen at supper, where, after the queen had put me upon a discourse of the discovery of our Lancashire witches, she answered it with a relation of a discovery of witches in Westphalia, where a whole village, all witches; and amongst

---

[1] Col. Goring commanded a regiment of foot in Holland at this time.   [3] See page 7.

[2] This probably refers to " The Wonderfull Discoverie of Witches in the Countie of Lancaster, with the Arraignment and Triall of nineteene notorious Witches, &c." Aug. 1612, before Sir James Altham and Sir Edward Bromley, by Thomas Potts, Esq. An advertisement prefixed, signed by the two judges, asserts that they "imposed the labour of this work upon this gentleman, by reason of his place, being a clerk at that time in court, imploied in the arraignement and trial." Sir Edward Bromley attests that he revised and corrected it.

F

them was the Bishop of Wurzburg's chancellor and his page, all whom deservedly burned. The queen, also inquiring of me touching the stocks of Bagmear,[1] reported that at Berlin, the Elector of Brandenburg's house, before the death of any related in blood unto that house, there appears and walks up and down that house like a ghost in a white sheet, which walks during the time of their sickness and until their death. Her majesty said that the Lady Leveston, then present, had seen it open the curtains. She also spoke (which Duke Bernard of Weimar averred unto her) that some ministers being at supper assembled together in a room of the house of Duke William of Weimar, which was troubled with spirits ; that being at meat, all their stools upon a sudden plucked from under them. A gentlewoman sitting there at supper, feeling something under her clothes, stabbing downwards suddenly with her knife, it came up all blood; her garter was taken off her leg, and tied under all clothes upon her bare arm.

Here I saw before supper the Rhinegrave, the son of Monsieur La Force, and after supper, Grave Henry Vandeberg, the Count of Culenberg and his lady, Vandenberg's sister. Here I was stayed supper with the queen's gentlemen, and wondrously kindly entertained.

The queen reported a great defeat given by Arnheim, the Saxon general, to the Imperialists,[2] in Silesia: four thousand slain in the place. Landgrave of Hessen hath likewise prevailed against Imperialists near Cullen. She also said that D. Bernard[3] was marched up into Upper Palatinate to fight with King of Hungary.

All the rooms in the Queen's house, walls, beds and all, covered with black.

The tulips which I had from the Prince of Orange's gardener cost five guilders the hundred, the best. They are to be set in

[1] Bagmere is a mere or small lake near Brereton Hall, wherein, according to ancient popular traditions, stocks or trunks of trees were seen floating for several days previous to the death of the head, or of the heir, of the family.

[2] Near Lignitz.

[3] Bernard, duke of Saxe Weymar, with the army of the Swedes and the Confederates, marched to attack the king of Hungary at the head of the Imperialists. The armies met at Nordlinguen, and the Swedes were totally routed, 26 Nov. 1634.

August or September. Many quails kept here in cages, which you may hear call in streets. Four churches in this town : two Dutch churches for the town, one for the prince's house, and one little poor church for the English. In the fairest church, which is fine, neat, and spacious church, are abundance, an infinite number, of arms hanged round about the church; and the pillars hanged round, yea even so thick as almost one covereth part of another; and in the chancel many fair arms placed betwixt the pillars. In this country, when they make a grave, they, finding a place where have been none buried before, make the grave as deep as possible, and bury one upon another. Their women never come to church with their corpse, save only their men, who march in ranks in good order, two and two together.

This 4 *Junii*, in morning, we went to LANDINA[1] by waggon, for which we paid three guilders: here are the basins wherein christened three hundred and sixty-five children of the Count of Henenberg's lady, who lies there, under the brass basins, interred:[2] here is also a monument of an English nobleman in this church. Here by the way we met two dromedaries, which were very unruly, and the horses much afraid. I leapt out of the waggon: the dromedaries are ugly creatures, bulches[3] behind and before, and betwixt them a

[1] Loosdruenen.

[2] Here is a church monument, where an earl and a lady are engraven with three hundred and sixty-five children about them, which were all delivered at one birth; they were half male, half female; the two basons in which they were christened hang still in the church, and the bishop's name who did it; and the story of this miracle, with the year and the day of the month mentioned, which is not yet two hundred years ago; and the story is this. That the countess walking about her door after dinner, there came a beggar woman with two children upon her back to beg alms; the countess asking whether those children were her own, she answered, she had them both at one birth, and by one father, who was her husband. The countess would not only not give her any alms, but reviled her bitterly, saying, it was impossible to have two children at once by one father. The beggar woman being thus provoked with ill words, and without alms, fell to imprecations, that it should please God to shew his judgment upon her, and that she might bear at one birth as many children as there be days in the year, which she did before the same year's end, having never borne child before.—*Howell's Letters*, sect. ii. lett. 13.

[3] Bunches. Dromedary, a sort of camel, having two *bunches* on the back. *Bailey, Dict.*

convenient seat for a man, where a man did ride when we met them.
They are as large as a camel I have seen. Here by the way we
observed the sea-sand, the shore to be much above us, and going up
unto the top of it, we went up an hill; herein to be admired the
wonderful providence of God, inasmuch as the sea doth not overflow the land, lying so much below it. These hills and banks of
deep sand are cast up and wrought by the sea, by the waves of the
sea, and here is barren dry sandy land as in Sherwood Forest, like
Bowden Downs,[1] save longer lank grass; and until the sea sand be
taken off and led away, the ground is nothing worth; this sea sand
is carried to Hage and other places, where they make firm foundations.   Here is poor rye on this sandy land.   A pretty jest of an
English boy, who said, " the dogs bark, the cocks crow, cows bleat
like English ones, and the men can speak no English." An Englishman sits here on a gibbet 'twixt Delph and Hage, who, being trusted
and left alone in the house, murdered the man's only son: he dwelt
in Shipley. He was put to a cruel death: first, one leg broken
by an iron mall; second, the other leg; then his thighs and arms,
one after another; then was given him a blow on the breast, and
his brains struck out. A late discovery of a murdering-inn near
Stralesound, wherein were slain eight hundred persons, and their
flesh pickled up. It was discovered by a post, who, meeting with
a scholar, and coming together on the way towards Stralesound,
when they came thither, the gates being shut, they were constrained
to lodge in an obscure inn. After supper the post was much distempered with the meat he had eaten, it did not well digest, so as
he could take no rest, and heard a lamentable crying out, and a
man's voice, which indeed was the scholar, who was tumbled out of
his bed through a false deceitful floor into a mighty deep cellar,
where the butchers presently slaughtered him, cut his throat, and
quartered him, whose quarters there found hung up and salted.
Thus it was discovered: the post rising early, it was enquired
where the scholar was; it was answered he was gone; hereupon the
post informs the magistrates of the town; they were apprehended,

---

[1] In Cheshire; now enclosed.

search was made, and all confessed, and that fat men were most useful unto them; none of whom escaped. These deservedly exe-cuted, as also those professed robbers, murderers, ravishers, blasphemers, and idolaters, who gloried in nothing more than committing notorious villanies; who, after they had stuprated a woman with child, cut her throat, ripped up her womb, took out her infant, and killing a bitch in whelp, took the young out of the bitch's belly and put them in the woman's womb, and sewed it up. These suffered at Prauge most tormenting deaths: first, in one public place in the city, their flesh of the one arm torn off, seared, to prevent bleeding to death; after one hour's intermission, the flesh on the back, breast, thighs, so excruciated; afterwards laid upon a wheel, and all their bones broken one after another, and so continued, some languishing two whole days more before they died, having been tormented before from eight in morning to four in afternoon; hereof Mr. Tomkins, who keeps the Blue Anchor in Hage, affirmed his eyes were witnesses. He also reported the former.

The 4 *Junii.*—At supper I paid for my ordinary twenty-six stivers.

The 5 *Junii.*—In morning I went to see some coys, whereof here are abundance. Six in my view; two whereof I saw, the former rented for two hundred and fifty gilders, the other for two hundred and twenty-five gilders a-year. Six here are within half a Dutch mile. They had both three pipes in one end and one in the other: two hundred flying smeaths belonging to one coy; abundance of pell-starts, and thirty pell-starts in one huck.[1] These coys near the highways; mighty high trees grow in both of them, so full of cover within the huck and without, as all ground, reed-seatings and all, covered with wood. Here a coy-duck brings up chickens; wood covereth some pipes so thick, as there is no net. Sometimes take two hundred on a day; sell them at Christmas for one shilling a duck; at other times, sometimes six-pence, seven-pence, and eight-pence, and nine-pence, as in season. Trees herein as high as birches; their ducks, smeaths, and pell-starts exceeding

---

[1] Hutch.

tame. By the way over against an heries[1] house planted about forty young trees for shade, preserved by four boards nailed square together, two yards high. Here a dainty garden of a plain man's, wherein portraited to the life in box all the postures of a soldier, and a captain on horseback. Herein a pond, wherein abundance of fish, which, upon the ringing of a bell and throwing in bread, come to the top to feed boldly. He said here were many sorts of fishes. The park all along the highway side boarded or walled with boards two yards high; and it is said that herein are both red and fallow deer. This belongs to the States-General. Prince Robert at Leyden told me there were many parks, and that it was a most pleasant, dry country about Reinberke, lately taken in by the States.

This 5 *Junii.*—We left Hage and came by waggon for LEYDEN, for which we paid twelve stivers a-man: we took waggon about four clock, came to Leyden about seven; it being three Dutch miles. Here near unto the Hage we passed through trees planted in good order, which belong under the inhabitants of Hage; afterwards we passed through a wood, wherein were many oak trees, said to be planted *per comitissam Johannam.* Here is a park belonging to the States, wherein is said to be both red and fallow deer. It is a park-like ground. Here, 'twixt Hage and Leyden, all (for most part) barren land and deep sands, which have been wrought and laid there by the sea, whose shore lies on left hand, seems to be much above you, and seem like high hills, so as though the ground you pass look much higher than the country below; yet there also, in respect of the shore above you, it seems a valley.

Here about Leyden is a more pleasant, sweet place than I have met with in Holland. This town (as also other towns) much of late enlarged, so as one of the ports,[2] the   port, stands now within the city. Here the daintiest curious gallows that ever I saw: three pillars of freestone neatly wrought, on which the beams are placed; upon the top of every pillar stands a large gilded ball, as big as your head. Here, when the poor beg, and when they will give them nothing, they give them this answer: God help you! God help you!

[1] *To herie* (obsolete), to honour. *Herse,* a canopy over a body lying in state; a temporary monument. A *heries-house* may be a kind of mausoleum.   [2] Gates.

Going about ten clock to see the princes (the Queen of Bohemia's children), and having kissed their hands, Prince Robert,[1] falling into discourse with me, asked me to stay and dine with them: I knew not what answer to make; he invited me a second time, and went away. Presently came a Frenchman, and was so importunate with me as he stayed me, and I dined with those princes. This Frenchman named them in this order: Prince Charles,[2] Prince Elector; Prince Robert; Prince Maurice, who hath lately been much disfigured by the small-pox; Prince Edward, the best face; next him Prince Robert; Prince Philip, and Prince Gustavus, so little as not able to sit at table. The queen's daughters: Elizabeth, Lodovica, Henrietta, Sophia. Here is brought up with them a cousin-german, their father's sister's son. After grace said by their pages, the Lord's Prayer said in English; two foul women.[3] Study from eight to ten, and then dance to eleven, and then dine; they return to their books at two, study till four; learn to fence to five. Here, in their stable, four dainty sorrel pied horses suitable. This house wherein their court is kept, lent them by the town, which seems to be larger and more spacious than any town I have yet seen; and although here be an university, yet no face nor presence of an academy. Here be only two colleges; in one about thirty students of divinity, who have their diets and twenty gilders a-piece, a square uniform little court or quadrangle: in the other, twenty students of divinity, who have therein their diets and fifty gilders a-piece; these only go in the habit of scholars: so as here is no face nor presence of an university. The scholars apparelled some as gallants, some like soldiers, some like citizens, some like

---

[1] Rupert.

[2] Charles Lewis, the prudent adherent of the parliament; Prince Rupert, celebrated for his precipitate valour, as one of his uncle's generals; Prince Maurice, another of Charles' generals. Of the other princes little is known, they probably died young: the male branches became extinct upon the death of Charles, the son of the above Charles Lewis. The Princess Elizabeth (see above); Lodovica, or Louisa, was distinguished as an artist, and some of her paintings are still highly esteemed, and adorn the walls of some foreign cabinets; Sophia, the well-known Electress-mother of George I, and one of the most accomplished women of her age. Of Henrietta little is known.

[3] Nurses?

serving-men; all in colours for most part. The schools here are very poor, mean things, in comparison of Oxford schools. Here are twenty-two professors, some of whom are continually reading from eight to twelve and from one to five: four professors of divinity: Joannes Polyander,[1] Antonius Thysius,[2] Constantinus Empereur,[3] Antonius Wallæus.[4] Doctors of physic: Adrianus Falcoburgius,[5] Ewaldus Serevellius,[6] Adolphus Vorstius,[7] Joannes Walæus.[8] Many civilians here. High Dutchmen most resort unto this university, because their universities in High Germany not so safe. Here more follow their pleasures than their books. Here, by the schools, we saw a printing-house, and the princes walking. Two things only which belong to this university memorable: the physic garden, wherein all manner of herbs and plants medicinable, though a small plot of ground not above half a statute acre.

Herein was I this night, *June* 6, when Adolphus Vorstius, Doctor of physic, read his lecture in this garden, which he is to perform twice a-week. His manner is to take a whole bed, four yards long and one broad, and to discourse of the nature and quality of every herb and plant growing therein, which he points out with his staff when he begins to speak thereof. He treated of the mastic-tree, which there grows, though it is but like a bush, and of no great stature: hereunto he ascribed much virtue. He also discoursed of lupins, of hyssop, and of hemlock, which he said was of a most venomous, somnifying, stupifying, and intoxicating quality; yea, if any man did but so much as touch it and rub it, that part that touched it would lose his natural heat: a young gentleman immediately before had been fingering it, and, upon hearing this, no little daunted and dismayed: another afterwards would needs

[1] Professor at Leyden in 1611, died in 1646.
[2] Born at Antwerp 1565, died at Leyden 1640.
[3] Professor of Hebrew from 1627 to 1648.
[4] Born 1573, died 1639.
[5] Adrian van Valckenburg born 1581, died 1650.
[6] Ewaldus Schrevelius succeeded Everardus Vorstius in the chair of Divinity, born 1576, died 1646.
[7] Born at Delft in 1597, Professor at Leyden 1624, died 1663.
[8] Rector of the Medical School in 1632.

touch it, an Englishman, but he confessed unto me that it cast such a savour, an offensive taste, to the brain, as he expected not. This doctor speaks good Latin, and expresses himself in very good language, and very fluently, and with much ease.

Here is likewise an anatomy school, wherein, besides the rarities mentioned in the Itinerary, are many more: an Egyptian king, a blackamoor, who is said to have died three thousand years ago, who was embalmed, and so preserved from putrefying to this day: his name was Pharaoh, brought hither within this thirty years. Here are the skins of men and women tanned: a man's much thicker and stiffer than a woman's. Here the anatomy of a woman executed for murdering her bastard child, and the child anatomized in her arms. Here we numbered the ribs in two anatomies of a man and a woman, and found eleven ribs in a man's side and twelve ribs in a woman's side.[1] Here is also an Egyptian king's daughter, a blackamoor, embalmed; the jaw of a whale, four or five yards long; the teeth of a whale, near half yard long one of them, twelve in number, the rest every two less than other; a young whale, cut out of his dam's belly, which lies below in the cellar, eight yards long. *Fulminis sagitta*, the dart of a thunderbolt, about the length and thickness of your little finger; under it is written, in Latin: "Existimant multi lactentes pueros, si herniis corripiuntur, lapide hoc cunis imposito restitui: aut, si non hoc morbo affliguntur, ab eodem preservari: De quo marbo, Dæus.[2] Qui caste gerit hunc e fulmine non ferietur; nec domus nec villa, quibus adfuerit lapis ille." Here are the anatomies of divers creatures, men, women, and children; bull, horse, stag, water-dog, goat, monkey, ape, baboon, fox, swine, musk-cat, house-cat, which hath fifteen ribs; divers other creatures whose ribs numbered (as bull, horse, dog) had but twelve; whale had seventeen ribs; greyhound, wolf, bear, swan, eagle, cock, stork, pigeon; the guts and maw of a man thirty-six

---

[1] This notion of inequality of number is among the vulgar errors noticed by Brown, book vii. ch. 2.

[2] Marbadæus, who wrote " De Gemmarum Lapidumque Viribus," printed at Cologne in 1539.

G

foot long; head of elephant, two tigers' skins stuffed; an Indian mole stuffed, as big as a cat: turtle shell, two yards every way; crab-fish, with an horn in the forehead about two foot; the body of a West India fowl, phænicoptoras,[1] three yards long, the body almost as great as a swan: short wings, red and black, long legs, long neck, crooked bill, feet like a goose; a cancer, East India, with a shell like a broad platter on her back; divers serpents, one great, one three yards long; a very great Roman urn, wherein they put the dust of their great persons dead, when their bodies are burned; a lamp, used [to be] placed by the Romans in their sepulchres, which is said to burn perpetually; the proportion of two crocodiles, one four yards long; caput alces; two Indian canes, nine yards long, half-yard about; many more rarities which I found in my book, and there pricked, and many more there are which are omitted.

In the physic-garden: an eagle fifty years old, white head and white train; another was here (now dead) which was a hundred years old; this inscription over her:—

> Sum celebris pennis, oculis, clangore, senecta;
> Spectator caveas pande, beabis, ave.

In this garden a tree, which hath such a strong venemous malignant quality, as, if one lie under all night, what creature soever, they are dead before next morning; hereof I broke a branch, which Ralph Brian rubbed but a little in his hand, and his finger burned and prickled. Herein divers plants and herbs, which cannot endure the wind or sun; these covered with glass. Here, in this little garden, fifty-six beds; all ordinary herbs, roots, and weeds, as well as rare herbs, and planted, to be found herein: tansy, French wheat, docks, hemlocks, alicampanum, bater-docks, &c. Many roots and plants set in pots, and prosper well. I bought a book, wherein are the names of all the herbs and plants in this garden, wherein more at large hereof in the book which sets down the nature and quality of the herbs and plants of this garden.

---

[1] Flamingo.

Upon *Saturday*, 7 *Junii*, we went to John's[1] father's in a waggon, by him sent. We went about six o'clock, and came to ALLIFEIN about half nine, which is nine English miles. This dorpe was burnt about fourteen years ago; the fire first took in rape-oil, suddenly flamed out mightily, and presently set on fire a stork's nest on top of church, and burnt the church and a great part of the town to the ground. It is rebuilded, and here is a dainty neat church new-built, wherein three great candlesticks hang over the middle aisle; one of them cost £25 sterling. We saw 'twixt this town and Leyden a neat gentleman's house (with a brave turret on top, which is a great grace) moated about, and a drawbridge to pull up most easily, an invention well deserving to be put in practice in England over all moats or dykes. Before ten hour, we came to John's father, and went with him to his coy, wherein wood excellently grown; apple-trees, plum-trees, and cherry-trees prosper very well, and shed forth abundance of wood.

The largest and neatest coy-house I have seen, lofted overhead to lay corn or hemp-seed, the pipes so straight, bending some little towards you; four pipes only until last winter, two in either end: one more, added last winter, of no use: here, by the help of a windmill, they can drown all the ground round about the coy. It is framed in this manner: a long piece of timber (such an one as in England we use to turn our windmills withal) is placed upon four stumps supporters, and it is laid slopewise, high with the head, whereon is fastened the four sails, and to the foot is joined a little wheel, which is turned by the wind turning the sails, which casteth out the water: this wheel is placed in deep narrow gutters proportioned unto it, and cut out for it to run in, out of which it throws the water into the land to be drowned.

Hence we went to see a rape-mill turned by an horse at Swammerdam, and by the way we passed by a pleasant and something higher ground, where, they say, was a city inhabited by those who

---

[1] John appears to have been his coyman. It seems not improbable that he was a Dutchman whom Sir W. Brereton had transplanted into Cheshire to manage his coys after the manner of Holland, where such matters were perhaps better understood.

were, one of them, as large sized and statured, and as strong, as two
or three Dutchmen now living. John my coyman reported it. We
saw the rape-mill turned by an horse, which drew about two
great mill-stones standing on the edge one by the other, which did
turn round upon a third mill-stone, upon which the rape-seed being
thrown was ground: near hereunto placed the pan, which of itself,
by the help of screws, turns about to be stirred, wherein they boil
the bruised rape, and thence put it into bags, which is put into a
press, which is beaten down with the mill also by virtue of a wheel
at the top thereof, which wheel turns and screws down the wedges
without any more labour save the mill going.

In my return I went in to see (at Allofein) the house of the Lord
Offerbeake, a great house promising much; but, entering into it and
examining the rooms, I found nothing answerable to what was expected: on the back side I saw a pool empaled, wherein were pell-
starts, smeaths, shovelars, teals, and others, and a straight poor pipe
to take fowl in. On this side the house spacious gardens and mighty
great orchards, and store of fish-ponds; on the other side of the
lane, and near unto the river of Rhine, most curious hedges and
walls covered; the first whereinto you enter two rood broad, near
twenty rood long; along the sides and ends whereof a strong frame
of timber, which guides and nourisheth a brave thick cover of a
kind of elms; this garden moated about; upon the top of this walk,
it is said, he intends to build a chamber, which may command and
overlook the river running by the side thereof, and may see many
brave ships and boats continually passing upon that river. Here
is a square plot converted into garden and walks, and most curious
hedges, and 'twixt every hedge and walk a dainty moat, which
seems to be full of fish. Towards the middle of the plot, the walks
rounded, and, 'twixt every walk, dubbed hedges kept in most curious
order; and in mid, round walks like a maze, the several plants:
1, box; 2, yew; 3, elm; 4, privett; 5, Geneva plant,[3] makes a thick
hedge almost like yew: 6, thorns, whereof a most dainty hedge is

---

¹ Juniper.

straight as a line the whole length of the plot; 7, cornowlee[1] makes an hedge like privett, but it is a broader and thicker leaf; 8, pear-tree hedges; 9, apple-tree hedges, both thick platted, and kept dubbed in good order; 10, wood of life,[2] which smells like worm-wood, grows to a good height, leaf in proportion resembles most holly fearon; 11, tamarisque, which is almost like savin; 12, red barbaries; the lowest of these hedges higher than any man can stride over, and, as I conceive, frames of timber guiding and supporting all of them.

Here in this village, on the back side of which runs the Rhine, I observed a chest bored full of holes, locked, which was placed in a dock prepared for it, which was with a pulley to be drawn out and let dry; herein were fish kept, to be always ready upon any sudden occasion to be taken, the ark being dry and empty of water; for this end I saw also twiggen round baskets at Hage to keep living fish in, hanging in the water, to draw out at pleasure.

We returned hence by water, being about nine English miles; it was about three hours' work, and cost us one gilder to hire a little sckuller boat to Leyden.

We stayed the Sabbath at Leyden, *June* 8, 1634, and heard Mr. Goodier (a worthy, honest man) in the English church, a little (yet neat) place, and not fully furnished with hearers. Hither also to this church we went in afternoon: came thither before two, yet sermon begun. After sermon,[3] all of that congregation desired to stay:[4] we departed. After this sermon ended we went to the Dutch church (St. Peter's), wherein are many scutcheons and arms, where we found them receiving the sacrament at a long table covered with white cloth, placed lengthways in an aisle which stands over across the church: the men, I imagine, had all received together at the same place; we only saw the women receive sitting; in the middle of whom, on the one side, was placed the minister (the predicant), who, after he had consecrated the bread and wine,

---

[1] Dogwood Cornel, *cornus sanguineus.*
[2] *Arbor vitæ.*
[3] *i. e.* in the morning.
[4] For the communion.

did administer the same unto those who sat next unto him, who conveyed, on both hands the predicant, the bread upon plates, and the wine in cups, to those who sat next unto them: they themselves broke the bread, being cut into long narrow pieces. When all these had received, they departed, and others succeeded; but, as it seemed unto me, this not administered with such decency and reverence as in England. After all had received, a psalm sung, and then some short prayer read, and so concluded. Here in this church all brass pillars 'twixt the middle aisle and the chancel. Here stayed in the church a great number of Dutchwomen, who resolved to keep their seats in the mid of the aisle (every of them sitting upon their own stool, brought and carried with them), until the next sermon, which was to begin about one hour afternoon. In this city, though it is said that there is about one hundred and forty thousand persons, yet not above three or four churches: St. Peter's, for Dutch, the principal; St. Mary's, for French; and the English church. Here is a brave ghuest-house, which now maintains seven hundred orphans; besides divers other ghuest-houses.

This is the largest and most populous city I have yet seen. Herein their greatest trade is fulling and making of wool: abundance of our English wool and fullers'-earth brought hither through Scotland by stealth; so as black cloths, far better dyed than ours, can here be afforded better cheap than at Delphe. This city governed by one scoute and three under-scoutes; four burgo-maisters, which make orders, laws, and constitutions for government of the city; eight sckepens give sentence upon all that break those laws, and are judges in matters of difference 'twixt party and party. The scoute (the sckepens present) execute what the burgo-maisters and sckepens order and judge.

June 9.—I went and advised with Dr. Warcoaste, a physician, touching my childrens' weakness. He directed that we should strip off the stalks the leaves of fern (*Latine appellebat Filix sic Dr.*) and dry them in an oven, and make a bed of it, and lay the child upon it; as also take the root, stamp it, and boil it in ale, and annoint the child's body all over therewith. "Aqua mellis distillata valet ad crinem robustiorem efficere, atque etiam crescere in vultus efficit barbam."[1] I gave this Dr. 2s. Dutch. I went afterwards to Dr. Florentius,[2] a most elegant and able man, speaks exquisite Latin, who prescribed rolling of both legs and the use of fern as aforesaid, and also to remove the obstruction, which perhaps occasioned that hardness of his belly and that swelling in the wrist-joints. He prescribed a scruple Cremoris Tartari to be taken twelve mornings in broth of veal or chickens; if this hardness proceed from the worms knit together, which is ordinary, then he prescribed six grains of corallin,[3] six of hartshorn, and one scruple cremoris tartari, "candidum, optimum abluatur" dixit " et foveatur crinis decoctu capillorum veneris,[4] ac etiam usu aquæ mellis distillatæ." I gave him also two Dutch s., his fee being but three stivers if you go to him, and six if he come to you; by order of States not to exact more; here the first degree they take is doctor, when the professors think fit, and the graduate deserving, sometimes at three or four years.

Mr. Goodier told me of a strange deliverance of this town besieged,[5] wherein the famine and pestilence raging, the town not being able to hold out any longer, the country was drowned by drawing up their sluices and cutting the banks, and the night following the wall in one place, convenient for the enemies to enter, fell down and broke down (a great breach); the noise whereof and the sudden eruption of the water took such impression of fear, and occasioned the apprehension of some further danger by some further design; whereupon they broke up their siege, and left the town. For this strange preservation a solemn day of thanksgiving kept yearly in this city. Here I heard a

[1] Distilled honey water is useful to make the hair grow stronger, and also to increase the beard upon the face.
[2] Wrote " De Peste" in 1814.
[3] *Corallina officinialis*, sea corallina, or white worm seed, at one time much used in medicine, now but rarely.
[4] *Adiantum capillus veneris.* The hair to be washed and nourished with a decoction of maiden hair, and also by the use of distilled honey water.
[5] By the Spaniards in 1574.

strange relation of bread-loaves of bread turned into stone. In the time of a very great famine, wherein a poor woman that had many children, and wanted bread, and came to her sister, who had much riches and store of victuals and bread, desired her sister to lend her one loaf of bread; she most falsely and profanely denied that she had any bread. Her poor sister pressed her further and was very importunate, and said she had bread. Her sister denied, and with this deprecation, wished if she had any bread, that it might be turned into a stone; and accordingly she and her husband supping and sending for bread, when it was brought, it seemed to be turned into stone, and all the loaves in the house also, which took such impression in her, as she fell sick and died. This was reported unto me, but I dare not report or justify the truth.

Here I saw the fairest and largest state-house, wherein was a lively description of the Day of Judgment.

About eight hour *Monday* 9 *June*, we went for Harlaim in the mart ship or passage-boat, and passed all along a dead water, about twenty roods over, until we came to a dorpe called Caghe, and then we passed Caghe-Meare, and so came to Harlaim Meare; it being a side wind, sometimes the boat rowled so much on one side, that it went within less than a quarter of yard of the water, the sail almost leaning into the water; and we met a little boat coming much against wind, so laviereing[1] as that the sail almost touched the water, and the water came within less than half a foot of running into the boat. This is a very large standing meare, whereon you may go almost from Leyden to Amsterdam: it is a mighty, vast, spacious thing. I saw it from the top of Harleim church steeple, and it can be no less than thirty mile long. Our passage was five stivers a-man from Leyden to Harlaim, by scute.

About one of the clock, we came to HARLAIM, the second city in Holland; and in the river, 'twixt the meare and the town, we passed by a ship loaden with beer, about the same distance, about the same burthen our ship was of. Here we laviered about twenty

---

[1] Tacking. *Laveer*, to steer a ship sometimes one way, and sometimes another.

times in this little narrow water, and saw another ship, a little before us, run ashore with laviering. Here before we came to the town we saw a dainty gallows: three pillars of brick, iron bars overcross, whereon hang two men in chains, all flesh consumed. A woman executed stands here fixed to a post: she suffered for murdering her own child. She was put to a most cruel death upon a wheel. Another man's proportion[1] stands here, lately erected and fastened to a new post. This man desiring an alms, which was not given, whereupon he threateneth revenge, and sets fire on that house, which burnt the whole dorpe; whereupon he was most cruelly burned. The sckipper that carried us said he went this passage every day in year (save frost.)

This city is the second town in the land, and one of the largest: it is conceived that there is about ten thousand persons inhabiting therein. The city is much decayed of late, because consisting most of weaving linen cloth and stuff (that being the greatest trade of this town), which doth not go off so well as formerly; making threads and lace, and witeing[2] the same in yarne-crofts. Brewing is a great trade in this town, the dorps hereabouts being supplied with this beer. Herein the Arminians suppressed. It is governed by one chief-scoute, one under-scoute, and one scoute that ruleth by night; four burgomaisters; seven sckepens, good-men, or friend-makers. The burgomaisters chosen thus: the sckepens and vorn-scapps (who are equivalent to our common-council men), choose and present unto the prince six of most sufficient, which are sent unto him by the senior sckepen, out of which number the prince selects and pricks two, which always serve four year. There are vornscapps, out of whom and by whom the sckepens are chosen.

Here is a most dainty curious old-man-house, which might well become lord in the land to live in: it is built in manner of a quadrangle, and most neat and uniform. In court four dainty suitable quarters in the court, which is most evenly paved with bricks; two gardens; two green quarters, to dry their clothes. Within the

[1] Body or figure.   [2] Bleaching.

II

house: a cloister, neat walk in sides whereof; convenient little neat lodgings, wherein placed two beds in wall, after Dutch fashion, for two persons: thirty of these chambers, which are capable of sixty persons. Here is a stately chamber for the fathers of the house, the governors of the house, which are four; another such-like room for the mothers of the house; a fair stately chamber, whereunto they are removed when they fall sick, where they are as well attended as though they were gentlemen. Here is also a curious neat hall, wherein they dine and sup: only such as dwelt here fifteen years can be admitted into this old-man-house.

In this town also a ghuest-house, for sick persons, be they strangers or others, to whom allowed their surgeons and doctors: a very rich, ancient house, which hath much lands and many houses to rent.

Here a wyes-house[1] for poor children, fatherless, whose parents have lived fifteen years in town.

A house of correction, to punish and set to work those that are able and will not work; out of the overplus of whose endeavours, those relieved that are needy and are of no congregation; whereas every congregation takes charge of and relieves their own poor. Here are also five or six old-women-houses, who are furnished with fine chambers and neat gardens.

Here is the fairest and most spacious market-place in the country (save Delphe); a very brave state-house hall, and over the scoute's-court door written in golden letters: "Audi alteram partem." Here a very fair, spacious, neat, long room, wherein are their shambles: all flesh, meat, mutton, veal, pork, and beef, sold by weight; a brave fish-market, the stalls curiously slated, an half-moon roof over the table whereon the fish is laid, beyond which the seller stands always dry; and so may be buyer: it is about sixty yards long, on either side such a roof or cover; in middle a neat and good broad walk.

Here is four churches of public use: the great church, St. Baves;

---

[1] Wees, i. e. orphan.

the Bacchanist[1] church, so called from that side of the town wherein it is seated, which is so called; St. John's church; St. Anne's church. The great church carries the name of the fairest, most spacious, in all Holland.

Here, in the monument, hangs three ships, armed before with iron saws, whereby they cut in pieces iron chains to bar up the haven of the castle Damiata,[2] wherein their lord was retained prisoner; whereby they released the lord of their town and country. The saws were placed in the belly of the ship, which was well followed and seconded by three or four that followed. In recompense of which good service their lord gave them two silver bells, which still hang in the top of their steeple, which I went to see, but would not be hired for them to take the same journey, there are such steep ladders, weak and narrow steps toward the top. Some say they took and found these bells in the town of Damiata.

As we were coming towards Amsterdam port, we saw a man about thirty-six years of age, not great-boned nor large-sized of himself, so stall-fed as that his legs were not able to support and carry his body; he was therefore constrained constantly to keep his bed: his companions, keale-bones[3] and checke-stones[4] to play with children. He is mighty fat on the sides. I never felt horse, nor beast, nor any creature, so thick and fleshy on ribs. He said he did begin to be thus pursle[5] and fat at fifteen years of age. He saith he hath been a prisoner in this manner this ten or twelve years. The lords of the town, at a great assembly, to feast and jovialize it, sent for this man, but his legs were not able to carry him home, so as they were constrained to cause him carried home upon a drag or sleade.[6] His legs in the calf as thick as a child's body, and in the small, as thick as any man's leg (as John Ward's)

---

[1] Baccheness, a district in Haerlem.

[2] This tale is sometimes differently told. It is said that during the siege of Damietta, in the second crusade, a party of Haerlemites constructed a vessel furnished with saws, and therewith cut through a chain which barred the entrance of the harbour, and so opened a way for the besiegers.

[3] *Keale* bones are kayles, kettlepins or ninepins. *Kegler*, Danish.

[4] *Checke* stones are chuck stones, or, as they are sometimes called, *duck* stones.

[5] *Pursle*, for pursy, fat, short-breathed.   [6] Sledge.

in the calf. We took the measure of the body of this monster, and, upon trial, found it did extend itself to compass my brother Rich., and Ralph Brian, and Will. Baylye: it was two yards and an half, wanting half a quarter. When he was thus measured, he sat up in his bed, and was in a thin bease[1] waistcoat.

Here I omitted the curious brass pillars in Harlaim church, which are neatly wrought; they are placed 'twixt the chancel and body of church; they are about forty-six in number: a curious brass border over them wrought in a work.

This city enjoyeth very great privileges, and is the only bridle to curb and prevent the increasing greatness of her neighbour, Amsterdam, who, of late, as in trade and addition of building, so in privileges, have much enlarged themselves: they have of late obtained a charter for a beast-market, which formerly was never there kept, but always at Anchusan.[2] They have recovered all the wind-mills which saw boards from Lardam.[3] They attempted, lately, to have walled Amsterdam strongly about, and for that end they began to make a strong wall towards Harlaim port and that side; but the inhabitants of Harlaim violently opposed themselves against them, and would not suffer them, but constrained them to desist.

Here, in Amsterdam, they have no power to execute any offenders, but are constrained to borrow and make use of the hang-man belonging to Harlaim, whose time they must wait and attend.

Having seen the churches in Amsterdam, I find that Harlaim church is the fairest and most spacious in this land; and then Leyden, Dort, Rotterdam, Amsterdam, Delph, &c. In Harlaim church four brave candlesticks, eight less; the fairest in all land, save four candlesticks in new church in Amsterdam, the greatest that I did ever see, worth fifty pounds at least.

This city is famous for those brave woods and walks belonging unto it, the like whereof not to be found in this province (except Hage). About six of the clock in the evening, entering a neat barge covered, which is a passage-boat, which are to go off at every hour's end, be there never so few passengers. One came with us

---

[1] Baize.   [2] Enckhuysen.   [3] Saerdam.

in this boat this day, and but four passengers in her. - They were twenty-six in number : thirteen from Harlaim, thirteen from Amsterdam, and know their order and turns, who, from five in morning to six at night, are, and do constantly go off at every hour's end. These barges are drawn with an horse in a most straight, curious, pleasant ditch, which was cut out within less than two years ; it was performed at the charge of the states of the towns ; it is said it cost them £20,000 sterling.

It was perfected in six months' time, though a troublesome and tedious work it must needs be, being about nine English miles long, some three or four foot deep, and about three rood broad.

It is said that out of the passage of every boat allowed to repay the money disbursed in this work about seven Dutch shillings.

Every footman passing on this bank 'twixt Harlaim and Amsterdam is to pay two stivers toll; every horseman, four stivers ; half to Harlaim, half to Amsterdam. So also the money paid by the scutes, which is for most part forty stivers ; two stivers for every person carried by scute, and ordinarily they carry twenty passengers ; when I came forty were in scute with me. Paid to the sckipper three stivers for every passenger, who pays in all five stivers ; so as at least every day (save two or three months' frost) they receive back, of the money disbursed, fifty-two guilders a day ; besides divers boats go off extraordinary, and in divers boats are many more than twenty passengers (which will much increase their receipts); and besides two stivers paid by every footman, or four stivers by every horseman ; this equally divided 'twixt Harlaim and Amsterdam, who were at the charge of this ditch ; so as at least this pays back every day six or seven pounds sterling.

Here along this passage are thirty-six stoopes[1] placed at equal distances; they are laid in oil, and figures are placed upon them ; here is likewise begun, by posts and boards nailed to the bottom, to part the way, whereon it is intended the waggons to go, from the way, which is also upon this bank, whereon the horses go

[1] A stoop is properly a vessel holding two quarts; here possibly it means a common cask.

that are to draw the scutes; which, finished, will be a stately work also. In the middle of this passage I observed and took notice of some of their sluices, which being drawn up, they may drown the whole land; and I saw the sea on one hand much higher than the meare below on other hand, and do believe that these were the sluices which were drawn up to drown the country and the enemy at such time as it was besieged; at which time this to be observed, that there came such a violent west wind as did much raise and increase the waters by bringing in the flood, and, after the enemy had raised his siege, the wind turned and was so forceable as it repelled the waters, and laid much of the country dry; for this deliverance a solemn day of thanksgiving held in Leyden every year. These extraordinary duties of thanksgiving and fasting better kept than with us, though their sabbaths much profaned. The prince, the king of Bohemia's son,[1] lost in the other passage over Harleimer Meire to Amsterdam, which, as is said, was principal inducement to cut out this passage. In the way they shewed me a dorpe, called Scloterdike, within an English mile of Amsterdam, wherein dwelt a Dutchwoman, and which house hangs up at this hour the picture of the woman and of her husbands.

This woman had twenty-four husbands; six of them drowned, two of them slain. She died about five years ago. She was a man-like woman. Stephen Offwood, our host, hath seen and known the woman; she died in this town. One of her husbands lived with her seven years, and she had divers children. This day 10 *Junii* I walked out of town to the house where she lived, wherein I saw her picture hanged up: her name was Frische Roomer; it is a tapp-house, and herein I drunk a can of beer.

[1] This was Prince Frederick, the eldest son of Frederick the Count Palatine and Elizabeth, daughter of James I. " Passing over Haerlem Mere, a huge inland slough, in company with his father, who had been at Amsterdam, to look how his bank of money did thrive, and coming (for more frugality) in the common boat, which was o'erset with merchandize, and other passengers, in a thick fog, the vessel turned o'er, and so many perish'd. The Prince Palsgrave sav'd himself by swimming, but the young Prince clinging to the mast, and being entangled among the tackling, was half drowned and half frozen to death.—*Howell's Letters*, sect. iv. lett. 10.

One thing memorable in the discourse of Harlaim omitted, that here they have a spacious coney-gree[1] which reacheth all along the sea-coast. Here during their kermes, which is their fair, and is now kept, every man privileged to kill with dogs, and carry away whatsoever he can kill. It is said here are upon these downs deer, which belong to the States, and no man suffered to kill them.

Arriving at AMSTERDAM 10 *Junii* about nine hour, we passed Harleimer Port and came into a fair street, wherein of late swarmed the most impudent whores I have heard of, who would if they saw a stranger, come into the middle of the street unto him, pull him by the coat, and invite him unto their house. One of the burgo-maisters coming through this street in a stranger's habit, was thus invited and assaulted, whereupon this street, which is above a quarter of an English mile long, which was stored with these hus-wifes, was about three or four months ago something purged; the scoute apprehended and banished about one hundred of them, the States paid the rent of their houses.

Junii 11.—We saw their Exchange, which, were it square, the walk underneath would resemble that of our Exchange in London,[2] but it is something narrower in the ends; it is not so stately and richly adorned in respect of the ornaments and pictures there, whereof this is naked overhead, where is their Exchange, which doth in proportion and form resemble ours, only the wares therein to be sold are but baubles and trifles in comparison of the old Exchange, London; the walk below and the room over-head is not square, but the ends shorter than the sides about a rood or two.

---

[1] *Coney-greys*, or *greeves*, rabbit burrows.—*Randall Holmes*, bk. ii ch. 9, p. 187.

[2] The original Exchange was built by Sir Thomas Gresham; the foundation was laid June 7, 1566 : it was completed Nov. 1567, and called the Bourse. This building was destroyed in the great fire; it was rebuilt, and opened with great ceremony Sept. 28, 1669.

In 1570, Queen Elizabeth went in great state from her palace at Somerset House to make Sir Thomas a visit at his own house. After dinner she went to the Bourse, visited every part, and then, by sound of trumpet, dignified it with the title of the Royal Exchange. All the upper part was filled then, and even to this century, with shops.

This is greatest and most flourishing city in this province, which
for trade is not inferior unto many in the world.

Tuesday 11 *Junii.*—We went into the house of Yantunus, who
hath been professor in Leyden of the Arabic language—a lusty old
man, whose beard reacheth his girdle. In this house he hath
erected a most curious water-work at an infinite charge; no room
without some rare invention for pleasure and delight; none for
lodging almost, but also contrived and furnished with several in-
ventions, and those all various to affect the outward sense, and
draw on ghuests to apply there. He is an Anabaptist, but a man
of most strange invention. This most rare invention, this water-
work, is erected in the top of his house, which is six stories high,
where having heard all sorts of music upon strings, upon wind-
instruments, and upon an instrument which did in a pleasant tune
and harmony make the bells to sound, playing thereon as you do
upon virginalls. Here we had three great glasses of their muddy
stuff, for which we paid (and for a dish of almonds and raisins) six
Dutch shillings. After this we were taken into a loft or gallery
in the same room: over against us stood upon a convenient place,
for that end prepared, the proportion of a woman milking a cow,
who seemed to move with her hand, and milked until the vessel,
whereinto the water distilled or was milked, ran over. Here was
another woman's proportion, as it were carrying away a vessel upon
her head, which, being filled with water, did also overflow. Afterwards here was an ox which p—— strongly, men tending the cow
and ox, as also digging; on the other side a bull which roared, a
cow and her calf which lowed, a cock stood overhead which crowed,
but hoarsely; we were then brought down to the water-work,
where was a ball tossed and danced two yards high by the strength
and force of the water-spout; proportion of the sun in water, but
before, the proportion of a globe, then of the sun, of the half-moon,
of a star much to the life, of a crown which was danced one yard
and dim high; two birds carried up, descended soaring; two boys

---

¹ Form or figure.

sat opposite one to the other about three yards distant, which ——————————— p—— stoutly one at the other, one upon the other; a woman out of whose breast water sprung; divers beasts placed upon the rails round about whereon we leaned, out of all whose mouths water strongly sprung, and was carried two or three yards: and in the mid, out of the very top of the work, the water did spring directly upwards three yards: in this work did the water issue at least in forty or fifty places. A lively representation of the five wise and five foolish virgins; the one having oil plentifully, the other wanting: the first received, the second repulsed. Adam and Eve, and the frogs and toads, which strongly spit out their venom; overhead a flat roof, on which placed a turret, to which you ascend by stairs made of iron-bars in a narrow compass, and so walk to a little cabin covered overhead, open on all sides, that the wind may not have over much power over it; and by a wooden ladder you ascend to the top of this also. Here is a commanding prospect twelve yards higher than the roof; this supported by four pillars, strengthened with some bars of iron.

June 12.—After we had dined with Mr. Pageatt,[1] where we had a neat dinner and strawberries, longest that I have seen, we went to a house called Dole-hoofe,[2] where we saw the pictures made in wax most livelyly of the Infanta standing, with her dwarf attending; 2. Henric the Fourth, Bourbon, King of France, and his Queen; 4. Gustavus Adolphus, the last King of Sweden, and his Queen, and the young Queen of Sweden, their daughter;[3] 8.[4] William, Prince of Orange,[5] in a furred and almost like alder-

---

[1] Probably the author of " A Defence of Church Government, exercised in Presbyterial, Classical, and Synodall Assemblies, &c. By John Paget, late able and faithful Pastor of the Reformed English Church in Amsterdam," 1641. To which was " prefixed an Advertisement to the Parliament, with some Animadversions on the Cheshire Remonstrance against Presbytery, by T. P." *i. e.* Mr. Tho. Paget, a minister in the diocese of Chester, who was prosecuted for nonconformity, and fled to Holland about the year 1621, where he probably died, but the time of his death is not known.—*Book's Lives of the Puritans.*

[2] Doole-house, vid. pp. 11, 13.   [3] The celebrated Christina.

[4] These numbers as in MS.   [5] William I, Prince of Orange, murdered July 1584.

man's gown, and a little round ruff about his neck; 9. Grave
Maurice;[1] 10. Prince Henry,[2] now Prince of Orange, his Princess,
Count Solmes[3] his sister, their son,[4] about seven or eight years of
age, an English nurse, and a new-born daughter, a little daughter
dead, laid in a cradle at her feet, and a page. Here also the picture in wax of the Maid of Meure,[5] who is reported to have lived
fifteen years without meat: all these so much to the life, as they
seem living as they sit. Here also was showed a work going upon
wheels, showing men in all postures, some mowing, some threshing,
some sawing, blowing the bellows, &c. Another show, representing the martyrdom of all the Apostles, some beheaded, some hanged
up by heels, some sawed to death, others crucified, &c. Here a
curious maze. Thence we went to another Dole-hoofe, where we
saw such another water-work as the day before, only it was on the
ground, and those who stood within a circle, and near unto the

[1] Grave Maurice, son of the above William I.

[2] Henry, brother and successor of Maurice. Maurice, just before his death in 1626,
charged Prince Henry to marry the Count of Solms' daughter, attending the queen of
Bohemia, whom he had long courted.—*Howell's Letters*, sect. iv. letter 15.

[3] This Count of Solms was son of John Albert, who in 1615 commanded a portion
of the army of the Prince of Orange, with which he relieved Brunswick, at that time
besieged by its own prince, with whom it had seriously quarrelled. He was grand-
master of the household of Frederic, king of Bohemia, to whose fortunes he adhered,
and whom he accompanied to the Hague, where he died about the year 1623. Grave
Maurice, a short time before his death, advised his brother Henry Frederick, his chief
heir, to marry Amelia, daughter to the Count de Solmes, who was then in Holland
with the Queen of Bohemia, and whose beauty and good carriage were accompanied
with a great deal of modesty and prudence.— *Vanloon*, vol. ii. pp. 95, 157; *Maurier's
Lives of Princes of Orange*.

[4] William, born 1626, died 1650, married the Princess Mary, daughter of Charles I;
was father of William III.

[5] It is probable that Meure is written by mistake for Bern, and that the following
statement relates to the young maid figured in that work.

"Here in the canton of Beerne, neere to Vrbs, wee went and saw a young woman,
who then had nigther cate, nor drunke, nor yet excremented for thirteene yeares,
being truly qualified by her parents, friends, and physicians, and other visitors. She
was alwayes bed-fast, and so extenuated, that her anatomised body carryed nought
but sinew, skin, and bones, yet was she alwayes mindeful of God. And the yeare after
this time, her body returned agayne to the naturall vigour, in appetite and all things;
and married a husband, bearing two children, dyed in the fifth yeare thereafter."—
Lithgow's Travels, ed. 1632, part viii. p. 347.

rails, were well washed: a woman well washed under her clothes once or twice. Here a show of ships sailing, which are moved by water; Actæon, turned into a hart, with horns, pursued by his hounds, Diana following in revenge. Here the show of the Pope going in procession, carried by his bishops, attended by cardinals, princes, abbots, monks, friars, and the devil following after them: here mass sung, the devil roars.

Yesterday, we bought four-score painted stones for one chimney; these postures of foot-men for the back of the chimney: care to be taken these to be placed half on one side of the hob, half on the other; half faces one way on the one side, and so the other side: drummers and officers to be placed in most eminent places. Horsemen's postures for an hearth: fifty to be placed with as much care and in same manner as the other. All these painted stones to be laid in water, until they be satisfied, before they be laid in sand in the hearth, or set on the back of chimney in lime and hair: they must be curiously placed, and in order disposed. For another hearth, fifty flowers; for another hearth, fifty birds. The horsemen and footmen cost nine gilders an hundred; the birds and flowers cost four gilders an hundred. I bought, this 12 *Junii*, the pictures of the Hen and Chickens, the Banquet, the Queen of Bohemia's picture, the Prince of Orange his picture ; all these four cost twenty gilders. The pictures of Dives and Lazarus, two of them, whereof one for Sr. Geo. Boothe;[1] Joseph standing before Pharaoh, and Christ's Ascension, for Sr. G. B.; these four cost twenty-six gilders: all eight together cost forty-six gilders. Two other pictures of Jeptah; the greater horseman for myself, the less for Sr. G. B.; both of one and the same price, cost eighteen gilders. Two postures of a man and woman, in plaister of Paris, the appurtenances at foot and over head, three pieces on either side: they cost eleven gilders; two chests, two gilders: these will take any gilding or colour in oil, and, I have observed, the foot coloured black; the mantle-trees unto all these wood lined with neat sieleing:[2] the mantle-trees all of wood. If any part of the corners

---

[1] Sir W. Brereton married Susan, the fourth daughter of Sir Geo. Booth of Dunham Massey, in Cheshire.   [2] Fine mortar, such as is used for ceilings.

break out, there is plaister of Paris powder, which is to be made as
it were pap, and instantly with point of a knife laid on : let it dry,
and when it is dry, form it and scrape it even with a chisel or sharp
knife.   To cleanse it and even it, use a piece of dog-fish's skin, or
for want thereof, hair-cloth.   The pictures of the seven Roman
Emperours, and three other pieces of the Goddesses, being in
plaister of Paris work, cost two gilders.   Hereof I had two dozen.

Bought eight gilt nobs, fair ones, cost six gilders ; eight painted
fair ones, cost forty-two gilders ; other four, less, about seven or
eight stivers a-piece ; six, less about five stivers a-piece.

The greater alabaster picture, five Dutch shillings ; the less cost
three shillings Dutch.   Wm. Daviseon offered to furnish me with a
couple of these perspectives, which shew the new-found motion of
the stars about Jupiter ; the price sixty gilders for both.

I agreed this day with Willm. Wrigtington, the Hull shipper,
to carry all my goods to Hull, and two servants, for which I was
to give him one pound ten shillings, whereof I gave him, in earnest,
a rix-dollar.

This day, being *Saturday, Junii* 14, is observed as the Jews'
Sabbath, who are about three hundred families seated in this town,
most Portugals.   A street they have called the Jews' street : they
have three synagogues here.   I was this day at their synagogue, from
nine to half twelve, then they concluded ; return at three, continue
until evening.   They have fifteen whom they call their Parnassus :[1]
these are the governors and judges.   They have all white mantles
of a kind of linen, but short : these they wear over their hats,
which they never put off during all their being in church.   They
have three sorts which perform their Divine Ordinances, their Levitical rites and ceremonies : the sons of Aaron, who represented the
priests, who carried their Alchoran, the five books of Moses, covered
with a cloth of gold, and whereon were divers little bells pendant,
placed in the form of a crown, which was fetched out of a little
cabinet ; this represents their tabernacle : these sons of Aaron are
their predicants, and also read the books of Moses ; the Levites sing

[1] Parnas, or Parnasim, a chief council amongst the Jews, especially of the Portu-
guese section.

the reading psalms of David in a tune; and the Parnassuses appoint of the Israelites such to read as they think fit. The sons of Aaron and Levites have longer white robes than the rest. Here in this congregation, no good order, no great zeal and devotion here appearing; much time spent in singing and in talking. We went hence to an Englishman and his wife, lately turned Jew, as is said, merely to enrich themselves: very obstinate and ignorant both. He is a merchant of tobacco. 'Tis said his wife, being an handsome woman, was a courtezan in London. They deny all the New Testament. Their men most black, full of hair, and insatiably given unto women: their wives restrained and made prisoners; their widows distinguished from all other women Jews by white veils hanging to their backs. They will not bury amongst the Gentiles, but have purchased unto themselves a peculiar burial-place, a field on the water-side, some three or four English miles from the town, wherein are erected their sepulchres; and when they remove, they remove also their bones thence away with them. Within this twenty years, they buried at Alchmoare; and when they changed their burial-place, their bones all were removed. This burial-place, at large described in the first leaf of the other book,[1] is placed by the side of the channel or water-passage leading from Amsterdam to Utrecht.

Junii 14.—I saw a late erected ox-market, without doors, wherein nine double stalls without doors; on both sides, one hundred yards long; a spacious paved walk behind them, and a walk railed out before them.

Another curious house slated, wherein places prepared to give the oxen meat; cratches and mangers both, a curious walk betwixt them dry; an open walk paved neatly behind them; nine also of these partitions, one hundred yards long a-piece.

Two fairs yearly at Luke-tide[2] and in April: they last three weeks or a month. Hither sent abundance of beasts out of Denmark and Sweden; paid for binding or tying up every beast, six stivers; and for excise paid to the town, the seventh part of the price for

---

[1] This other book, here referred to, is not now known to exist.
[2] The middle of October : St. Luke's day, Oct. 13.

every beast, sheep, hog, or calves, bought or eaten : the buyer pays
one-half, the seller the other half.

Excellent windmills to saw boards, placed near a navigable ditch ;
the windmill wherein I was, four stories high ; herein these, being
double mills, will employ sixteen saws at least, and will cut
through, will saw, a piece of timber of twenty yards long in an
hour. The labour and iron-work hereof was said by a wheelwright
would cost fourteen hundred gilders, besides wood and those
materials.

I viewed a spacious piece of ground (which was about three years
ago water, six or seven foot deep, called Deimer Meare), about four
English miles in compass, which was drained in this manner. First,
they made a strong bank forty foot broad, upon firm land round about
it, upon which firm land placed three windmills to throw out the
water on either side ; six in all ; which mills are placed in the lowest
part of the land, so as all the water may fall unto them ; ditches
and trenches made to receive the water, which cast out the water so
plentifully, as in one summer it was laid dry. By help also of two
overcross ditches, which receive all the water, and convey it unto
these windmills, which are spacious and neat dwelling-houses ; only
the roof of them is to turn with the wind, the lower part immovable.

This land the first year sowed with rapes, to settle it ; the
second year built upon and planted, with curious orchards and
gardens. We saw the house of Mr. Jacob Paw, a rich merchant,
which shows bravely, and richly, and sumptuously, and yet most
slight, all composed of boards painted in curious works in oil-colours,
the boards not laid cross, but set upon the end, and neatly jointed
one into the other. Within we found divers mantle-trees of wood,
cut in the form and proportion of marble mantle-trees, and painted
in mantle-colours ; this most ordinary, and with such pictures of
plaister of Paris work as I bought. Here a long and neat orchard
planted with trees in order. Here a curious and neat hen-house ; and
house for tame coneys : his kitchen, dining-room, and houses of office,
on one side of the court, a distinct pile from the other, which is only
a house for pleasure, delight, and lodging ; and to answer this other
pile wherein are houses of office, another is built on the other side of

court opposite unto this; (both of boards, and but slight and laid in oil): in this house the hen-house, coney-house, stable, coach-house, &c.

Sunday, Junii 15.—I was at English church, a long narrow edifice, which lately belonged unto a nunnery there. Here I received the sacrament; all receivers coming up and sitting at a long table whilst they received; all the men first successively, and then the women, and when they have received, return to their places. When the sacrament of baptism is administered, no god-fathers required nor admitted, only the parents of the child are to answer to these three questions: 1. Whether they conceive their child born in original sin, and to stand in need of Christ a Re-deemer; 2. It is demanded whether they believe the doctrine of the Old and New Testament to be the word of God, and that the religion professed in these reformed churches (*id est*, whereof he is a member) is grounded upon the word of God. 3. It's required that he should employ his best endeavours to train up his child in this faith; to all which an affirmative answer being given, the child is baptized without any ceremony, in name of Father, Son, and Holy Ghost, &c. Marriage likewise solemnized by the English and Dutch reformed churches, without the use of the ring or any ceremony, only an admonition precedes, directing how these married persons should demean themselves each to other, and for that end those scriptures read hereunto most pertinent; as also a large discourse precedes, touching the institution of this sacred ordinance, and those texts hereunto pertinent also read. The mar-riage of cousin-germans absolutely and generally disallowed of, and prohibited in all these churches, and by all sects and religions here.

Sermon being ended, in afternoon, we went to the Lutheran church, which is the neatest church, one of them, that I have seen in this land. It's a new church, and built after a new fashion; the pulpit placed in middle of the great aisle, and with greatest advan-tage for the hearers. Here is the greatest assembly in the town; and in this church two fair spacious vaults or galleries, one above the other, which go round about the church, save in one end, wherein placed the greatest. I admired to find no pictures in their

windows, and enquiring into their opinions, I could not discover
any difference at all twixt our church and theirs in matter of
religion, save only in matter of consubstantiation; for the greater
number of them will not allow of the use of images in any sense,
the rest only for ornament, not for adoration: herein I was the
rather confirmed because no images at all extant in their church
and windows. Here baptized after sermon fourteen children, the
water not sprinkled upon their faces, but the predicant doth pull
back the cloth and dressing upon the head, so as all the skull of
child's head is bare, and holding the face downward, he is sufficiently prodigal of water, pouring divers handfuls upon child's
head, and holding his hand upon child's head, rubbing the same
during all the time that he is pronouncing the words of baptism,
which as I conceived were equivalent to these of ours: "I baptize
thee in name of Father, Son," &c., using as long a speech whilst he
held the child in his arms, as our ministers do. I observed diligently, and he used not the sign of cross, which all the Dutch
churches reject. Here were no godfathers; those that brought
and carried the children gave the name unto the predicant, and all
these were women that held and brought the children. Immediately after these baptized, succeeded a couple to be married, who
used the ring, and it was as long in solemnizing as our marriages,
but I saw no other ceremony used but the ring and joining hands;
after this concluded, all the bride's kindred, friends and acquaintance
that are present, or meet with her, kiss her, even in the church,
where groom leaves her, and her own friends bring her near his
house, where he meets her, salutes her, and receives her. Amongst
the Lutherans I observed that they bowed always at the name of
Jesus, so often as it was used in the solemnity of their marriage,
which was very often.

These sects allowed which have churches. Protestants, Dutch,
English, French, have churches; Lutherans, Arminians, Brownists, have also their churches; and the Anabaptists, whereof 'tis
said are above thirty several sects, have their churches; the Brownists divided, and differing amongst themselves; Mr. Canne being
the pastor of one company, and one Greenwood, an old man, a

tradesman, who sells stockings in Exchange; I saw him there; he is the leader of another company. The Jews have three synagogues here, but, methinks, their ceremonies much differ and degenerate from those instituted in the Levitical law. The Papists, Arians, Socinians, and Famielists of Love, have also their public meetings in houses turned into churches, and that without control; but these swarm not so much as rest.

The customs and excise here very great, but I could never attain to an exact knowledge thereof, though I applied myself to enquire; but this I heard, that this town affords as great revenues, to maintain the wars to the States, as four provinces—Zeland, Utrech, Over-Isell, and Friseland. A mighty revenue derives out of the excise paid for beer and wine by tap-houses and wine-sellers: for every barrel of beer they pay seven gilders and dim. excise, and for every barrel of English beer, Bremen beer, and Rostacher beer, and spruce beer received into their houses, they pay ten gilders a barrel. The burgers and burgomaisters pay for small beer two gilders, and one stiver excise; and for strong beer, fifty-six stivers. For every Winchester measure of rye ground at the mill, five stivers; and for wheat, ten stivers. For all flesh, the seventh penny, as also for fish about the same proportion; and whatsoever is here spent, they must pay excise for: but this encouragement here given to strangers and merchants, that what goods they bring hither and hence export to other countries are excise free (except tobacco); or, if the merchants bring any commodities and sell them in the town, they pay no excise, but the buyer pays excise.

An infinite number of ships not to be numbered lie here. Last week, five hundred sail of ships went out of the Tarcle[1] upon one day. From this town to every town in this province a daily passage-boat mart-ship; for Zeland twice a week; for Over-Isell, Utrecht, or Friseland, Gronneing[2] and Zutphen and Gilderland, every day; and although this be a most flourishing city, which maintains as great a trade as any city in Christendom, yet most inconveniently seated in many respects, the air so corrupt and unwholesome,

[1] Texel. [2] Groningen.

especially in winter-time, when most part of the country round
about overflowed. Here no fresh-water, no water to brew withal,
but what is fetched from Weesoppe,[1] six English miles distant.
Hence they have much beer, as also from Rotterdam, Harlaim,
Delph, and Utrech: no water to wash withal but rain-water preserved in rain-bags;[2] little fire to be afforded in this country, except
turf: for every hundred baskets (every basket containing about
three bushel) the excise paid is six gilders: excise paid also for
milk, butter, cheese, cherries, and all fruit and roots. The most of
the wood burnt brought out of Denmark, Norway, which is here
used: the coals come from Newcastle, for which the excise paid is
six gilders for a chaldron. And although here they now build
most glorious and spacious houses, yet it must needs be at a most
excessive charge, as not only wanting all materials within themselves, no timber nor stone in the land, no brick burnt near them,
but they are constrained to undergo a great addition to these
charges in making firm and secure foundations in this boggy,
mareish soil. They are enforced to drive trees to the head, which
are fourteen or sixteen yards long, a yard distant round about the
ground whereupon is intended the house to be built; upon the
heads of these trees placed planks, whereupon the walls and foundation are erected; this are forced into the ground by a great
heavy piece of wood, which is drawn up in a frame for this end
contrived, and the weight thereof falling upon the tree drives into
the ground. This is the work of no less than thirty or forty men,
who will in half an hour drive to the certain one of these long
trees. Here mighty expensive in their buildings, especially in
their floors; sometimes they will bestow seven hundred or eight
hundred gilders upon one floor.

One thing I omitted touching the placing of my posts,[3] which
are made of plaister of Paris: they are to be placed to the wall,
and set straight by a plummet of lead, and with good store of white
lime to be joined to the wall, and all the three pieces to be one
joined to another, by being set in lime and hair; no weight to be

---

[1] Weesp.   [2] Rain bags, backs, large tubs or vats.
[3] Postures he calls them elsewhere. See pp. 58, 59.

laid upon them, nor they must not attempt to make any impression in them to fasten them: this only to be observed, that a mantle-tree to be placed upon the head of these posts, which is to be wood, and is here used to be of slight pieces of timber; they go out into the room about three-quarters of a yard, and are faced with some neat sieleing; underneath the end of the mantle-tree placed a board, under which board, and twixt which and the head of the post, that part next unto the chimney-wall, is placed a wedge twixt the board and head of the post, which doth hold fast together all the pieces of the post: some of these covers in wood which are framed like mantle-trees of marble, and are laid in marble colours in oil, and these in divers works in Jacob Paw's new house in Die-meere.[1]

The names of the churches in this town: the Dutch churches, 1. The old church; 2. The new church, a dainty fine thing, wherein four great pendant candlesticks of brass, and eight lesser fair candlesticks; 3. The Southern church, a neat church erected within thirty years; in the windows of this church the pictures of the arms of the companies of every trade. 4. The Heylighe-stee,[2] this most ancient, save the two former; herein preach the High-Dutch. 5. The Northern church, alias Crucekerk, built in form of a cross, and in mid round. 6. The Western church, the neatest church of all, lately finished; it was thought and was so purposed that here should be made the highest steeple in town, if the foundation will bear and sustain it. 6. Here is another in a remote place called Odulph's-Capple;[3] herein they preach once every week. 7. Here allowed by the state one French church. 8. One English church; these two churches prepared by the state, and the ministers maintained by them: allowed unto Mr. Pageatt 1100 gilders, £110 sterling per annum. 9. The Lutherans have a fair church lately built, this only connived at, but a mighty congregation, and a capacious church. 10. The Arminians' church, a dainty fine thing, connived at, though not so public as the Lutherans, nor so great a congregation; this built on the back-side.

---

[1] Diemermeer.   [2] Heilige Stede.   [3] St. Olof's chapel.

11. The Jews have three synagogues connived at; one of them I saw, a neat place, an upper room. 12. The Anabaptists have three meeting-places, which are connived at, these resembling barns, so they term them: amongst these Anabaptists, some Arians, some Socinians; of these Anabaptists 'tis said there are thirty-three sorts. 13. Here are some few Familists of Love, which have a meeting-place. The Papists have not any constant meeting-places known; these most restrained, yet they are connived at, and meet often in great men's houses.

In this city a most curious dainty Corn Market, square on three sides, covered neatly about three yards wide, made arch-wise, and painted overhead; a dainty fine walk when it is empty, and in the middle a capacious place to set corn in. A curious fish-market, and two fair houses wherein the flesh-market is kept; shambles on both sides, and a fair clean walk in middle; these places made clean once or twice a day.

The fairest and most curious streets in this city: the Heres Graff, bravest buildings herein, only on one side; the Cæsars Graffe, this most uniform graffe, built alike on both sides, not so stately buildings as the Heres Graffe; the Princes graffe; the Single. In the middle of these streets fair, broad, navigable channels, but no ships carrying sail here admitted to come in; and trees that bear a good shadow placed close by the water-side, and in so good order as all day long on one side the street you may walk in shade. Within twenty or thirty years this town has much enlarged, and made as large again as before; then were added these fairest graffs, the Heres, Cæsars, Single, Princes Graff, and divers others, which are the fairest in all the town. Here a stately stone bridge, made with iron rails, whose foundation stands not upon the ground, but upon piles of wood; it consisteth of eight arches; three iron-rails placed one above another, supported by iron posts fastened into the stone; this I conceive to be for lightness.

Memorand.—Received from Mr. Bayneham about 4 Junü, as appears by a note under his own hand. . . .

I say four hundred gilders　　.　　　.　　　　400 gilders

Received by Raph Brian of Mr. Bayneham 5 June one hundred gilders

Received by John Ward 16 June from Mr. Bayneham two hundred gilders

Hereof lent unto my brother Rich. at Delph . . £5 0 0

To Mr. Davenport of Woodford's son . . . 2 10 0

To my brother at Amsterd. 1 10 0

Parcels of goods committed to the custody of Will. Wrightington of Hull: Six baskets of stones for floors to be placed three black ones for one white; the points to be placed towards the door, three black ones for one white. There are ninety white stones; black ones two hundred and seventy, which cost, the black ones, 15 gilders an hundred. For seventy-five white marble stones and two hundred and twenty-five black ones I was to pay 70 gilders, and so proportionably for the rest. To make these smooth or clean, a Gothland stone herewith sent, to be used to take out any stain or spot. These disposed of into six baskets. In one basket, sixty-six black stones; in two, fifty white stones; in the third, forty white stones, fourteen black; in the fourth high basket, seventy-four black; in the fifth, fifty black stones; in the sixth, there are sixty-six black stones; the less of these stones, rubbed with water, is to take out a stain or spot, the greater to make them smooth and even. Two great chests, wherein two pictures, poasts of plaister of Paris, with all the appurtenances. One basket, wherein painted stones for hearths. One great wooden box, wherein ten pictures. Two gammons of Westphalia bacon loose. One coy-dog. One pair of turtle-doves and an half, one trunk, one great white box, hemp-seed and French water to be given them, the powder of freestone to be given them in their cage to cleanse their maws. The three white turtle-doves cost 4 gilder 10 stivers with cage. The two dun ones cost 3 gilders. A dainty tansy of gooseberries[1] at Geor. Huitts, made by Mris. Cave.

[1] The dainty reader will, we hope, thank us for discovering the following receipt for a tansy of gooseberries.

" Take a quart of green gooseberries, top and tail them, and boil them in clarified butter in your frying-pan till they are enough done; then pour into them the yolks of

Touching the present condition of the state of Holland, observe that by reason of the two late expensive and chargeable sieges of Buss,[1] and especially Maestricht, these states are much indebted; nevertheless they maintain at sea and land one hundred thousand men. Eighty sail of ships, men of war, to guard the seas, some say many more; the watchman on Dunkirk steeple told us that he numbered a hundred and twenty States' men of war pass by that haven, many whereof we saw lying in that road at anchor, touching the further particulars whereof, quære the observations touching Dunkirk, fol. 90, in the other book. Eighty sail of less ships, men of war, to guard the rivers of the Maze, the Wall, the Isell, the Tarcell,[2] the Skell,[3] and the drowned lands in Holland, Zeland, and Brabant; divers of these we saw and took notice of. Twixt Dort and Williamsteed,[4] and not far from the Teele, where we lodged all night, we saw one of their little gallies, which was rowed with oars (being slaves sentenced to the gallies) in calm weather.

Their poorest towns supported by placing garrisons in them; the country maintained by soldiers, who spend twice so much as the States allow them. No man persecuted for religion, nor scoffed at, be he never [so] zealous.

a dozen or fifteen eggs, being well beaten, with half a pint of cream, and a suitable quantity of sugar; when it is baked enough, strew over it rose water and sugar, or sack and sugar."—*Middleton's Five Hundred New Receipts*, 8vo. 1734.

[1] Bois-le-duc. [2] Texel. [3] Scheld. [4] Willemstad.

THE SECOND YEAR'S TRAVEL THROUGH SCOTLAND AND IRELAND.

1635.

Junii 11.—WE came from Handf.[1] and took horse about eight in the morning, and came to WAKEFIELD about seven. We baited at Bostockes at Woodhead,[2] where we paid two-pence a pint for ale, and 3*s*. 8*d*. for victuals; and at Wakefield at the Bull, where we lodged, we paid 5*s*. for supper and breakfast; it is an honest and excellent house. Here next morning I gave my bay mare garlic and butter for her cold, but it wrought nothing with her, nor did the drench, which I usually give, which I gave her at Yorke next morning. But by the way I observed a coney-warren walled about with stone, containing about one or two acres of land, and not far from Yorke I went about half a mile out of the way to take a view of Bishopps-thorpe, the Archbishop's palace, which is about a mile or two distant from Yorke, placed sweetly upon the bank-side of the river Owes.[2] It is the poorest and least capacious house which I have found in England belonging to any bishoprick, a very little poor hall, and no fair rooms in the whole house. In the chapel I observed the table representing the altar placed in the lower end of the chapel; a stone building which seems to have

---

[1] Handford, the residence of Sir W. Brereton, between Wilmslow and Cheadle.

[2] Woodhead is a very small village seven miles from Mottram Longdendale in Cheshire, "a place well known," says Aikin, "to the weary travellers who have crossed the hills above in their way from Yorkshire. It consists of three public and a few private houses." "The public-houses depend upon travellers, few of whom pass without calling, and, indeed, it would be imprudent for them to neglect feeding their horses there, as they have no other opportunity of doing it for a considerable distance, especially on ascending to Brentland edge, which lies on the way to Wakefield."

[3] Ouse.

been an old chapel converted into a dove-house, which hath two tunnels. The church, which is the parish church called Bishopsthorpe church, is the least and poorest church I have met withal in England; here is only a curate maintained to say service. The bishop's cellar here well furnished with thirty-two hogsheads of good strong beer, and eight pipes of the same; we tasted of it.[1]

12.—We lodged on Friday at Msis. Keyes in Cunnie-street in YORKE, where we had excellent entertainment, and very reasonable, and next morning, 13, taking another view of the Minster and Chapter-house, I observed the round roof hereof (for which it is most famous) to be framed of wood and boards painted. In the chapel, wherein the bishop is installed, sitting in St. Peter's chair, which is an old, little, decayed chair, and famous for nothing but the antiquity thereof, there was a decayed monument for St. William,[2] the residue of whose bones were taken by the sexton, 1633, and laid carefully up, and this, as he said, was done by the king's special command; the man shewed us a rich gilt basin and ewer, and two fair bowls with plates to cover them gilt; these made use of when the sacrament of the Lord's supper is administered, and as he said they cost the king £300 or £400. Here is a draw-well, called St. Peter's well, which the sexton much magnified.

A very stately organ lately erected in the minster-quire, under which is written : " Benedictus Deus Patrum nostrûm, qui dedit in corde regis ut adornaret domum suam."

On the north or north-east side of this minster, seated Sir

---

[1] This account of Bishopsthorpe is not now correct. Considerable alterations and improvements were made by Archbishops Dawes and Gilbert, but these were effected to the greatest extent by Abp. Drummond, between the years 1763 and 1769, and " the whole palatial structure and its dependencies are, in their present state, well adapted to those purposes of dignified hospitality which are incumbent on the Primate of England." Abp. Drummond restored the archiepiscopal chapel ; and at his instigation, and chiefly at his expense, the parochial church of Bishopsthorpe was rebuilt.—*Storer's Cathedrals.*

[2] William, consecrated 1144 ; deprived 1147 ; restored 1153. A man of great piety, canonized one hundred and twenty years after his death (June 4, 1154), when his bones were removed to the nave of the cathedral.

Arthur Ingram's[1] house, and brave garden, whereof not a third part furnished with flowers, but disposed into little beds, whereon placed statues; the beds all grass; very fair, high, spacious walls round about this garden, and large fair trees, but nothing well furnished with fruit. Here I observed a sloping border, a full yard high, placed to the trees, which hath brought forth roots out of the lower part of the body of the tree; this border is kept green, but the gardener conceives it no advantage to the trees, which are now cut and dubbed, but the gardener dislikes that course. To keep in order and to weed, and maintain this garden; another spacious orchard wherein are many walks; and to keep a fair stately walk upon the city walls, which do bound and compass this orchard; to tend and dispose of his fish, to keep which he hath divers fish-ponds in this ground; and to breed and bring up young pheasants, there is only allowed him per annum; and Sir Arthur to be at no more charge. The pheasants are bred in this manner; when the pheasant hens begin to lay, their eggs are taken from them, kept in bran, and set and hatched under an hen, fed with pisimers, and kept in an house. Four cisterns here are made of brick, about a yard deep and square, to keep pikes, breames, tench, and carp; water is pumped into these, but I do not expect these to succeed well; they are placed in an open house walled, but the roof sufficiently open, and yet under lock and key. This gardener conceives that mingling muck with soil, and placing it to the tree roots, is very good, but not muck alone.

Monday, Junii 5.—I went to see S. J. Hob,[2] with whom I had

[1] Sir Arthur Ingram, of Temple Newsom, Co. York, high-sheriff of the county 1630, father of Henry, first Viscount Irvine, died 1655.

[2] It is not improbable that the person here intended was Sir John Hotham, who with other northern gentlemen, were most angry with the Earl of Strafford.—*Clarendon*, book iii. p. 188.

He had received some disobligation from the Earl, and continued the invective against him, which was commenced by Pym in Parliament in the debate upon his impeachment, mentioning many particulars of his imperious carriage.—p. 173.

The Earl's quarrel with the gentlemen of Yorkshire seems to have been caused by his succeeding Sir John Hotham as Custos Rotulorum in 1615.

much discourse circa quend. nob, whom he had found a most dangerous man[1] to discourse with in private, and therefore this was
always his answer, when his opinion or advice was required, that
he would consider of it, and return his answer in writing; some
things charged and fathered upon him which he never spoke; instance given of a most dishonest practice in P. W. unto whom was
delivered in Channell-row-house[2] a great book of two sheets of parchment subscribed by W. D.,[3] wherein were feoffees in trust, Comes
Sarisburiens.[4] Sir Gualter Cope and others. A fine there is still
extant leading to this book, which he finding, repaired presently ad
Com. Sarisb.,[5] and said unto him: " You and some others are
feoffees for such an estate, enquire, 1 beseech you, into your father's
evidence;" whereupon search being made by him, he found the
book, and delivered it unto him, whereby W. Comes D.[5] conveys
over lands and goods ejus Comitis, reserving only Bidst[6] and £1000
per annum. In this, provisio facta per Dom. R. S. this book delivered
in loco predicto to P. W., with this charge and command; that
the same should be most carefully kept and laid up against his
coming that summer ad L.,[7] where was then D. de T.[8] This was
received by P. W., and it was promised; but at his coming ad L.,
and that he was desired to peruse the evidence in Eagl. Tow. So

[1] This certain noble person and dangerous man was probably Sir Thomas Wentworth, afterwards spoken of as P. W., or President Wentworth; he was made President of the Council in the north of England in Mich. Term. 1628, Deputy of Ireland
1631, afterwards Lord-Lieutenant of Ireland and Earl of Strafford.

[2] Channel, or as it is now called, Canon-row, Westminster. In this row was the
residence of William, Earl of Derby.—*Pennant's London.*

[3] William, sixth Earl of Derby, who succeeded his brother in the earldom in 1594,
and died in 1642. He married Elizabeth, daughter of the Earl of Oxford, and niece
to Robert, Earl of Salisbury.

[4] The Earl of Salisbury was the celebrated Sir Robert Cecil, who was attended upon
his death-bed by his friend and co-trustee Sir Walter Cope.

[5] William, second Earl of Salisbury.

[6] Bidston is situated in Cheshire, near the mouth of the river Mersey. This, and
adjoining manors, belonged to the Earls of Derby, by whom it was alienated in 1653.

[7] London.

[8] Probably the Duke de Tremouille, whose daughter, the celebrated defender of
Lathom House, was married to James, son and successor of the above-mentioned
William, Earl of Derby.

soon as he came thereinto, he spoke thus to P. W. "Let us begin where we last left; where is that book I gave you at Lond. in loc. predicto?" He answered, in such a box; where searching, no such thing was to be found; every box, till, and corner searched, but it was not to be found in that house: quære utrum nil negatur super sacrament. P. W.

This man[1] the most understanding, able, and industrious justice of peace in this kingdom. No warrant granted out, but he takes notice thereof in a book; and at sessions an account demanded of all those warrants sent out, which, if the constables, to whom they are delivered, do not execute nor return, and give an account, they are called upon at the sessions; or, if those that require and procure the warrants keep them in their hands and make use of them for their own ends, and do not deliver them to be served, they are bound over to the sessions. This day, a widow by him ordered to be committed, because she refused to pay the money, which was five pound, committed to her husband as overseer of the poor of the parish, whose stock this was, she being his executor; this he said might be justified, and that the law thus directs.

To cure a strain of the back sinews, Raph Hungate's receipt, practised upon old cripple and many other horses with good success: receive of euphorbion three pennyworth, as much cantharides; let these be bruised and mingled with oile de bay, three pennyworth; or for want thereof with swine's grease rendered, whereof you make an ointment or salve; if it be a great, or an old strain, you must add unto it one or two pennyworth of white mercury (more or less to be used as in discretion you think fit, and according to the strain). This being mingled with the former, to be applied thus: when all the hair is clipt off where the swelling and strain is, then also shave it with a sharp razor, and afterwards, with a pen-knife sharp and well-wetted, lance it down the back and swelled and strained part of the leg in three or four long razes; and the ointment with your hand is to be rubbed and chafed upon

[1] Sir J. H.

the place shaved and lanced; if your horse be unruly, he must be
cast; then take a fire-shovel red-hot, or a red-hot iron plate, and
hold before the place thus anointed until the ointment sink
and drench into the skin. These cautions to be observed: first,
the horse is to be tied so short as that he cannot reach it with his
mouth, lest he gnaw when it smarts, and be poisoned; after
twenty-four hours thus tied, you may turn him out of doors, for
he must not stand still in the stable; this, being thus anointed, will
blister within half an hour or an hour. Secondly, observe whether
it swell upwards and towards the body, which, if you discern,
speedily with milk anoint, and with your hand stroke the swelling
downwards 'twixt his brisket and his knee. He must be diligently
watched and attended, and after five or six days you must anoint
the same with fresh butter.

Junii 18.—I went from ALERSTONE to ELLENTHORPE in five
hours, where discoursing about the great storm, I was there credibly
informed that upon Ribstone Moor (which is near Sir Henry Goode-
ricke's[1] in Yorkshire) there perished seven persons in the storm not
twelve score from their habitations, and one woman near Gooles-
borrow,[2] Judge Hutton's,[3] that attained to the door of her husband's
house, being shut, one of her maids saw her at the door through
the window, but she being spent, sat down upon a block before the
door: they went unto and opened the door in all haste, and found
her quite dead. Sea-fish upon the coast of Lanckashire perished in
the storm fifty cart-load together.

Great complaint here, at Fail-kirk in Scotland, as of the last
winter's extremity of cold, frost, and snow, wherein perished many
in their houses for want of relief, divers and many houses being

[1] Sir Henry Goodricke, Knt. was born 1580, died 1641. He was father of Sir John
Goodricke, the first baronet, who received that honour in 1641.

[2] Goldsborough.

[3] Sir Richard Hutton, a man learned in the law, was appointed one of the justices
of the Common Pleas, March 3, 1617. One of his daughters married Mr. Dawney of
Cowich, Yorkshire, and was mother of the first Viscount Downe. He was the Serjeant Hutton of Goldsburgh to whom Judge Davenport addressed the letter with an
account of a trial for a murder discovered by an apparition.

buried in the snow, and could not be found but by the smoke of the chimneys. Many sheep and cattle perished in this storm, so now they are mightily punished with extreme drought, which, as it keeps down their summer, so also doth it hinder the winter, corn from shooting freely.

[A most extreme winter also hath here been in Ireland, and such drought and extreme heat here at Ennercoffie and Washford, as doth burn up all their corn and grass. These heats began *Jul.* 7, and it was as extreme violent hot weather as ever I felt in my life from this day; it did exceedingly distemper us to travel in the heat of the day, or indeed any time of the day, except there were some cooling refreshing wind; during this time the wind stood most easterly. This extreme hot scorching weather did continue in Ireland until about 21 *Julii*, upon which day was much rain, and it continued dropping weather until we left Ireland, *Jul.* 25. In all high field grounds much want of hay and grass, which is burnt up, insomuch as Mr. Ward, mine host at Waterford, affirmed that where he had two load of hay last year, he had scarce one this year. Here also they had extreme storms of frost and snow, and when I came into England, *Julii* 26, I found the like wants and complaints in England. I paid at Bristol twelve pence day and night hay, and at Bath ten pence a night for hay; and a minister affirmed unto me, coming 'twixt Bath and Bristoll, that where they had twenty load of hay last year, they had not four load this year. About this time here was much dropping weather.][1]

Mightyly punished in this country by drought, and much more in the south: here they are constrained to put their milch-kine into their meadows; no rain to speak of hath fallen here since the storm, and in the bishoprick no grass almost to be found, nor any low meadows.

Ju. 19. — We left Ellenthorpe: whence to CATERICKE BRIG is

[1] This paragraph, here inclosed within brackets, is written in a rather darker ink, and was probably inserted at a later period upon a space that chanced to be blank, at the foot of the page, as connected with the previous remarks upon the state of the weather, which had been introduced by his " discoursing" at Ellenthorpe.

twelve miles, fair way; Leemeing Lane, seven long, as straight, level way as is Wattling Street from the Cross,[1] 'twixt Hintley[2] and Lutterworth to Adderstone.[3]   From Caterigg Brigg to Peirs Brigg[4] seven miles,[5] a straight way also; thence to Bishoppe Auckland, seven mile.   We lodged at Newton, two miles out of the road, and from Peirs Brig, with generous Mr. Henry Blackistone, younger brother to Sir W. Blackstone of Gibsett,[6] whose eldest son married my cousin[7] Mary Eggert.   Here I was kindly and neatly entertained, and this gentleman brought me to Aukeland, invited me to his brother's, and his nephew Wren's, Mr. Linsley Wren, who married Sir W. Blackstone's daughter, a fine gentlewoman,[8] very lively, and of a free carriage, &c.   Here he lodged all night, and (upon his return to Auckland next morn) staid with me until evening.

Junii 20.—We went from this good family upon Sat. 20 *Ju.*, and by the way in his grounds he showed good marle; he breeds about twenty calves yearly.   I saw handsome wellikeing stirks of his, about twenty.   This morning I tasted pure white honey out of the last year's comb.   Here bees prosper well, though it be so much north; here is about eighteen hives; none perished last winter; the mouths stopped in winter close up; only to admit air, let a little hole be made with a stick.   The hives were only

---

[1] Now called High Cross.   [2] Hinckly.   [3] Atherstone.

[4] Pierce bridge, over the Tees, connects the counties of York and Durham.   It is twelve miles from Catterich bridge.

[5] Twelve miles.

[6] This eldest son of Mr. Henry Blakiston, was a distinguished loyalist, and knighted at Oxford, 12th April, 1643, by King Charles I, in whose service he held the rank of colonel, and was desperately wounded in the attack on Massey's quarters, Sept. 1644.

[7] Cousin is here used merely as indicative of some relationship, not in the sense to which it is at present restricted.   Richard Egerton of Ridley married Margaret, only sister to Sir William Brereton; his sister, Mary Egerton, the lady here mentioned, married Sir William Blakeston of Newton, Co. Durham.

[8] Barbara, fourth daughter of Sir William Blakiston, was contracted to marry Lindley Wren, son and heir of Sir W. Wren, Knt. of Binchester, 27th Sept. 1622, when she was only about sixteen years of age.   This lady's lively and free carriage provokes some further remarks from Sir W. Brereton.

covered on the top with a clod of earth, and are indeed very strong and substantial. In some places in this country they remove their hives in winter into their houses; they yield most profit and purest honey if they live not above two or three years, and then may be drowned. A good hive worth about one pound ten shillings or two pound per annum, so much were their bees worth. Here I saw the most and best purest honey that I ever met withal; one great pot worth five or six pounds; greater profit herein than in any other commodity, and with least trouble and charge.

This day at BISHOPPE-AUCKLAND with Dr. Moreton,[1] Bishop of Durham, who maintains great hospitality in an orderly, well-governed house, and is a very worthy reverend bishop, whose importunity I could not resist, who, when I offered to take leave, brought me into my chamber. This castle, as it is a stately, pleasant seat of great receipt, so is it of great strength, compassed with a thick stone-wall, seated upon the side of an hill, upon a rock, a river running below, and good store of wood (though little timber) encompassing above.

Here is a very fair, neat hall, as I have found in any bishop's palace in England. Two chapels[2] belonging hereunto, the one over the other; the higher a most dainty, neat, light, pleasant place, but the voice is so drowned and swallowed by the echo, as few words can be understood. The tower is made use of upon Sabbath-days, where, 21 Junii, Dr. Dod,[3] now Dean of Ripon,

[1] Dr. Thomas Morton, Bp. Chester 1616; Lichfield and Coventry 1618; Durham 1632. Born 1564, died 1659.

[2] Not many years after the date of this journal, the chapel was completely destroyed by the blasphemous and traitorous wretches who espoused the same cause as Sir William himself; the materials were used for a private dwelling, which after the restoration was pulled down by Bishop Cosin, who employed the same materials again to assist in erecting the present enlarged chapel.

[3] Thomas Dod, D.D., nephew of John Dod the Decalogist, was chaplain to King Charles I, Archdeacon of Richmond, Dean of Ripon, and Prebendary of Chester, Rector of Astbury 1607, and of the lower moiety of Malpas 1623. He preached before the king at Nantwich in his progress through Cheshire in 1617. He died Feb. 10, 1647-8. He was twice married; in 1604, to Thomasine, daughter of Thomas Coller, his predecessor as rector of Malpas; in 1619, to Dorothy, daughter of Hugh Bromley of Hampton.

made an excellent sermon; great resort hither on Sabbath by the neighbourhood; one sermon in morning and prayers in the afternoon.

Here are three dining-rooms, a fair matted gallery, wherein there was placed on both sides these pictures: Jo. Huss, Hierom of Prauge, Luther, Zuinglius, Cranmer, Latymer, Whittakers,[1] Wickliffe, Calvin, Beza, Perkins,[2] Bullinger, Jewell, Pagius,[3] Ridley, Bradford,[4] Zanchius,[5] Bucer, &c. And none but of this strain.

A dainty stately park, wherein I saw wild bulls and kine, which had two calves runners. There are about twenty wild beasts, all white; will not endure your approach, but if they be enraged or distressed, very violent and furious; their calves will be wonderous fat.

Apud prandium, this 20 *Junii*, a discourse per ipsum Epis., of a petition or supplication presented to the Queen Eliz., by a girl of twelve or fourteen years of age, whose father was injuriously committed to prison by the means and greatness of my L. Hundson, then L. Chamb., who, being committed, sends for a daughter, a child of pregnant wit and parts, and gives her money to pay for her fraught, directs her to take presently a pair of oars to Greenwitch, and to go directly to the Queen, and not to impart

---

[1] William Whitaker, a strenuous controversialist against the errors of the Church of Rome, was born at Holme in Lancashire, and died in 1595. Bishop Hall said of him, " Never a man saw him without reverence, or heard him without wonder."

[2] William Perkins, of Ch. Coll. Camb., born at Marston, Warwickshire, author of many learned works, which, as he was lame of his right hand, were all written with his left. He was deprived by Abp. Whitgift for puritanism. He died at Cambridge, 1602.

[3] P. Franciscus Fagins was a Jesuit, executed at Tyburn, 30th Ap. 1602, but this can scarcely be the person intended, as he was by no means of a strain with the others mentioned.

[4] John Bradford, one of the most eminent preachers of his time, of exemplary piety, and of true Christian charity, was burnt in Smithfield, July 1, 1555.

[5] Jerome Zanchius, born 1516, a disciple of Peter Martyr, was professor successively at Strasburgh, and Heidelburgh. He died 1590 having the character of being one of the most learned of the reformers, as also one of the most pious, and of the greatest moderation in controversy, combined with proper firmness.

unto any her errand, only she was by her father directed to answer all that questioned her, " I have a supplication to her Majesty." She was brought up into the Presence where the Countess of Oxford personated the Queen and deceived the child; afterwards being brought before the Queen, my Lord Hunsdon present, who, seeing her, said, " This is a pretty supplicator;" who, being commanded to deliver her message, said, " A supplication to your Majesty; my Lord Hunsdon hath committed my father, like a thief, to prison for seeking his own." The Queen, much displeased, said, " My Lord, ex ore infantis you are condemned; let this be reformed." He was thereby set at liberty.

Some other facetious discourses I remember. Archie's[1] answer to Don Olivaries[2] (when there was a solemn procession and great adoration of the Host in the streets), who demanded whether he did not believe that Christ was there really and personally present? He answered, " No; for he had heard it said, that, when he was upon the earth, the whoreson thieves crucified him, therefore he will come no more amongst them." Herewith Olivaries, much taken, asked him another question, " Dost not thou believe that the Pope's Holiness is guided with such an infallible spirit, as that he cannot err, so as if he say, ' Your red coat be black,' you are bound to believe him?" to which he answered, " What saith your Excellence?" He repeated the same question. After he had a little paused, and stammered, he answered: " If the Pope say so, he is ill of eye-sight." These answers reported to the king and queen of Spain, who were much affected therewith, and then was there conferred, and is still continued, a pension of £100 per annum.

I demanded from him,[3] " Whether bowing at the altar were enjoined and commanded by any canon, or left free and arbitrary?"

[1] Archibald Armstrong, court-fool to kings James I and Charles I. He was the last but one who held that official situation. Cromwell had little taste for wit or fun, and the courtiers of Charles II, averse to a monopoly of such articles, became themselves purveyors to his Majesty, and rendered an official fool unnecessary.

[2] Count-Duke of Olivarez, prime-minister of Spain, and favourite with the king at the time of King Charles I's visit to that country.

[3] i. e. from Bishop Morton.

M

He answered, " It was left free and arbitrary ; it was not bowing to the altar now in use, but towards the east, as Daniel pray ; and it was not to be accounted an altar, but the communion-table."

A certain person seeing some sit above the communion-table in St. Nichol. Church in Newcastle, said, " It was not fit that any should sit above God himself."

This Bishop assured me that fair spring-water, in the morning received into your mouth, and there kept until it be lukewarm, and then swallowed, is an excellent medicine to cure the cholick and stone, and that he himself hath been hereby cured, and also Sir William Blackstone of Gibsett ; the reason hereof, by him appre-hended, was, that the fasting-spittle was herewith swallowed, which hath an excellent virtue fasting, even to kill a serpent. He said he knew some, who would never part with any spittle, but swal-lowed it down.

Here we rested the Lord's-day, and were very generously and nobly entertained. Here dined with him this day Mr. Linsley Wren of Winchester, and his wife, a mighty gallant, a fine dainty gentlewoman,[1] if she knew but how to value and prize the perfec-tions God hath given her ; whose husband hath impaired his estate in maintaining   at so great height.

Junii 22.—Upon Monday morning early, Dr. Dod and myself hence departed, and I delivered unto his servant my packet of letters for Cheshire. I went hence to the city of DURHAM, which is seven miles from Auckland Castle, where I gave, in rewards to the officers, ten shillings and sixpence.

We saw Durham hence, which stands high upon divers hills, and is a stately and delightful prospect, especially the minster and the Bishop's Palace, which is built castlewise, and is a place of great strength, and is in good repair, wherein the bishop doth winter ; which is not large as Auckland, but very stately and convenient. He is Bishop of Durham and Earl of Sadberrie. In this there is a very little chapel, and no great hall, and three dining-rooms, and a

---

[1] See above, p. 78.

little gallery, wherein are the arms of all the gentlemen of this country of Bishoprick.

The minster is as neatly kept as in any in England, built like unto Paul's; wherein are, in the body of the church, on either side, eight great and stately pillars as great as Paul's: herein the daintiest font that I have seen in England, the body or font-stone and foot of pure marble, over which is placed a cover or canopy folding of wood, curiously carved, wherein described the history of Christ's baptism. Herein a stately pair of double organs, which look both into the body of the church and chancel; a stately altar-stone, all of fine marble, standing upon a frame of marble pillars of the same marble of the font. When the communion is here administered, which is by the bishop himself, here is laid upon this altar, or rather communion-table, a stately cloth of cloth of gold; the bishop useth the new red embroidered cope, which is wrought full of stars, like one I have seen worn in St. Dennis in Fraunce; there are here other two rich copes, all which are shaped like unto long cloaks reaching down to the ground, and which have round capes.

In the higher end of the church, above the chancel, stood[1] the shrine of St. Cuttbert, which doubtless was very large and rich, inasmuch as before it, and on either side, you may discern the stones whereupon you tread much worn, and great cavities made by the scraping of those that came to worship and offer to this saint; and, betwixt this shrine and the higher end and wall of the church, there is a cross aisle, which doth also encompass the chancel. Here still appears where there were formerly nine altars, which are now demolished. In the window there is placed the picture of St. Cuttbert praying in the holy isle, the water flowing up to his chin; the picture also in glass of a friar correcting a nun, and turning down the bed-clothes to her middle. Here in the chancel, which is very neat, is a most stately desk of brass, which was the ninth part of a candlestick, which at the dissolution was thrown into an obscure place, and found but of late; this was a most mighty vast candlestick. In the lower end

---

[1] *i. e.* previous to the Reformation.

of this minster (which is called St. Cuttbert's) is St. Marie's chapel, which was erected and added unto the church by Bishop Langley;[1] herein is now the consistory kept, and herein also is a tomb and monument of Bede: " Hic jacet in fossa Bedæ Venerabilis ossa." In the churchyard is the tomb of him that was the steward, and disbursed the money when the church was erected; of whom it is reported that, all his money being paid over night, his glove was by a spirit every night filled and supplied, so as though it was empty over night, yet was replenished next morning; his hand is made holding a glove stuffed with money; and by this means was this great work built; the name of steward of the work was Hubbapella.

Upon the highest hill within this town is seated this minster and palace, and those parts of the streets of this town which are seated upon the same hill are within the walls, which are eucompassed with the wall of the city. This minster is endowed with mighty large revenues, 'tis said no less than £7000 or £8000 per annum. Twelve prebends belong hereunto, worth £200 or £300 per annum. The deanery worth about £1400, and twelve petty canons about £10 per annum. This hill, whereon seated the minster and castle, is almost compassed round with the river Weare, over which there are placed two fair bridges. There are four or five other streets of the town and suburbs, placed straggling one from another upon the hill tops. Some reasonable handsome houses in this city, which is but poor by reason here is no trade. This city is compassed about with much higher hills than it is built upon.

Hence in the afternoon; going toward Newcastle upon [Tyne] we saw Lumley Castle, which belongs to my Lord Lumley;[2] it is

[1] St. Mary's chapel is an addition to the cathedral, situated in front of the west end, and is termed the Galilee. It is said to have been built by Hugh Pudsey, bishop from 1153 to 1195, and to have been repaired and altered by Bp. Langley. Thomas Langley was consecrated bishop of Durham, Aug. 8, 1406, made cardinal June 1, 1411, and twice held the office of lord chancellor of England. He died in the year 1437.

[2] The ancient barony of Lumley became extinct in the year 1609. Richard Lumley, descended from a branch of the family whose succession to the family honours had been barred by an attainder, was knighted by King James I, 1616, and created Lord Viscount Lumley of Waterford in Ireland in 1628. He adhered to King Charles I, and bore arms in his cause, having fortified his residence, Lumley castle.

in reasonable good repair, though of no great strength; near hereunto, and about three mile from NEWCASTLE, there is a town placed, called Chester-in-the-streete. The suburbs of Newcastle on this side the bridge are in the Bishoprick, and it is said that the counties of Bishoprick and Northumberland divide upon the middle of Tine bridge.

This is beyond all compare the fairest and richest town in England, inferior for wealth and building to no city save London and Bristow, and whether it may not deserve to be accounted as wealthy as Bristow, I make some doubt. It is seated upon the river Tine, the mouth of which river affords such a narrow channel at low water, as it is said not to be above forty yards broad; and at the mouth there is a great shelf and bank of sand, so as at a high water also it is most dangerous passage for strangers, inasmuch as they must pass near to that side of the haven which lieth close by and near under the command of Tine-mouth Castle; which is a dainty seated castle, almost compassed with the sea, wherein hath been the fairest church I have seen in any castle, but now it is out of repair, and much neglected: it belongeth to the Earl of Northumberland. This river conveys a navigable channel from the sea to Newcastle, which is about seven miles, and it doth flow about six or seven miles (as I was informed) above the town into the country: this river is very plentifully furnished with salmon,—and over the same, 'twixt Bishoprick and Northumberland, there is erected (except London Bridge over Thames, and the bridge at Barwick over Tweed) one of the finest bridges I have met with in England, consisting of eight arches. London contains eighteen arches; Barwick bridge, fifteen; and this of Newcastle, eight arches. Rochester bridge over Medway hath six large arches, erected with most difficulty, and over the deepest channel; and it is a neat bridge, which hath iron bars placed on both sides.

This town of Newcastle is governed by a mayor, a recorder, a sheriff, and ten aldermen: it hath great revenues belonging unto it (as I was informed), at least £5000 or £6000 per annum, besides great collieries employed for the use and supply of the commons and poor of the town. Herein are five churches; and St. Nichol. church, which is the fairest, is as neat pewed, and formed with as much uniformity, as any I have found in England, and it is as neatly kept and trimmed. This town was assessed to pay £3570 towards the building of the late ship;[1] and Yorke taxed £1800; and some towns of the country contributed with them, and paid £700, part of £1800 taxed. There is every day a market here kept, and in a dainty market-place. Tuesday and Saturday, a mighty market, and much provision comes out of Northumberland; infinite store of poultry. This town (a great part of it) placed upon the highest and the steepest hills that I have found in any great town; these so steep as horses cannot stand upon the pavements,—therefore the daintiest flagged channels are in every street that I have seen: hereupon may horse or man go without danger of sliding.

Resting here 23 *Jun.* I took boat about twelve clock, and went to TINE-MOUTH and to the SHEELDES, and returned about seven clock; it is about seven miles. Here I viewed the salt works, wherein is more salt works, and more salt made, than in any part of England[2] that I know, and all the salt here made is made of salt-water; these pans, which are not to be numbered, placed in the river-mouth, and wrought with coals brought by water from Newcastle pits. A most dainty new salt-work lately here erected, which is absolutely the most complete work that I ever saw; in the breadth whereof is placed six rank of pans, four pans in a

[1] The tax of ship-money was first imposed in 1630. A writ was directed to the sheriff of every country "to provide a ship of war for the king's service, and to send it, amply provided and fitted, by such a day to such a place." Leave was given to commute this for a sum of money. The tax was abolished in 1641.—*Clarendon*, bk. i. pp. 120, 504.

[2] "As early as 1489, iron salt-pans are mentioned as having been constructed by Lionel Bell, of South Shields. The salt-pans are frequently mentioned in the reign of Elizabeth, and seem betwixt that period and the reign of Charles I to have attracted several settlers to South Shields. In 1667, there appears to have been one hundred and twenty-one salt-pans. In 1696, when the salt trade had reached its height, one hundred and forty-three. From that period this branch of trade has been gradually decreasing, and at present (1820) only five salt-pans remain."—*Surtees' Durham*, vol. ii. p. 95.

rank; at either outside the furnaces are placed in the same manner as are my brother Boothes,[1] under the grate of which furnaces the ashes fall, and there is a lid or cover for both; and by the heat of these ashes, there being a pan made in the floor betwixt every furnace, which is made of brick, for which also there is a cover, there is boiled, and made into lumps of hard and black salt, which is made of the brine which drops from the new-made salt, which is placed over a cistern of lead, which cistern is under the floor of the store-house, which is in the end of the building: these great lumps of hard black salt are sent to Colchester to make salt upon salt, which are sold for a greater price than the rest, because without these at Colchester they cannot make any salt.

These twenty-four pans have only twelve furnaces and twelve fires, and are erected in this manner, all being square and of like proportion. They are placed by two and two together, one against the other: the six pans in the highest rank, the bottom equal with the top of the lower. The highest pans are thrice filled and boiled till it begin to draw towards salt; then a spiggot being pulled out, the brine thus prepared runs into the lower pans, which brings it to a larger proportion of salt than otherwise, gains time and saves fire, because it must be longer boiled in the other pans, and would spend fire, which is saved by reason of the heat which derives from the furnace of the upper pan, which by a passage is conveyed under the lower pan, which passage is about half a yard broad in the bottom, and is, at the top, of the breadth of the pan, which rest upon a brick wall which is of the thickness of one brick at top; and this concavity under the lower pans is shaped slopewise like unto a kiln, narrow in the bottom and broad at the top; and this heat, which is conveyed under and makes the lower pans to boil, comes, together with the smoke which hath no other passage, under these pans through loop-holes or pigeon-holes, which is conveyed into a chimney (a double rank whereof is placed in the middle of this building), betwixt which is a passage for a man to

---

[1] Sir William Brereton married, for his first wife, Susan, daughter of Sir George Booth, of Dunham. "Brother Booth" was probably William, the eldest son and heir of Sir George, and father of the first Lord Delamere. He died the following year, 1636.

walk in. In the middle of every these chimneys is there a broad iron-plate, which is shaped to the chimney, which, as it stops and keeps in the heat, so it being pulled out abates the heat.

It is to be observed that the twelve lower pans are only to be drawn twice in twenty-four hours, and by that time they are ready to be drawn; the brine in the higher pans will be sufficiently boiled and prepared to be let into the lower, which are only to be drawn, and that twice in twenty-four hours; they .yield every of them every draught two bowls, which is worth 2s. a bowl, and sometimes 2s.4d., so every pan yielding every day four bowls at two draughts, which comes to 8s., all twelve pans are worth every day 4l. 16s.; so as all the twelve pans in a week make salt worth 28l. a week; which in the year amounts unto £1400, accounting fifty weeks to the year. Two men and one woman to get out ashes, and one to pump their brine, manage and tend this whole work. The men's wages is 14s. a week, besides he that pumps. This salt is made of salt-water, which out of a brine pit made, which is supplied at full sea, is pumped, and by pipes of lead conveyed into every pan: the wall of this house is stone, and the roof of this and all the rest of the houses wherein are brine-pans, are boards. Touching the proportion of fuel here spent, and some other particulars, Dobson's letter [1] is to be perused, and some further directions are to be received from him.

Here at the Shields are the vastest salt works I have seen, and by reason of the conveniency of coal, and cheapness thereof, being at 7s. a chaldron, which is three wain load. Here is such a cloud of smoke as amongst these works you cannot see to walk; there are, as I was informed, about two hundred and fifty houses,[2] poor ones and low built, but all covered with boards. Here in every house is erected one fair great iron pan, five yards long, three yards and a half broad; the bottom of them made of thin plates nailed together, and strong square rivets upon the nail heads,

---

[1] Dobson appears to have been the agent or manager of some of these salt-works, and we cannot discover that this letter was a published one.

[2] This seems to be a very considerable exaggeration. See note, p. 86.

about the breadth of the batt of your hand: these pans are three quarters of a yard deep; ten great bars there are placed on the inner side of the pan, three square, two inches thick; every of these great pans, as Dobson informed me, cost about 100*l*. and cannot be taken down to be repaired with less than 10*l*. charge. Every pan yields four draughts of salt in a week, and every draught is worth about 1*l*. 10*s*.   Spent in coal: ten chaldron of coal at 7*s*. a chaldron, which amounts to 3*l*. 10*s*. in coals; deduct out of 6*l*. there remains 2*l*. 10*s*. besides one man's wages. So as in these 250 pans there is weekly spent in coals 775*l*., every pan yielding 6*l*. weekly, being 250: total of the worth of the salt made in them amounts to 1500*l*.; gained 735*l*.; deduct of this 120*l*. workmen's wages for making it, 120*l*.; clear gain about 600*l*.[1] a year. A wain load of salt is here worth about 3*l*. 10*s*., and a chaldron of coals, which is worth 7*s*. is three wain load.

Here, at NEWCASTLE, is the fairest quay in England I have met withal, from Tine-bridge all along Towne-wall, and almost to the glass-works, where is made window-glass. Divers havens of stone wall erected to cast out their ballast upon, and they pay for every ton cast out 6*d*. This is a spacious haven, now naked of ships, but sometimes thronged.

The fairest built inn in England that I have seen is Mr. Carre's, in this town: we lodged at the Swan, at Mr. Swan's, the post-master's, and paid 8*d*. ordinary, and no great provision.   He is a very forward man to have a coy here erected.

This town unto this country serves instead of London, by means whereof the country is supplied with money; whereas otherwise so much money is carried out of the country to the lords and land-lords, as there would be neither sufficient money to pay the tenants' rents, nor would the country be supplied with money. This town is also famous for the walls which compass round the town, about which you may walk, and which is strengthened with strong towers placed upon the wall at no great distance. Hence to Car-

[1] There is an error in this calculation. 775 ought to be 875, and 735 ought to be 625; then the clear gain will be £5Q5 a-year.

lisle was there erected the Picts' wall, which was the ancientest monument I have heard of in England. It was the work of the Romans: in some places, it is said to be above twenty yards broad towards Carlisle; the people go to market upon it, and it may well be owned by the Romans, as being the bravest and best deserving work of greatest industry and charge, and the strongest fortification that I have ever met in England, reaching, as here it was reported, from this town to the city of Carlisle, which is said to be sixty miles. It was made against the incursions of the Picts; many inscriptions upon divers of these stones, which perpetuate the fame and memory of the Romans.

Junii 24.—We left Newcastle, and came to MORPETH, which is twelve miles, and is the post-town; and by the way, about seven miles from Newcastle, we took notice of a convenient seat of a coy in Point Island, which belongs unto Mr. Mark Arington.[1] We found at Morpeth a fine little castle, in good repair, which belongs to my Lord William Howard;[2] a market-town, but poor houses. We dined at post-master's, and paid 12d. ordinary, and 6d. ordinary. Thence to ANWICKE is fourteen miles, where we lodged at the post-master's house; 6d. ordinary, and good victuals and lodging. Here we saw a mighty great castle belonging to the Earl of Northumberland, wherein were all houses of office, many of them now in decay; but my lord is repairing the same by degrees. Great revenues paid unto him out of this country; at least eight horse-load of money. He hath four castles in this county, viz. this castle, Warp-weth[3] castle, Tin-mouth castle, and [Prudhowe castle.]

Great lands he hath in York-shire, at and about Toppliffe, where he sometimes lived, whence he rose in the rebellion in the

---

[1] "Mark Errington married the heiress of Sir Brian Stapleton, who married one of the co-heiresses of Viscount Beaumont. Errington's son took the name of Stapleton, and the Beaumont peerage is now in abeyance between his descendants and the other co-heir."—See Sir N. Harris Nicholas' *Synopsis of the Peerage.*

[2] Lord William Howard was the celebrated Bald Willy or Belted Will Howard, Warden of the Western Marshes. He was great grandfather of the first Earl of Carlisle, and died 1640.   [3] Warkworth.

North,[1] and upon a moor near Burrough-bridges, which belongs unto Mr. Mallorye, of Studdley, there assembled the forces, and there met him the Earl of Westmerland.

Two horrible, and most cruel, detestable murders· have of late been committed in Bishopp-ricke and Northumberland. Mr. Lampton of Whittle, near Chester-street, which is three miles from Newcastle, an ancient gentleman of 300*l.* or 400*l.*[2] per annum, is now prisoner in Durham gaol, for poisoning two wives: his first wife was Mr. Heath's, of Kepeir,[3] daughter, by whom he had five sons and daughters. He sent one of her maids to New-castle to buy mercury, arsenic, and stybium, which, it should seem, by some means, he procured his wife to receive, (a day or two after she was churched); who, as she died suddenly and unex-pectedly, so was she as suddenly and secretly buried. He hath

---

[1] This alludes to the insurrection attempted in 1569 by the Earls of Northumberland and Westmoreland, who united their forces, amounting to nearly six thousand men, with the expectation of being joined by all the Roman Catholics in England. They issued a manifesto, declaring that they intended nothing against the queen, their sole aim being to re-establish the Roman Catholic religion, and remove evil counsellors. Elizabeth acted with her usual judgment and prudence, and despatched an army under the Earl of Sussex, before whom they slunk away and dispersed. Northumberland was taken, imprisoned, and ultimately beheaded at York, Aug. 22, 1572.

[2] Edward VI granted the possessions of the dissolved house of Kepyear, in Eyton parish, to John Cockburne, who speedily conveyed it to John Heath, who again speedily disposed of a part of it to John Watson of Newcastle. This John Heath was probably ancestor to one of the supposed victims in this sad tragedy. See Surtees' *History of Durham*, vol. ii. p. 267.

[3] Mr. Surtees gives the pedigree of Lambton of Trebley, and sometime of Whitehill:

Susan, d. of John Groves, Ald. of York, sister to Frances, wife of Sir John Conyers, Bart.	=	Ralph Lambton, of Trebley, Gent. bapt. 14 Jan. 1592-3, living 1657.	=	Elizabeth, d. of —— Glover, widow of Ralph Sympson, of Piddingball Garth, Gent. marr. at Pottington 19 May 1633, buried there 4 May 1635
Ralph—John—William—Henry—James.				Mary—Elizabeth.

There cannot be any doubt that the above Ralph is the person charged with the murders; but the author was probably misinformed as to the name of the first wife,— for, by the Chester-le-Street register, it appears that Ralph Lambton and Susan Groves were married June 16, 1618, and Mrs. Susanna, wife of Mr. Ralph Lambton, died about 1629.—*Information of Sir Cuthbert Sharp.* Surtees does not make the slightest allusion to the tale here recorded. See Surtees' *History of Durham*, vol. ii. p. 201.

since given to this maidservant, and assured unto her during her life, a pension of 2*l*. per annum. This trusty servant he hath since made use of as an engine to effect and accomplish the like design: and, as is now proved by the apothecary, in Newcastle, of whom the poison was bought, (all whom my Lord Bishop commanded before him by warrant): it appears, by his testimony upon oath, that this maid came divers times unto him, in her master's name, for mercury, arsenic, and stybium, which he refused to furnish her withal: hereupon, Mr. Lampton himself came to the apothecary and expostulated with him. The apothecary answered, except he sent a note under his hand, that he might be assured it was for him, he would send none: hereupon, he sent a note under his hand (which was produced), and mercury, arsenic, and stybium were, by the same maid, sent him the day before his wife's death, who was a rich widow (Raph Simpson's, a grazier wife), who brought him 3000*l*. and 300 or 400*l*. until her son came to age: this 3000*l*. was left unto the younger children; which her eldest son coming to age, and sueing Mr. Lampton, hereupon some dislikes were conceived by him against his wife, who, not being well and having taken physick, and sending for a captain, who was left in trust by her former husband, and sending for ale for him, whereof one bowl full was left undrunk, when she went to bring him down stair: in the meantime, her husband stays in the chamber and puts this poison into the cup, and invites her drink it at his return, which (after she had put sugar into) she drunk, and presently fell into great extremity; accused her husband to have poisoned her; sent for the captain, who, immediately returning, found her at point of death, whose last words were: That she took it upon her death, that her husband had poisoned [her], and withal she related the manner, and so died, desiring that her children and this captain would see her death revenged. After her death, her body was viewed by the physicians, and all of them unanimously affirm that she was certainly poisoned. He is committed to Durham gaol, but pleads himself.

Junii 25.—We lodged at the post-master's, at Anwick, last

night, where we were well-used : 6*d.* ordinary supper, and 4*d.* breakfast; good lodging, and neat. Hence to Bellford, which is next post-town, twelve miles. Here, losing our way, we wandered thence to Fennam, four or five miles; whence, over the sands to the HOLLY ISLAND, is two miles: in this island, there was formerly a fair abbey dedicated to St. Cuttbert, to the abbot whereof belonged great revenues. In this Holly Island, as they here report, St. Cuttbert inhabited in winter, and in the summer season in the islands of Ferne, which you may hence discern, which are reported to breed abundance of fowl. This whole isle, which is seven miles about, though now it is not worth more than 100*l.* a year, besides the warren, which is 40*l.* per annum, all belongs to my Lord Suffolke: this church and abbey ruinated; only the walls and pillars of it remain, and they are very fair pillars, and resemble Durham. There is another little church now used, and in repair, which stands near to the abbey church, whereunto resort the inhabitants of Fennam, a village placed on the other side the island. Here, touching the sea intermitting her course of flowing on the Sabbath-day, 'twixt 9 and 12, and so, in the afternoon, I have heard much and often, and applied myself to enquire the certainty hereof. I spoke with Capt. Rugg, Captain of the Fort, and with Mr. Joanes, an inhabitant here, an intelligent gentleman, an Oxford: as also I did enquire of our host and our guide, and divers other inhabitants of the isle, who all, *una voce,* concurred, no man dissenting, in the assertion that there was nothing supernatural therein to be observed: for although they acknowledged it to be most true that it is always passable over those sands at nine a clock, so as those that live and reside upon the main land may, every Lord's day, come over those sands to church about that hour; this is, by those that are popishly affected, superstitiously applied and imputed to the merit and effect of St. Cuttber's prayers, whereas, indeed, there is nothing extraordinary therein. They give this natural reason: it always so falls out

---

[1] Theophilus, second Earl of Suffolk, son of Catherine, so celebrated for her beauty and unprincipled rapacity.

that at the change and full of the moon, the flood is at the height at or about three o'clock, and then *par consequence* it is low water, and the sands are dry, at or about nine oclock; so as then it is most easy to pass: when it is full sea at three clock, it must needs be low water at nine clock: and when it is no spring-tide, you may ride over the sands (if you be well acquainted with them, as those are that inhabit near, and resort to church there) at full water, and this is not only ordinary upon the Lord's day, but upon all other days of the week. Thus did our guide affirm that it had been ordinary in his practice; if, therefore, it should so fall out as to be full water upon the Lord's day, at or about nine oclock (which cannot often happen) yet may it then be passed, because it is low and ebb floods as well, and no otherwise than upon other days of the week.

In this island, in a dainty little fort, there lives Captain Rugg, governor of this fort, who is as famous for his generous and free entertainment of strangers, as for his great bottle nose, which is the largest I have seen. This is a dainty little fort, built tower-wise upon the top of a little round hill, which is a rock; this planted with ordinance; below, on very top of the hill, a neat flagged and walled court before the door, where are two brass ordinance, the one brought from Cales, and three iron ordinance; one of them came also thence. There are neat, warm, and couvenient rooms in this little fort.

Here in this island was brought unto us a young seal, or, as some call it, a sea-calf, which was this morning left upon the sands dry; they nourish it with milk. It hath an head and eyes like a calf, and hath two fins before like feet, and two behind, which it cannot draw up like fins, whereby also it is enabled to move in a creeping manner, and that slowly, yet constantly and restless; it hath a navel, and cries. Hence to Barwicke, seven miles, whereof three miles is upon the sand.

Junii 25.—We arrived about five clock at BARWICKE, where we passed a very fair, stately bridge over Tweede, consisting of fifteen arches, which was built by king James, and, as it is said, cost

£17,000. This river most infinitely stored with salmon, one hundred or two hundred salmons at one draught; but much more was reported by our host, which is most incredible, that there were two thousand salmons taken since Sunday last. This town seated upon the main sea, the Northern Ocean, and seems to be almost environed with the sea.

The haven is a most narrow, shallow, barred haven, the worst that I have seen; it might be made good, a brave and secure haven, whereas now only one little pink of about forty ton belongs unto it, and some few fishing-boats. There being, therefore, no trade in this town, it is a very poor town, many indigent persons and beggars therein. Here were the strongest fortifications I have met with in England, double-walled, and out-works of earth, and the outer walls like unto Chester walls, and without the inner walls a deep and broad moat well watered; the inner walls of invincible strength, stone wall within, and without lined with earth about twenty yards thick, with bulwarks conveniently placed to guard one another, like unto the Buss,[1] Bergen, Antwerpe, or Gravelin: these were begun by Queen Mary, finished by Queen Elizabeth, but something in decay: these walls environ the town.

A stately, sumptuous, and well-seated house or castle was here begun by the last Earl of Dunbar,[2] where the old castle stood; but his death put an end to that work. Here was a most stately platform propounded and begun; a fair long gallery joiced, not boarded, wherein is the largest mantle-tree I have seen, near five yards long of one piece; this leaded over, which gives the daintiest prospect to the sea, to the town, to the land, and the river. This, with much lands hereabout, was bestowed upon him by king James, who left all his lands to his daughter and heir, who married the now Earl of Suffolk. This town is seated on the north

[1] Bois le Duc.

[2] George Hume attended king James from Scotland; was created Lord Hume of Berwick in England, and Earl of Dunbar in Scotland. He died in 1611, leaving only one child, who married Theophilus, the Earl of Suffolk.

side of Twede, and is placed upon the sloping of a steep hill. They speak of three hundred and sixty salmons taken at one draught, and ordinarily about eighty, and one hundred, or one hundred and twenty, at one draught. We lodged at the Crown, were well used; 8*d.* ordinary, and 6*d.* our servants, and great entertainment and good lodging, a respective host and honest reckoning.

26 *Junii.*—Upon Friday we departed from Barwicke, which, though it be seated in Scotland, yet it is England, and is annexed to the crown of England by act of Parliament, and sends two burgesses to the Parliament-house, and here the country is not reputed Scottish, until you come to a town, four miles distant from Barwick, called ATEN,[1] which belongs to the Lord Aten, who hath there a pretty castle placed on the side of an hill; hence you pass (after you leave a few corn-fields near the town) over the largest and vastest moors that I have ever seen, which are now dry, and whereupon (in most parts) is neither sheep, beast, nor horse. Here is a mighty want of fire in these moors; neither coal, nor wood, nor turf; only the cutt and flea top-turves with linge upon them. These moors you travel upon about eight miles, and then come to a village called Apthomas,[2] and not far hence you leave the castle and town of Dunglass[3] on left hand, which is pleasantly seated, and seemeth to be in good repair, and not far hence is there an high-built house or castle, called Anderwick,[4] belonging to Mr. Maxwell of the bedchamber.

[1] Ayton is situated about nine miles from Berwick; but Berwick bounds, which comprise all that is attached to England, extend only about two miles from the town. Of Ayton Castle not a vestige now remains; a modern house was built upon its site, but this too has disappeared, having been consumed by fire in 1834.

[2] Of this Welch-like name I am unable to offer any explanation. I find no Scotch village with a name resembling it, unless perhaps Old Cambus.

[3] The castle of Dunglass was a stronghold of the Earls of Home, and afterwards of the Douglases; it was destroyed by the Protector Somerset in 1548, but afterwards rebuilt and enlarged, so that it was capable of entertaining King James I and his retinue on his way to take possession of the throne of England. This too has been destroyed, and the site is occupied by the beautiful seat of Sir James Hall.

[4] Anderwick is probably Innerwick Castle, at one time a stronghold of conside-

Enquiring the way before, how far to Dunbar, it was answered, it was three miles. I demanded whether so far; he said, "Yes, it was three bonnie mile." About a mile from Dunbar, we observed this husbandry; the grass, weeds and wreck, brought by the sea and with the tide, and left upon the sands, was carried and laid thick upon the ground. This used for corn.

Here is my Lord Rocksburne's[1] house or castle, seated with [in] six score of the main sea, where groweth and prospereth many kinds of wood; the highest thorns that I ever saw; this I admired, because I have observed all the sea-coasts whereby we passed, almost an hundred miles, and could not find any manner of wood prospering near the sea-coast. Here, in the village, we observed the sluttish women washing their clothes in a great tub with their feet, their coats, smocks and all, tucked up to their breech.

We came from Barwicke about seven clock, and came to DUNBARR about twelve, which is twenty English miles : it is not improperly called Dunbarr, because it is so environed with shelfs, bars and sands, as there is no manner of haven, though the main sea beat upon the town, which indeed is not seated upon any river, which might furnish it with an haven or a navigable channel; only here is an haven made of great stones piled up, whereinto at a spring-tide a ship of one hundred ton may enter, but not without much hazard. Six miles hence in the sea (though it be a far shorter cut by land) is the island of Bass,[2] which is here very conspicuous; a mighty high

rable importance, the property of the Stewarts, which afterwards passed into the hands of the Hamiltons, and was destroyed by the Protector Somerset. Sir James Maxwell, father of Sir James, created a baronet by king Charles I, married Isabel, the daughter of Sir Alexander Hamilton, of Innerwick.

[1] Sir Robert Ker, of Cesford, accompanied James I to England, and was created Lord Roxburgh ; in 1616, he was promoted to the dignity of Earl of Roxburgh ; 1637, made lord privy-seal ; adhered to the fortunes of Charles I. Died 1650, aged eighty.

[2] The Bass Island was a very ancient possession of the family of Lauder, who disposed of it, in 1671, to king Charles II, who used it as a state-prison. John Blackadder and Alexander Peden were imprisoned there. It was the last fortress in Britain over which the flag of James II waved; and its defence against the troops of William III was singularly heroic.

rock placed in the sea, whereinto there is only one passage, and that for a single person. This is now fortified, and inhabited by the lord of the Bass. It is about one English mile about. Herein are kept sheep, and some kine and coneys; abundance of fowl breed here, solem-geese, storts,[1] scoutes,[2] and twenty several sorts of fowl, which make such a noise as that you may hear them and nothing else a mile before you come to them. These solem-geese (as it is reported of them), when their eggs are sufficiently sitten, they stamp upon them with their feet, and break them; they breed in the sides of the rocks, and there is fowl (said to be) sold here, taken in this island, worth £200 per annum. Here is excellent fresh water in this isle, a dainty pure spring which is to be the more admired. The isle of May is not hence above three leagues, and it is easy to be discerned, wherein also abundance of fowl breed.

From Dunbarr to Edenburgh we came this day in the afternoon; it is called but twenty miles, but it is twenty-five or twenty-six miles at least; and by the way we observed very many stately seats of the nobles. One we passed near unto, which is the Earl of Winton's,[3] a dainty seat placed upon the sea. Here also is apple-trees, walnut-trees, sycamore, and other fruit-trees, and other kinds of wood which prosper well, though it be very near unto, and within the air of, the sea. In this house the king lodged three nights; and in this earl's chamber at Edenborough, in Mr. William Callis his house in the High-street near the Cross, I lodged, and paid one shilling and sixpence per noctem for my lodging.

About six or seven miles from this city I saw and took notice of divers salt-works in poor houses erected upon the sea coast. I went into one of them, and observed iron pans eighteen foot long and nine foot broad; these larger pans and houses than those at the

[1] Probably the cormorant, which in Scotland is called *scart*.

[2] Scoutes, guillemots, *colymbus troile*.

[3] Seaton House, built by George, third Earl of Wintoun, where he entertained James I and Charles I. He died in 1650, aged sixty-five. Upon the attainder of the last Earl in 1719, the property was sold, the house was allowed to fall into decay, and entirely pulled down in 1790.

Sheildes. An infinite, innumerable number of salt-works here are erected upon this shore; all make salt of sea-water. About four miles hence stands MUSSLEBORROW, touching which they have this proverb: Mussleborrow was a borrow when Edenborough was none, and shall be a burrough when Edenborough shall be none.

About nine o'clock at night we came into EDENBOROUGH, where, by reason of the foot-boy's negligences, we were put upon great straights, and had our lodging to seek at ten o'clock, and in conclusion, were constrained to accept of mean and nasty lodging, for which we paid one shilling and eight-pence; and the next morning, *Saturday,* 27 *Junii,* we went to the Towle-boothe,[1] where are the courts of justice, which are six: 1. The Court wherein meet the Lords of the Privy Council, whereof are most of the eminent nobles of the land. 2. That Court[2] wherein there are fifteen judges sit attired in purple gowns, turned up with velvet of the same colour; hereof the President is Sir Robert [Spottiswoode].[3] As it is here reported, if any of those fifteen be absent hence any day, they incur the forfeiture of, and pay, one pound a day for absence. The Archbishop of St. Andrewe's, Lord Chancellor of Scotland, is the prime man in this kingdom. 3. There is another inferior Court near adjoining hereunto, wherein sits weekly and successively every of these fifteen judges alone; this court takes only cognizance of inferior causes, and of less importance: and, as

[1] The Tolbooth was built in 1561, and was destined for the accommodation of Parliament, the courts of justice, and the confinement of prisoners. From the year 1640, however, when the present Parliament-house was built, till 1817, when it was pulled down, it was used only as a prison.—*Heart of Mid-Lothian,* note to ch. vi. ed. 1831.

[2] The Court of Session was established by king James V, in the year 1532, to consist of fourteen and a president. This office was held by Sir Robert Spottiswoode from the year 1633. He was second son to the Archbishop mentioned below, and secretary of state in Scotland. After the defeat of Montrose in 1646, he was taken prisoner and put to death by the rebellious covenanters, his crime being his having delivered to Montrose the king's commission to be captain-general of Scotland.

[3] John Spottiswoode, the historian of the Church of Scotland, at the very early age of eighteen succeeded his father as parson of Calder, in Mid-Lothian; was made Bishop of Glasgow in 1603, Archbishop of St. Andrew's in 1615. He held the office of lord chancellor of Scotland from the year 1635 to the time of his death in 1639. He was born in the year 1565.

it seems unto me, is erected in favour and ease of the rest fifteen judges; and if any intricate cause or of greater consequence occur, the present judge then propounds unto and consults with the rest of the fifteen judges. In this court I observed the greatest rudeness, disorder, and confusion, that ever I saw in any court of justice; no, not the like disorder in any of our sessions; for here two or three plead and speak together, and that with such a forced, strained voice as the strongest voice only carries it; yea, sometimes they speak about two or three several causes at one and the same time, which makes an extraordinary disorder and confusion, so as no man breathing can hear distinctly or understand any thing so promiscuously spoken. 4. There is an Exchequer, or court of the king's revenue. 5. There is a court below, under the beforenamed courts, wherein sit the judges touching criminal matters and misdemeanours. 6. The Consistory, which takes only cognizance of ecclesiastical affairs.

In this kingdom the clergy of late extend their authority and revenues. Archbishoprick of St. Andrewes is Lord Chancellor of Scotland and Regent here. And, as I was informed by some intelligent gentleman, it is here thought and conceived that they will recover so much of that land and revenues belonging formerly to the Abbeys, as that they will in a short time possess themselves of the third part of the kingdom.[1] The Duke of Lennox and Marquis Hamilton are possessed of the largest proportion of Church-land: it is expected that they should resign and deliver up their interests and rights therein to the Church, whose example it is thought will induce the rest of the nobility to do the like. And to the end that they may carry some sway in Parliament, it is now endeavoured (as some here informed

---

[1] Sir W. Brereton seems to have here fallen into the society of spirits congenial to his own, and to have listened credulously to the falsifications and exaggerations of some not kindly disposed to the Church. To the Archbishop's praise be it spoken, that he did endeavour to regain some of the property of which the Church had been sacrilegiously deprived. That it was not personal wealth he sought for, may be safely presumed, as it was upon his own petition that the property of the see of St. Andrew's lying south of the Forth was appropriated to the endowment of a new Bishoprick, to be seated at Edinburgh.

me, Mr. Calderwood[1] and Dr. Sharpe) to restore abbots, and to invest them in the revenues and seats of abbeys: hereof they say there are forty-eight which are intended to be established, who are all to sit and carry voices in Parliament; which, if it can be effected, then there will be always in the parliament-house so strong a party for the king, considering those officers that have an immediate dependance upon him and the bishops and abbots, as that they will be able to sway the whole house. Divers of the clergy incline this way, and many also are mighty opposite and averse hereunto.

This *Saturday*, after dinner, I took a view of the castle here, which is seated very high and sufficiently commanding, and being able to batter the town; this is also seated upon the top of a most hard rock, and the passage whereunto was (as they there report) made through that hard and impregnable rock, which cannot be touched or hewed, and it is indeed a stately passage, wherein was used more industry, pains, art, and endeavour, than in any place I have found amongst the Scotts. It is but a very little castle, of no great receipt, but mighty strength; it is called Castrum Puellarum, because the kings of the Picts kept there virgins therein; upon the wall of the castle, towards the top, is this insculpsion, part thereof gilt,—a crown and sceptre, and dagger placed under it cross-wise, with this superscription: " Nobis hæc invicta miserunt 106 Proavi:" the same arms and inscription is placed upon the front of the abbey, which is the king's house. Out of the court of this high-seated castle, there was one that watched (a soldier in his turn) in a little wooden house or cabin, which by a whirlwind was taken and thrown down both together over the castle wall and to the bottom of this high and steep rock, and the man not hurt or bruised, save only his finger put out of joint. Hence you may take a full view of the situation of the whole city, which is built upon a hill nothing oversteep, but sufficiently sloping and ascending to give a graceful ascent to the great street, which I do take to be an English mile long, and is the best paved street with bowther

[2] Calderwood was a strenuous opponent of king James's efforts in favour of the Church. He published, in 1623, a celebrated work called " Altare Damascenum, seu Ecclesiæ Anglicanæ politia Ecclesiæ Scoticanæ obtrusa," &c. He died in the reign of Charles I.

stones [1] (which are very great ones) that I have seen: the channels
are very conveniently contrived on both sides the streets, so as
there is none in the middle; but it is the broadest, largest, and
fairest pavement, and that entire, to go, ride or draw upon.

Here they usually walk in the middle of the street, which is a fair,
spacious, and capacious walk. This street is the glory and beauty
of this city: it is the broadest street (except in the Low Countries,
where there is a navigable channel in middle of the street) and the
longest street I have seen, which begins at the palace, the gate
whereof enters straight into the suburbs, and is placed at the lower
end of the same. The suburbs make an handsome street; and indeed the street, if the houses, which are very high, and substan-
tially built of stone (some five, some six stories high), were not lined
to the outside and faced with boards, it were the most stately and
graceful street that ever I saw in my life; but this face of boards,
which is towards the street, doth much blemish it, and derogate
from glory and beauty; as also the want of fair glass windows,
whereof few or none are to be discerned towards the street, which
is the more complete, because it is as straight as may be. This
lining with boards (wherein are round holes shaped to the proportion of men's heads), and this incroachment into the street about
two yards, is a mighty disgrace unto it, for the walls (which were
the outside) are stone; so, as if this outside facing of boards were
removed, and the houses built uniform all of the same height, it
were the most complete street in Christendom.

This city is placed in a dainty, healthful, pure air, and doubtless
were a most healthful place to live in, were not the inhabitants
most sluttish, nasty, and slothful people. I could never pass
through the hall, but I was constrained to hold my nose; their
chambers, vessel, linen and meat, nothing neat, but very slovenly;
only the nobler and better sort of them brave, well-bred men, and
much reformed. This street, which may indeed deserve to deno-
minate the whole city, is always full thronged with people, it being
the market-place, and the only place where the gentlemen and
merchants meet and walk, wherein they may walk dry under foot,

[1] Bowlder stones, fragments of rock rounded by the action of water.

though there hath been abundance of rain. Some few coaches are here to be found for some of the great lords and ladies, and bishops.

Touching the fashion of the citizens, the women here wear and use upon festival days six or seven several habits and fashions; some for distinction of widows, wives and maids, others apparelled according to their own humour and phantasy. Many wear (especially of the meaner sort) plaids, which is a garment of the same woollen stuff whereof saddle cloths in England are made, which is cast over their heads, and covers their faces on both sides, and would reach almost to the ground, but that they pluck them up, and wear them cast under their arms. Some ancient women and citizens wear satin straight-bodied gowns, short little cloaks with great capes, and a broad boun-grace[1] coming over their brows, and going out with a corner behind their heads; and this boun-grace is, as it were, lined with a white stracht cambric suitable unto it. Young maids not married all are bare-headed; some with broad thin shag ruffs, which lie flat to their shoulders, and others with half bands with wide necks, either much stiffened or set in wire, which comes only behind; and these shag ruffs some are more broad and thick than others.

This city of Edenborough is governed by a lord provost (which is equivalent to a lord mayor) and two or three bailiffs, who execute the office of sheriffs, who, as they assume no extraordinary state, only some few officers attending them, so they do not maintain any great houses and hospitalities; and when any occasion of greater consequence and importance occurs, they then call unto them and consult with, as assistants, some of those that have been formerly lords provosts. The people here are slothful, that they fetch not fresh water every day, but only every other day, which makes their water much worse (especially to drink), which when it is at best is bad enough. Their houses of office are tubs or firkins placed upon the end, which they never empty until they be full, so as the scent thereof annoyeth and offendeth the whole house.

I was this day with an intelligent, understanding man, who told

[1] *Bongrace* was a sort of hood, or the broad band in front of the hood, which projected far, and preserved the face from being sunburnt.

me there were above sixty back-lanes or streets, which were placed
in the side of this street, and went out of it; narrow and inconvenient straight lanes, some wider, some narrower, some built on
both sides, others only on one side; and enquiring what number of
persons might be in this city, I found that it was generally com-
puted that they were no more than sixty thousand persons, because
there are only four parish churches in this city, and it is observed
that there are no more than about four thousand communicants in
every parish.   Here is a dainty hospital erecting, not yet finished.[1]
I took notice here of that common brewhouse which supplieth the
whole city with beer and ale, and observed there the greatest,
vastest leads, boiling keeres,[2] cisterns and combs,[2] that ever I saw:
the leads to cool the liquor in were as large as the whole house,
which was as long as my court.

   Junii 29.[3]—We went this morning to behold and take a view of
LEITH, where is the haven belonging to this city; which is a pretty
little haven, neither furnished with near so many ships as it is
capable of, nor indeed is it a large haven capable of many ships.
There are two neat wooden piers here erected, which run up into
the river, but not one ship saw I betwixt them.   There are two
churches in this town, which belongs unto and is subordinate to
the city of Edenborough.   This town of Leith is built all of stone,
but it seemeth to be but a poor place, though seated upon a dainty
haven: the country 'twixt this and Edenborough, and all hereabout this city, is corn, is situate betwixt the hills and the sea.

   [1] Heriot's Hospital.   George Heriot, goldsmith and jeweller to kings James I and
Charles I, died in 1624, leaving great wealth, the residue of which, after many be-
quests to relations, friends and servants, he left to the magistrates of Edinburgh, to
found and endow a hospital " for the maintenance, relief, and bringing up, of so many
poor and fatherless boys, freemen's sons of the town of Edinburgh, as the same should
be sufficient for."   This building, one of the most interesting ornaments of the city of
Edinburgh, was begun iu 1628, after designs of Inigo Jones, and was not completed,
as we see here, in 1635.   In 1650 it was nearly finished, and used by Cromwell as a
hospital for his soldiers; at length, Monk removed the soldiers, and in 1659 it was
opened for its original purpose, and the building was completely finished in 1660.
   [2] *Keeve*, a large vessel, in which the liquor is placed to work.   *Comb*, a large wooden
vessel or tub ; a measure of four bushels of corn is in some districts called *a comb*.
   [3] Junii 27.

Upon the top of the Toole-bowthe stands the head of Gawrie. Here are pies (whereof I have had some this day to dinner) which are sold twelve for a penny English. Here upon the Tole-boothe stands the head of Earl Gawrie.[1] Many Highlanders we observed in this town in their plaids, many without doublets, and those who have doublets have a kind of loose flap garment hanging loose about their breech, their knees bare; they inure themselves to cold, hardship, and will not diswont themselves; proper, personable, well-complectioned men, and of able[2] men; the very gentlemen in their blue caps and plaids.

The sluttishness and nastiness of this people is such, that I cannot omit the particularizing thereof, though I have more than sufficiently often touched upon the same : their houses, and halls, and kitchens, have such a noisome taste, a savour and that so strong, as it doth offend you so soon as you come within their walls; yea, sometimes when I have light from my horse, I have felt the distaste of it before I have come into the house; yea, I never came to my own lodging in Edenborough, or went out, but I was constrained to hold my nose, or to use worm-wood, or some such scented plant.

Their pewter, I am confident, is never scoured; they are afraid it should too much wear and consume thereby; only sometimes, and that but seldom, they do slightly rub them over with a filthy

[1] The Earl of Gowry was one of the chief conspirators who seized James I in 1582, and kept him under constraint for about a year, when he escaped. The conspirators were, upon submission, pardoned; but the Earl of Gowry was tried the following year upon some new charges, and executed. It was probably not the head of this earl which then remained upon the Tolbooth, but that of his son, who, in the year 1600, conspired with his brother to lure king James to his house at Perth, and then assassinate him. The plot so far succeeded, as to draw the king to the house, and even into a private chamber, where the earl's brother and a servant were prepared to commit the bloody deed. The king contrived to struggle with the assassins, and to rouse his attendants, who rushed to his assistance, and put both the earl and his brother to death upon the spot. Though this occurred upon the 5th of August, their bodies were brought to the Parliament-house on the 15th of November following, when they were hanged upon a gibbet, dismembered, and the heads cut off and affixed upon the top of the prison-house.—Abp. Spottiswoode, *Hist. of Scotland*, pp. 320, 462.

[2] Sic in MS.

dish-clout, dipped in most sluttish greasy water. Their pewter pots, wherein they bring wine and water, are furred within, that it would loathe you to touch any thing which comes out of them. Their linen as it is sluttishly and slothfully washed by women's feet, who, after their linen is put into a great, broad, low tub of water, then (their clothes being tucked up above their knees) they step into the tub and tread it, and trample it with their feet (never vouchsafing a hand to nett[1] or wash it withal) until it be sufficiently cleansed in their apprehensions, and then it looks as nastily as ours doth when it is put unto and designed to the washing, as also it doth so strongly taste and smell of lant[2] and other noisome savours, as that when I came to bed I was constrained to hold my nose and mouth together. To come into their kitchen, and to see them dress their meat, and to behold the sink (which is more offensive than any jakes) will be a sufficient supper, and will take off the edge of your stomach.

Julii[3] 28.—*Lord's day.* Touching the government and orders of the church here established. It is governed by pastors, elders, and deacons; there are about twelve elders, eight deacons, and two pastors in every parish, (as Mr. Wallis, a judicious merchant informed me:) these deacons, their employment and office is to provide for the poor; the elders take notice and cognizance of all misdemeanors and offences committed in their parish, unto every of which elders there is proportioned and allotted a part of the parish, which is under their care and charge, who take notice of all fornications, adulteries, thefts, drunkards, swearers, blasphemers, slanderers, extortioners, and all other scandalous offences committed in their parishes: these (by virtue of their offices and strict vows, and protestations,) are to present all these offenders unto the minister and church-officers, who proceed to ecclesiastical censure; it is the duty of these to provide bread and wine for the parishioners at the communion, and this upon the parish charge; these also are assistants to the pastors in the administration of the sacrament. All

---

[1] *Nett*, to clean, from the French *nettoyer*.   [2] *Lant*, chamberlye, urine.   [3] *Junii* 28.

these officers are yearly changed, and chosen by the parishioners, and are proclaimed in the church, to be designed for those places a year before they are invested with those places, that so if any just exception can be made against them, they may be put by that office and others elected.

Once every week, the pastors and elders, and sometimes the deacons, assemble and meet together, to consult upon and consider of the affairs of the parish; they are most strict in their censures against fornicators and adulterers; those that commit fornication under colour of intended marriage, and after promise of marriage, are enjoyned to sit upon the stool of repentance one day. This stool is a public and eminent seat, erected towards the lower end of the church about two yards from the ground, either about some pillar, or in some such conspicuous place, where the whole congregation may take notice of them; this seat is capable of about six or eight persons. Here this day, 28 *Junii*, I was at sermon in the Gray Friors, where there stood three women upon the stool of repentance, who are admitted to sit during the sermon. Those other fornicators are enjoined three days penance on this stool; adulterers are censured to stand every Lord's day upon this stool during twelve months in a sheet of hair, and this enjoined them in divers churches. This day, after sermon, the preacher admonished some who had persevered in a course of impenitence and uncleanness, and had often been admonished and enjoined to give testimony of their repentance, and to make satisfaction to the congregation; this hath been delayed, and is not performed. He said, he wondered that people were not ashamed to sin against God and against their brethren, and against their own souls, and yet they were ashamed to make satisfaction unto the church, which had conceived just matter of offence against them, for so great scandal thereby given. He added, that they had proceeded with much remissness against them, and forborne them not one year but two, but if at the next meeting they did not make their appearance, the next Lord's day they would publish their names to the congregation. They proceed in their ecclesiastical censures with all meekness, endeavouring a reformation first by those means, and

very rarely, not once in many years, do they denounce any excom-
municate.   There are some officers made choice of to take notice
of, and to apprehend all those that loiter in the streets upon the
Lord's day, during service and sermon-time; these are punished
by being committed to the Toll-bowth; and if any are found in
any house tippling, or gaming in church-time, they are committed
to prison.   Those also called to account that are met walking from-
wards the church, and are detained in durance until they be brought
before the bailiffs of the town, who punisheth them severely.

Good provision is here made by the deacons, the church officers,
for the poor, a collection and contribution every Lord's day before
sermon ; every well-affected parishioner doth receive the alms and
bounty of those who come to church (all which give something), in
box; hereunto they are chosen and designed by the church officers;
this they receive at the church door, and there is also a monthly
taxation and assessment laid upon all the inhabitants of the parish,
towards the relief of the poor, so as none beg, nor are suffered to
wander upon and down the parish ; but though many poor people
swarm and abound here, and more than I have met with in any
part of the world, yet these most abound here, and the most
miserable creatures in the world.

Bought in Edenburgh ; Thanksgiving Sermon upon birth of
Prince, and the Itinerary of Scotland and Ireland: two pair of pistols,
which cost eight rix-dollars, which is £1. 18s. 4d., a dudgeon-hafted
dagger and knives, gilt, 3s. 8d.

Divers earls' and lord's houses here in Edenburgh, as mean
buildings as gentlemen's and knight's in London and England.
Here I saw the Earl of Trequheres' house, who is deputy treasurer
under my Lord Morton ; he was made earl when the King was
last here.   I paid here for my horses two rix-dollars, and for our

---

[1] Sir John Stewart was appointed treasurer-depute, and created lord steward of Traquair, April 1628. In 1636, he was appointed high treasurer of Scotland, having been
before raised to the dignity of Earl of Traquair, Lord Lintown and Caherstoun, June
1633, when king Charles I. was at Holyrood. He was of a very timid disposition, but
firm in his allegiance to his sovereign, in whose service he suffered an imprisonment of
four years, and upon his liberation returned home, and lived in extreme poverty until
his death in September 1659.

lodging for six persons, three beds, every night 1s. 6d.; for victuals Saturday 7s. 2d., Sunday, Monday, Tuesday, breakfast about £1. 5s.; washing, 1s. 8d.; rewards to the maid and cook, 2s.

The College of Edinburgh, called King James his college, was founded by the citizens about seventy years ago, by the direction of Mr. Rollock, the first principal thereof, and minister of the college church. The order that is observed in the worship of God is this; upon the Lord's day, they do assemble 'twixt eight and nine hour in the morning, and spend the time in singing psalms and reading chapters in the Old Testament, until about ten hour; then the preacher comes into the pulpit, and the psalm being ended, he reads a printed and prescribed prayer, which is an excellent prayer; this being ended, another psalm is sung, and then he prays before sermon, and concludes his sermon betwixt eleven and twelve hour; and during the intermission, many continue in the church until the afternoon's exercise, which begins soon after one, is performed in the same manner as in the morning, save the chapters then read out of the New Testament, and they conclude about four hour. I was in the morning at the Gray Friors, where I heard a very worthy man, Mr. James Sherley: in the wall of the yard of this church, I observed very fair tombs and monuments, erected in memory and honour of divers merchants and others interred in this church-yard; which custom, if they continue, in the revolution of a short time the whole wall will be most gracefully adorned with

¹ In 1580, application was made to king James VI to grant a charter for the foundation of a university at Edinburgh, and the whole arrangements were completed in 1582. The college was built, and the various offices maintained, at the expense chiefly of citizens of Edinburgh. Robert Rollock commenced his education under Mr. Thomas Buchanan, and prosecuted his studies at St. Andrew's. In 1583, he was made first Principal and Rector of the university at Edinburgh, where, by his lectures of divinity in the schools, and his sermons to the people, he came to be greatly esteemed. He was a person of great worth and learning. He wrote commentaries on the Psalms and some of the prophets; and some sermons and pieces of devotion were also published by him. A rare example of holiness he was, both in his life and death. He was much weakened by his exertions in the troublous times in which he lived; he was naturally of an infirm body, and grievously pained with the stone, whereof at last he died in February 1598, in the forty-third year of his age.—*Abp. Spottiswoode, Hist.* p. 455.

tombs, which are most stately ornaments round about the same.
In the afternoon I went to the College Kirk, where I heard a blind
man preach, much to be admired. Here I saw the sacrament of
Baptism administered in this manner:—the preacher standing in the
pulpit, and there being placed and fastened into the same a frame
of iron, shaped and proportioned to a basin, wherein there stands
a silver basin and ewer; here the minister useth an exhortation of
gratitude for God's great goodness, in admitting them to this
privilege, &c., and demanding from the witnesses (which are many,
sometimes twelve, sometimes twenty), according to a printed form
of Baptism, the parent receives the child from the midwife, presents
the same unto the preacher, who doth baptize it without any manner of ceremony, giving a strict care of Christian and religious
education, first unto the parent, then to the witnesses.

When the sacrament of the Lord's Supper is administered, a
narrow table is placed in the middle aisle, the whole length of the
aisle, about which the most of the receivers sit, as in the Dutch and
French churches, but now the ceremonies of the Church of Eng-
gland are introduced, and conformity is much pressed, and the ges-
ture of kneeling is also much pressed.

About twenty years last past, by virtue of an Act of Parliament
made in this kingdom, there was every year once assembled a
national council, consisting of one burgess for every burough, one
baron or elder in every presbytery, and two or three ministers or
pastors for a presbytery; but these meetings were dissolved and
taken away about twenty years last past, and now that Act of Parliament is made void and abrogated.

The discipline of the Church of England is much pressed and
much opposed by many pastors and many of the people. (Quære
touching aire 77.) The greatest part of the Scotts are very honest
and zealously religious. I observed few given to drink or swearing;
but if any oath, the most ordinary oath was, " Upon my soul."
The most of my hosts I met withal, and others with whom I conversed, I found very sound and orthodox, and zealously religious.
In their demands they do not so much exceed as with us in England,
but insist upon and adhere unto their first demand for any commodity.

I observed few bells rung in any of their churches in Edenborough, and, as I was informed, there are but few bells in any steeple, save in the Abbey Church steeple, which is the king's palace. Herein is a ring of bells erected by king Charles immediately before his coming into Scottland, anno Dom. 1635, but none here knew how to ring or make any use of them, until some came out of England for that purpose, who hath now instructed some Scotts in this art. In most of the eminent churches in this city, the king hath a stately seat placed on high, almost round about some pillar opposite to the pulpit.

June 30.—About twelve hour we left Edenborough, and came to LIGHT-GOAW, twelve miles from thence. This seems to be a fair, ancient town, and well-built, some part of it of stone. Here is a fair church, and a dainty conduit in the middle of the street. Here the king hath a very fair palace, built castle-wise, well-seated, so as it may command the whole town, which is governed by a provost and bailiffs, who have power to punish with death offences committed within their liberties. By the way, I observed gentlemen's (here called lairds) houses built all castle-wise. We lodged this night at FAIL-KIRK, whence about seven miles distant (which we discerned as we came) is seated the best house or castle of his Majesty in this kingdom, called Sterlin, which is placed upon an high commanding rock and hill, and not far from the fair navigable river Frithe, near adjoining whereunto this is situate. Here is another of his Majesty's houses, an abbey called Drumfarmalin, which is not above ten miles distant hence; and his Majesty's most pleasant and gallant houses are Falkeland, and Sterlin, and Luthgow; and there is also another palace in the abbey of Scune, where the kings formerly were crowned.[2]

---

[1] The palace of Dunfermline is said to have been the birthplace of King Charles I. That monarch, during his visit to Scotland in 1633, held a court here; and in this palace Charles II signed the Solemn League and Covenant. It has since that time been neglected and alienated; and scarcely a vestige remains beyond one chamber, called the king's kitchen.

[2] The last coronation at Scone was that of King Charles II, in 1650.

All along the shore of Frithe are placed, even almost to Sterlin, from beyond Mussleborough, salt-pans, wherein a mighty proportion of salt is boiled, which cannot be estimated and guessed, because the works are not easily to [be] numbered, which are placed all along the shore, at least thirty English mile.   The conveniency of coals gives greatest encouragement to the erection and pursuit of these works; coals abound all along the shore, yea, it is conceived that the vein lies all under the river, seeing it is found on both sides as it were reaching towards the other.   Here the chief charge is the getting, which is not easy, seeing the vein lies sometimes sixteen or twenty fathom deep.   The greatest part of salt here made is transported into Holland.   Here now are some of their ships, which are also supplied with coals hence, now the rather, because the custom of 4s. upon a chaldron being increased, they decline the trade there, and none or few of them are there to be now found.   Coals are sold for 3s. or 3s. 6d. chaldron, and carriage 2s. 8d.   Here was (about seventeen hundred years since) a great stone and earth wall, called Grhames Wall,[1] leading from Forth, six mile below Leith, over the main land to Dumbarton, which is upon the West Sea; which wall was thirty-two miles long, and gave bounds to the kingdoms of Scots on the south and Picts on the north; at every mile's end was there erected a tower for the watchmen, and a castle at every two miles' end, wherein was a strong garrison.

About half mile hence was there a cruel battle fought betwixt the English and Scotts, in anno 1298, in Julii 22.[2]   Then was there slain, which here are buried in the churchyard, and whose monuments are still extant, Stewart of Butts[3] (out of which house

[1] Antoninus' Wall, or Grahame's Dyke or Grime's Dike.

[2] The battle of Falkirk, where the Scottish army was so signally defeated by Edward I.

[3] Sir John Stewart, styled of Bonkyll, from his marriage with Margaret, the heiress of that name and place, was second son of Alexander, high steward of Scotland, who died in 1283.   In the battle of Falkirk, while giving orders to his archers, he was thrown from his horse and slain; and his archers crowding round his body, perished with him.   The want of entire confidence in the pedigree of the Stewarts, which seems to

it is said his majesty that now is hath descended) and Sir John Grahames,[1] both brave men. About fourteen miles hence is a meare or lake called LOEMUND,[2] in Perth, wherein are the flitting islands, which move (my host, Mr. Fleemeing, affirmed he hath seen it): it is most rough in calm weather; the fish are without fins. There is in CARICKE a rock three yards long and one broad, upon which if you tingle with your knife, it will ring like brass pan : this is called the Ringing Rock, and is near the highway, about sixteen miles from Port Patrick. Strange footsteps[3] in the cave of Caricke, wherein (as my host here affirmed that he had often seen it) are always to be seen and found the prints and footsteps of men, women, and children, of dogs, cats, sheep, kine, horses, deer, and all manner of beasts; yea, he further protested that he had seen it, that though the sand were overnight sifted, yet these impressions were to be found next morning. And whereas some write and some report of a deaf rock, it is but a fable, so I was informed by very judicious men. Here we paid 6s. English supper for seven persons, and lodged in Mr. Fleemeing's house, who is a very intelligent, proper, complete, and well-bred man.

There is a great Earl of this country; his name is Fleemeing,

have existed in the time of Sir W. Brereton, long continued ; and with a view to settle the disputed point, Mr. And. Stuart, in 1798, published his *Genealogical History of the Stewarts.*

[1] Sir John Graham was second son of the third Sir David Graham. He was the faithful friend and companion of Wallace; and, being slain in the battle of Falkirk, was buried in the chapel of that place, with the following epitaph, which still remains:

"Mente manuque potens, et Vallæ fidus Achates,
Conditur hic Græmus, bello interfectus ab Anglis."

[2] Loch Lomond was long proverbially famed for three wonders, "Waves without wind, fish without fins, and a floating island." Waves without wind, or at least without wind apparently enough to create the swell which sometimes occurs in lakes, is not very uncommon ; the fish without fins are supposed to be vipers, which are said to be occasionally seen swimming from one island to another. The floating island is a wonder which has been ascribed to other lakes, and variously accounted for. One account states that it was artificially constructed about the fifth century, of huge pieces of timber, strongly united together by one Keith Macindoile, and then covered with soil, and planted.

[3] Page 122.

and his title Weghkton,[1] whose house or palace we saw; but there
was so much wood encompassed the same, as we could not discern
the same. Here we were shewed by Mr. Guordon a meadow of
his, reputed the fairest meadow in Scotland. I would not give in
exchange for it the Broad Meadow, though it be much larger;
one acre of the Broad Meadow worth two of this. I paid for hay
here 6d. per noctem, and 12d. peck per oats.

Julii 1.—Hence I departed, and about twelve miles hence there
is a town called Cuntellen.   *   *

Here by the way, we were showed the relics of a stately wood
cut down, which belonged to this Earl of Weghkton. There is
very little or no timber in any of the south or west parts of this
kingdom, much less than in England. I have diligently observed,
but cannot find any timber in riding near one hundred miles; all
the country poor and barren, save where it is helped by lime or
sea-weeds. Limestone here is very plentiful, and coals; and where
there are no coals, they have abundance of turves. Poorest houses
and people that I have seen inhabit here; the houses accommodated
with no more light than the light of the door, no window; the
houses covered with clods; the women only neat and handsome
about the feet, which comes to pass by their often washing with
their feet.

About one hour we came to the city of GLASGOAW, which is
thirty-six miles from Edenburgh, eighteen from Failkirke. This
is an Archbishop's seat, an ancient university, one only college
consisting of about one hundred and twenty students, wherein are
four schools, one principal, four regents. There are about six or

[1] John Fleming, Lord Fleming, was advanced to the dignity of Earl of Wigtoun by
King James VI, in 1606.

seven thousand communicants, and about twenty thousand persons in the town, which is famous for the church, which is fairest and stateliest in Scotland, for the Toll-boothe and Bridge.

This church I viewed this day, and found it a brave and ancient piece. It was said, in this church this day, that there was a contribution throughout Europe (even Rome itself contributed), towards the building hereof. There is a great partition or wall 'twixt the body of the church and the chancel; there is no use of the body of the church, only divine service and sermon is used and performed in the quire or chancel, which is built and framed church-wise; and under this quire there is also another church, which carries the same proportion under this, wherein also there is two sermons every Lord's day. Three places or rooms one above another, round and uniformed, like unto chapter-houses, which are complete buildings and rooms.

The Tole-boothe, which is placed in the middle of the town, and near unto the cross and market-place, is a very fair and high-built house, from the top whereof, being leaded, you may take a full view and prospect of the whole city. In one of these rooms or chambers sits the council of this city: in other of the rooms or chambers, preparation is made for the lords of the council to meet in: these stately rooms. Herein is a closet lined with iron; walls, top, bottom, floor, and door, iron; wherein are kept the evidences and records of the city: this made, to prevent the danger of fire. This tole-booth said to be the fairest in this kingdom: the revenues belonging to this city are about 1000*l.* per annum. This town is built: two streets, which are built like a cross, in the middle of both which the cross is placed, which looks four ways into four streets, though indeed they be but two straight streets; the one reaching from the church to the bridge, a mile long,—the other which crosseth, that is much shorter.

Two archbishops; of St. Andrewes, Spotswood, Chancellor,

---

[1] This under church was in the crypt, which was appropriated as a parish church, in 1560, to the Barony parish, which was created out of a district in Glasgow. It continued to be used as such till about the year 1801, when a new parish church was built.

Regent: the other of Glasgoaw, Dr. Lindsey. Bishops, above twenty.[1]

The prime cities in Scottland: Edenborough, St. Andrewes, Dondye, Aberden, Glasgoaw, Perth or St. Johnstone, Lightgow; Aire, Sterling, Dumbarton, Erwing, Don Frise,[2] Haddington, Dunbarr, Erwin, Elgin, Murray, Banffe, Enverness, Boughan.

Fairest bridges in Scottland: 1. Done, which is in the north, under which, as Mr. Guerdon informed me, that a ship of fifty or sixty ton may pass with her sails full spread. This is but one arch, placed on a high rock, upon either side much above the water. A very fair bridge at Glasgoaw, over Cleyd the river; St. Johnstones is a gallant bridge, stands upon Tay; Aberden. Glasgoaw is a fair bridge, consisting of seven or eight fair arches, which are supported and strengthened with strong buttresses: this river is now navigable within six miles of this city; it ebbs and flows above the bridge, though now the water is so shallow, as you may ride; under the horse belly. Beyond this river there is seated pleasantly a house, which was Sir George Elvinstones, and is to be sold to pay his debts: the revenue thereunto belonging is above £300 per annum. The price offered by this city, who are about to buy it, is £6000, the suburbs and privileged places belonging unto it induce them to buy it.[3]

---

[1] The bishopricks in Scotland were not so numerous as stated by Sir W. Brereton. There were two archbishops and twelve bishops. Archbishops: St. Andrew's and Glasgow. Bishops: Edinburgh, Dunkeld, Aberdeen, Moray, Brechin, Dunblane, Ross, Caithness, Orkney, Galloway, Argyle, The Isles. These were all deprived after the rebellion of 1688, by the new government. Dr. Patrick Lindsay was translated from Ross to Glasgow, 1633. He was deprived by the Covenanters in 1638, and retired to Newcastle, where he died 1641.

[2] Dumfries.

[3] The Gorbals are a suburb of Glasgow, lying on the opposite side of the river Clyde; in early times it was the compulsory retreat of persons affected with leprosy, and peculiar privileges were attached to it. The right of barony and regality belonged to the archbishop of Glasgow, who in 1607 alienated it to Sir George Elphinstone. The treaty mentioned in the text does not appear to have been concluded before 1647, when the authorities of Glasgow purchased from the representatives of Sir George Elphinstone this property, with all the rights, privileges, jurisdictions, and powers of baron and superior.

We lodged in Glasgoaw, in Mr. David Weyme's house; his wife's name is Margrett Cambell (the wives in Scotland never change, but always retain, their own names), no stabling hereunto belonging; in the town we were constrained to provide stabling, I paid 5d. for pease straw, for my straw; no hay would be gotten. We paid for victuals, dinner, and breakfast, seven persons, two rix-dollars.

There is a good handsome foundation propounded and set out, to to add a good fair and college-like structure to be built quadrangular; one side is already built, and there hath been collections throughout Scotland towards the building of this college, and much more money is collected than is needful to the building hereof.[1] Here the library is a very little room, not twice so large as my old closet; that part of it which is now standing is old, strong, plain building. This college is governed by one principal, four regents, and about one hundred and twenty students. Here the scholars may be distinguished from others by gowns (in Edenborough they use coloured cloaks), though coloured, some red, some gray, and of other colours, as please themselves.

Here I visited the Archbishop of Glasgoaw's palace, which seems a stately structure, and promises much when you look upon the outside. It is said to be the inheritance of the Duke of Lennox, but the archbishops successively made use of it.[2] Here I went to see the hall and palace, and going into the hall, which is a poor and mean place, the archbishop's daughter, an handsome and well-bred proper gentlewoman, entertained me with much civil respect, and would not suffer me to depart until I had drunk Scotch ale, which was the best I had tasted in Scotland, and drunk only a draught of this ale in this kingdom. One fair house is here lately built, he that built it died before he finished it. Upon the way hence to

---

[1] The university of Glasgow was founded about 1460, and had undergone several vicissitudes before 1577, when, being in a very low estate, it was revived by a royal grant of lands, a new constitution, and considerable private subscriptions; in consequenco of which, the new buildings alluded to were undertaken. We suppose them to have been the buildings which were taken down in 1811, to make room for the range then erected from the designs of Peter Nicholson.

[2] This building was very near to the cathedral; but little, perhaps nothing, of it now remains, and the site is occupied by the infirmary.

Erwin, we discerned many islands, and, amongst the rest, the great isle of Arran, belonging to the Marquess Hamilton.[1] Many more islands hence appear, and indeed the isles, belonging and annexed unto this kingdom, are said to be more land than half the main land of this kingdom. Mr. Guerdon informed me that they were above three hundred in number.

One more remarkable isle, hence shows itself at forty miles' distance; this is placed in the sea about sixteen miles from shore. It is a mighty high rock, seeming very steep and high, round at the top; the name of it is Ellsey, and it belongs to my Lord Castle:[2] not inhabited, but with abundance of fowl, and two eareis of goose-hawks, this year stolen by some Highlanders. This rock or island was in our view three days, whilst we travelled betwixt sixty and seventy mile, and when you are at a great distance, it presents itself in shape like a sugar-loaf, and when you approach nearer, it seems lower and flatter at the top, but it is a much-to-be-admired piece of the Lord's workmanship. In this isle of Ellsey, which is my Lord Castle's, there breed abundance of solemne (solan) geese, which are longer necked and bodied than ours, and so extreme fat are the young, as that when they eat them, they are placed in the middle of the room, so as all may have access about it; their arms stripped up and linen cloaths placed before their clothes, to secure them from being defiled with the fat thereof, which doth besprinkle and besmear all that near unto it.

Julii 1.—I came from Glasgoaw about eight hour, and came to Erwin about twelve hour, which is sixteen mile. We passed through a barren and poor country, the most of it yielding neither corn nor grass, and that which yields corn is very poor, much

[1] James, Marquis of Hamilton, created Duke of Hamilton in 1643. In 1648, the army he commanded was put to flight, and himself compelled to become prisoner upon articles of capitulation. On the 9th of March 1649, he was murdered, at Westminster, by the self-styled high court of justice.

[2] Ailsa is a very rocky island, about two miles in circumference, and nine hundred and forty feet high. The proprietor at this time was John, sixth Earl of Casselis, a man of great honour and integrity, of uncompromising loyalty to Kings Charles I and his successor. He died 1668.

punished with drought.   We came to Mr. James Blare's in Erwin, a well affected man, who informed me of that which is much to be admired: above ten thousand persons have within two years last past left the country wherein they lived, which was betwixt Aberdeen and Ennerness, and are gone for Ireland; they have come by one hundred in company through this town, and three hundred have gone hence together shipped for Ireland at one tide : none of them can give a reason why they leave the country, only some of them who make a better use of God's hand upon [them], have acknowledged to mine host in these words ; "that it was a just judgment of God to spew them out of the land for their unthankfulness."

This country was so fruitful formerly, as that it supplied an overplus of corn, which was carried by water to Leith, and now of late for two years, is so sterile of corn as they are constrained to forsake it. Some say that, these hard years, the servants were not able to live and subsist under their masters, and therefore, generally leaving them, the masters being not accustomed, nor knowing how to frame,[1] to till, and order their land, the ground hath been untilled ; so as that of the prophet David is made good in this their punishment: "a fruitful land makes He barren, for the wickedness of them that dwell therein ;" for it is observed of these, that they were a most unthankful people : one of them I met withal and discoursed with at large, who could [give] no good reason, but pretended the landlords increasing their rents : but their swarming in Ireland is so much taken notice of and disliked,[2] as that the Deputy hath sent out a warrant to stay the landing of any of these Scotch that came without a certificate.   Three score of them were numbered returning towards the place whence they came, as they passed this town.

---

[1] *To frame* does not seem to be used by mistake for *to farm*, which expression, as we now use it, was perhaps scarcely known at this time, but means to arrange the course of cultivation in a methodical manner.

[2] Our traveller seems to have been misinformed; this emigration had been encouraged by James I and Charles I, and by their successive governors in Ireland, above all by Strafford, with a view to the gradual introduction of obedience to law, and the encouragement of art and industry.

Some of them complain of hard years (the better to colour and justify this their departure), but do withal acknowledge that corn is as cheap with them as in this town; but in the distraction and different relation of themselves, there may be observed much matter of admiration; and, doubtless, *digitus Dei* is to be discerned in it.

Here we were well used, and paid about 4*s.* 4*d.* for our dinners. Here I exchanged Mr. Hobbye's nag with Mr. James Blare, for the white nag, and paid £1. 6*s.* 8*d.* to boot.

This town of Erwin is daintily situate, both upon a navigable arm of the sea, and in a dainty, pleasant, level, champaign country; excellent good corn there is near unto it, where the ground is enriched and made fruitful with the sea-weeds or lime: the other ground which lies at too great distance to be thus helped, either very poor corn, if it be sown; or if it lie, no grass at all. The minister of this town is Mr. David Dike, a worthy man; and upon further conference with my host, I found him a right honest man of approved integrity, who is also part owner of the best ship belonging to this town, wherein I spoke with a merchant, who came lately from West Chester, and performed the journey in five or six miles (days), being about one hundred and eighty miles:— from hence to Don Frise forty-four miles; thence to Carlile twenty-four, and so to Pereth, &c. Hence to Dublin by sea is about forty hours' sail with a good wind. Hence they trade much into Bourdeaux in France, and are now furnished with good wine. Not far hence, about two miles, lives the Earl of Egglington, at Killwining, he hath a dozen or sixteen halls or houses hereabouts, and sways much in these parts.

---

[1] Sir Alexander Seton became sixth Earl of Eglinton, upon the death of his cousin in 1612. He attached himself to the Parliamentary party, and was present at the battle of Marston Moor. He was, however, extremely dissatisfied at the murder of the King, and suffered imprisonment and sequestration for the cause of Charles II. He was restored in 1660, but survived only a short time, dying Jan. 7, 1661. The sixteen halls or houses were attached to the family estates by his predecessor, who obtained a grant for erecting the property of the dissolved abbey of Kilwining into a temporal lordship, with the patronage of the churches of Kilwenny, Irvine, Dunbarton, Kilmarnoch, Loudon, Androssan, Kilburny, Daley, Dunlop, Beith, Stewartoun, Stevenson, Dreghorn, Pearston, Kelbride, and Kilmachornal.

Hence we came to AIRE, which is eight miles upon the sea coast, a most dainty pleasant way as I have ridden, wherein you leave the sea on your right hand; here we taught our horses to drink salt-water, and much refreshed their limbs therein. Coming late to Aire, we lodged in one Patrick Mackellen's house, where is a cleanly neat hostess, victuals handsomely cooked, and good lodging, eight[1] ordinary, good entertainment. No stable belonging to this inn; we were constrained to seek for a stable in the town, where we paid 8*d.* a night for hay and grass for an horse, and 1*s.* a peck for base oats. This also is a dainty, pleasant-seated town; much plain rich corn land about it; and better haven, there being a river, whereon it is placed, which flows much higher than the bridge, which is a great and fair neat bridge, yet nevertheless it is but a bare naked haven, no pier, nor defence against the storms and weather. Better store of shipping than at Erwin. Most inhabiting in the town are merchants trading unto and bred in France.

Enquiring of my hostess touching the minister of the town, she complained much against him, because he doth so violently press the ceremonies, especially she instanced in kneeling at the communion; whereupon, upon Easter day last, so soon as he went to the communion-table, the people all left the church and departed, and not one of them stayed, only the pastor alone.

Julii 2.—Hence we went to the cave of CARICK, which is about eight miles from Aire, where there dwells a laird, Sir Alexander Kendrick of Cullen,[2] who hath a pretty pleasant seated house or

---

[1] Sic in MS.

[2] Cullen or Colzean Castle, in the early part of the fifteenth century, was the property of the Kennedy (not Kendrich) family, afterwards ennobled under the titles of Kennedy and Cassilis. The rocks underneath the castle are penetrated with several deep caves, which the natives have peopled with fairies. Burns, in his *Halloween*, commemorates their pranks:

"Upon that night when fairies light
On Cassilis downans dance,
Or owre the lays, in splendid blaze,
On sprightly coursers prance;
Or for Colzean the route is ta'en
Beneath the moon's pale beams,
There up the Cove to stray and rove
Amang the rocks and streams
Unseen that night.

castle, which looks full upon the main sea; hereinto we went, and there found no hall, only a dining-room or hall, a fair room, and almost as large as the whole pile, but very sluttishly kept, unswept, dishes, trenchers and wooden cups thrown up and down, and the room very nasty and unsavoury. Here we were not entertained with a cup of beer or ale; only one of his sons, servants and others, took a candle, and conducted us to the cave, where there is either a notable imposture, or most strange and much to be admired footsteps and impressions which are here to be seen of men, children, dogs, coneys, and divers other creatures. These here conceived to be Spirits, and if there be no such thing, but an elaborate practise to deceive, they do most impudently betray the truth; for one of this knight's sons and another Galloway gentleman affirmed unto me that all the footsteps have been put out and buried in sand over night, and have been observed to be renewed next morning. This cave hath many narrow passages and doors, galleries also, and a closet and divers rooms hewed with mighty labour out of an hard limestone rock. Herein are two dainty spring wells, whereof I tasted; a foul, slippery, dark passage is thereinto, and it was first framed and intended for a stronghold or place of defence, no way to be offended or annoyed by any assault, if the port be made good; though one door looks towards and conveys light from the seaward, yet these seas are so guarded with rocks all along the shore of Caricke (such terrible rocks and stones I never saw) as no ships dare nor do frequent those seas.

This day we were exceedingly punished for want of drink and meat for ourselves and our horses, and could not meet with any good accommodation in riding forty long miles; the entertainment we accepted, in a poorer house than any upon Handforth Green, was Tharck-cakes,[1] two eggs, and some dried fish buttered; this day, as many days before, I drunk nothing but water, and divers of our horses; and Will. Baylye almost fainted for lack of relief. This day we passed up and down many high and steep hills, which

---

[1] *Thar-cakes*, oat-cakes.—*Cole's Dict.*

you cannot ride, and very much hard and stony beaten way, exceeding much moorish barren land.

We came into GALLOWAY about six miles from the chapel, and therein observed one of the widest, broadest, plainest moors that I have seen; it is much moss, but now so dry, as it is good hanking.[1] Coming off this moor, we observed an eminent stone, and tried it with our knives, and it did ring and sound like metal. About eight hour we came to this long desired chapel,[2] the town is thence denominated and so called. This is situate upon a long loch, four miles long, wherein the sea ebbs and flows. Here we found good accommodation (only wanted wheat bread) in Hughe Boyde's house; ordinary 6d., good victuals, well-ordered, good wine and beer, lodging, and horse meat. This house is seated four miles from the Port Patrick, whence it is to Carlingworke[3] 32 miles; best lodging there is Tho. Hutton; thence to Don-Frise 28 miles; best lodging is John Harstein; thence to Carleil 24.

Julii 4.—We went from hence to the PORT PATRICK, which is foul winter way over the mossy moors, and there we found only one boat, though yesternight there were fifteen boats here. We hired a boat of about ten ton for five horses of ours, and for five Yorkshiremen and horses; for this we paid 1l. and conditioned that no more horses should come aboard, save only two or three of an Irish laird's, who then stayed for a passage, and carried his wife and three horses. His name is Levinston,[4] laird Dun Draide.

---

[1] *To hank* is to form into hanks, and hanks are withys or any rude material twisted into a double loop, to fasten gates. This word may possibly have had more general signification, which we have been unable to detect.

[2] By the epitome of Sir W. Petty's survey by Philip Lea, it appears that chapel now hears the name of Stranraer; later maps and modern directories omit to notice this change of name.

[3] Carlinwark, a small town, now called Castle Douglas, situated on the borders of a lake between Kirkcudbright and Dumfries.

[4] Sir William Livingston, of Kilsyth, had charters of the lands of Duntreath, the place perhaps here called Dundraide. He died in 1627, and was succeeded by his grandson, who was included by name in the grant of the above lands. He suffered in the royal cause, and was created Viscount of Kilsyth and Lord Campsie in August 1661, and died in September following.

Here we shipped our horses two hours before we went aboard. It is a most craggy, filthy passage, and very dangerous for horses to go in and out; a horse may easily be lamed, spoiled, and thrust into the sea; and when any horses land here, they are thrown into the sea, and swim out. Here was demanded from us by our host, Thos. Marsh-banke, a custom of 2s. an horse, which I stumbled at, and answered that if he had authority to demand and receive it, I was bound to pay it, otherwise not; and therefore I demanded to see his authority, otherwise I was free to pay or refuse: herewith he was satisfied, and declined his further demand. Here is a pretty chapel lately built by Sir Hugh Montgomeries,[1] laird of Dunskie on this side, where he hath a castle, and of Newton de Clanyboyes on the Irish side, where he hath a market-town.

The boatman that carried us in a bark of about fifteen ton, his name was David Dickie, who hath a dainty, fine, pretty, nimble boy to his son, who will make a good sailor. The boat is a good sailing vessel, and good expert mariners, but not manned with sufficient number of men. She took in four horses more than we covenanted, and was so much overthronged with passengers, as we had not every man his own length allowed to lie in at ease. Our horses were shipped about two hour, the wind being north-west; but turning into the south-west, or rather west-south-west, we went not aboard until after three hour; the wind then being so much averse and so directly against us, as that we could not get out of the haven, so as they were constrained to haul out with a cock-boat a good way. We were got clear out of the haven about four hour; and before we had sailed a league, the wind was more averse; but presently favouring us something more with a full gale of wind, we had so speedy a passage as that by six hour we were within sixteen miles of the coast of Ireland. The wind then failed, and was sometimes

[1] The family of Montgomery were large landed proprietors in Scotland and in Ireland, and were ennobled by the title of Earl Mount Alexander in Ireland, which became extinct in 1758. Sir James Hunter Blair married the heiress, and his repre-sentatives now possess the Scottish portion of the property, including Dunskey Castle, situated about half a mile from the town of Port Patrick.

very weak and poor, and sometime due west and directly averse, yet we passed on though slowly, and about eight or nine mile from the coast of Ireland we passed the Strangawre, which is a mighty high running channel, where there is a concurrence and confluence of three strong tides, which run about nine or ten mile in length, and about two mile in breadth; these occasioned by the islands and points of land; but when we passed them, the wind was so weak, as it was there more calmed and less troubled than in any other part of our passage. We had no sooner passed the Strane-gawre, but (although when we went aboard it was very calm and like to be fair weather, which gave encouragement to them to hazard a passage by night) the wind failed us, and we were much affected with the apprehension of the inconvenience of lying at sea all night, because the tides are so strong as they would carry us with the ebbing water down towards the isles of Scottland, the wind also being either so averse as to bring us back to the shore of Scott-land, or to concur with the tide to carry us down towards the isles of Scottland; but then suddenly arose a strong wind and storm of rain, which did come out of the west and from the landward, which did much perplex the sailors, so as they were constrained to take down, and did in all haste take down the lower part of the main-sail and the fore-sail, which they call the main bowline or main bonnet. Two or three of these showers and storms did follow one another, which though they did increase and renew our fears, yet it pleased God (who knows better what might conduce unto our safety than ourselves) to make these storms the instruments of bringing us to harbour about two hour upon the coast of Ireland, under the Black Rock, which is in the island of Mague;[1] hereby we were sheltered all night from most cruel, violent, and tempest-uous storms, which did much affect and discourage us, though we lay at anchor and under the shelter of a high hill. Here we took up our lodging in this open boat, and suffered a wet cold lodging, yet it pleased God that I took no cold, nor did any other distemper

[1] Magu.

seize upon me, save only a faintingness when I came on shore, and
an extreme purging, although the sea wrought effectually and
plentifully with me, and purged me more by vomit only when I
was at sea, than ever formerly, so as my stomach was not only
cleared and discharged of phlegm, but also of abundance of choler
and green stuff.

'Twixt Erwin in Scottland and Colrane[1] in Ireland are the
highest running seas about the sound of Raughrick,[2] which is an
island belonging to the Earl of Antrem.[3]   The shortest passage
'twixt Scottland and Ireland is from Mule Kenteir,[4] a rock or
point of the Highlanders in Scottland, which is sixteen mile to
the Faire-head or Marble-head in Ireland: this is only a passage
for the Highlanders: from Port Patrick to Carick-Fergus is about
nineteen leagues, and to Donoh-a-Dee[5] or Groomes Port about
fifteen leagues, as one of the sailors informed me.

At our landing in Ireland, the ship came as near the shore as
she durst, and all the horses were thrown into the sea, and did
swim to land, and climb a great steep rock.

Julii 5.—Upon the Lord's day in the morning we went ashore
the coast of Ireland, in the Isle of Mague, where we were landed
upon the rock, whence we found a difficult and tedious passage;
and at the top of the hill we were very civilly and courteously
entertained by a Scotch gentleman, who lives in a mean, poor
house, hath good store of corn, milk, calves, and kine: hence
we went to Carick-Fergus, corruptly called Knock-Fergus, which
is four miles, and came thither about two hour.   Took up our inn
in Mrs. Wharton's house, who is a Chester woman, a neat woman
in her house; good lodging and usage, 6*d.* ordinary, 4*d.* a night
hay and oats, 6*d.* peck provender.

This town, so called from one Fergus, who built the castle, and
from Carick, which in Irish signifies a rock; and indeed the town
may well take his denomination from the castle, which is seated

---

[1] Coleraine.   [2] Rathlin.
[3] John, second Earl and only Marquess of Antrim, born 1609, died 1682.
[4] Mull of Cantire.   [5] Donaghadee.

upon a rock, and commands both town and haven. Almost all the houses in this town were built castle-wise, so as though the Irish made spoil of and burnt the town, yet were they preserved unburnt. This is but a pretty little town within the walls of a very small extent and capacity; the only grace of this town is the Lord Chichester's[1] house, which is a very stately house, or rather like a prince's palace, whereunto there belongs a stately gate-house and graceful terrace and walk before the house, as is at Denton my Lord Fairfax house.[2] A very fair hall there is, and a stately staircase and fair dining-room carrying the proportion of the hall: fine garden and mighty spacious orchards, and they say they bear good store of fruit. I observed on either side of his garden there is a dove house placed one opposite to the other in the corner of the garden, and 'twixt the garden and orchards; a most convenient place for apricots or some such tender fruit to be planted against the dove-house wall, that by the advantage of the heat thereof they may be rendered most fruitful, and come sooner to maturity, but this use is not made thereof. Very rich furniture belongs unto this house, which seems much to be neglected, and begins to go something to decay. It is a most stately building, only the windows and rooms and whole frame of the house is over-large and vast; and in this house you may observe the inconvenience of great buildings, which require an unreasonable charge to keep them in repair, so as they are a burthen to the owners of them.

There is maintained in this town two companies of soldiers, the one a troop of horse, the other of foot, consisting of fifty in either company, under the command of my Lord of Chichester's eldest

[1] Sir Edward Chichester, second Baron and first Viscount Chichester in Ireland, a very worthy and eminent person, well accomplished for peace or war, and very serviceable in the wars in Ireland. He died 1648. This magnificent house, called Joymount, was built upon the site of a ruined monastery, by Sir Arthur Chichester, the first peer, and several times Lord Deputy of Ireland.

[2] Ferdinand, Lord Fairfax, an eminent leader among the Parliamentarian generals, and father of the still more eminent Sir Tho. Fairfax. He died of a gangrene in his foot, in 1648.

son.[1] The troop of horse were lately sent to attend my Lord Deputy, in this progress very completely furnished, well horsed, and in red coats all suitable.

, It is reported of this town that they have been always loyal and faithful to the state of England. This is seated upon a loch which comes from the sea, and is navigable with the tide for small vessels to the quay. This loch runs all along to BELLFAST, which is eight mile from Carick-Fergus, and is thither also navigable; it is about three or four miles broad, well furnished with fish, and also with fowl in winter. Here upon that part of this loch next to Bellfast I observed a convenient seat.

From Carickfergus to Bellfast you ride all upon the Lock-side; it is most base way, and deep in winter and wet weather, though now it is hard and dry.

July 6.—This town of Carick-Fergus is governed by a mayor, sheriff, and aldermen, endowed with great privileges, and is the shire town. At Bellfast my Lord Chichester hath another dainty stately house (which is indeed the glory and beauty of that town also) where he is most resident, and is now building an outer brick wall before his gates. This not so large and vast as the other, but more convenient and commodious, the very end of the Loch toucheth upon his garden and backside; here also are dainty orchards, gardens, and walks planted. Near hereunto, Mr. Arthur Hill (son and heir to Sir Moyses Hill[1]) hath a brave plantation, which he holds by lease, which still is for thirty years to come; the land is my Lord Chichester's, and the lease was made for sixty years to Sir Moyses Hill by the old Lord Chichester. This plantation is said doth yield him a £1000 per annum. Many

---

[1] Arthur, the eldest son of Viscount Chichester was, in March 1647, created Earl of Donegal in his father's lifetime for his fidelity to his prince, affection to his country, and activity against the rebels. He was born in 1606, and in 1627 succeeded Lord Valentia in the command of his troop of fifty horsemen. He died in 1675.

[2] Sir Moyses Hill was associated with the Earl of Essex, in 1573, to suppress O'Neile's rebellion, and was subsequently made governor of Olderfleet Castle, which guarded the harbour of Larne. He then served under Arthur, the first Lord Chichester, Lord Deputy of Ireland; and in 1603 was made first Provost Marshal of Carrickfergus. He died Feb. 1630.

Lanckashire and Cheshire men are here planted; with some of them I conversed. They sit upon a rack rent, and pay 5s. or 6s. an acre for good ploughing land, which now is clothed with excellent good corn. From Bellfast to Linsley Garven is about seven mile, and is a paradise in comparison of any part of Scotland. LINSLEY GARVEN is well seated, but neither the town nor country thereabouts well planted, being almost all woods, and moorish until you come to Drom-moare.[1] This town belongs to my Lord Conoway,[2] who hath there a good handsome house, but far short of both my Lord Chichester's[3] houses, and this house is seated upon an hill, upon the side whereof is planted a garden and orchard, and at the bottom of which hill runs a pleasant river which abounds with salmon; hereabouts my Lord Conoway is now endeavouring a plantation, though the land hereabouts be the poorest and barrenest I have yet seen, yet may it be made good land with labour and charge.

From Linsley Garven to DROM-MORE is about seven mile. Herein we lodged at Mr. Haven's house, which is directly opposite to the Bishop of Drommore[4] his house, which is a little timber house of no great state nor receipt. His chaplain's name is Leigh, born in Manchester. This is a very dear house, 8d. ordinary ourselves, 6d. our servants, and we were over-reckoned in beer.

This town, as it is the seat of the bishop of this see, so he is lord of it, and it doth wholly belong unto him. In this diocese, as Mr. Leigh his chaplain reported, this is the worst part of the kingdom, and the poorest land and ground, yet the best church livings, because there are no impropriations.

At my coming to Carick-Fergus, and being troubled with an extreme flux, not as yet come to so great height as a bloody flux, my hostess, Mris. Wharton, directed me the use of cinnamon in

[1] Dromore.
[2] Edward, second Viscount Conway, succeeded his father in 1630, and died in 1655, leaving an only son, at whose death in 1683 the title became extinct.
[3] See page 127.
[4] Theophilus Buckworth occupied the see of Dromore from 1613 to 1652.

burnt claret wine, or rather red wine, as also the syrup and conserve
of sloes well boiled, after they have been strained and mingled
according to discretion with sugar; they are to be boiled with sugar
until they be cleared, having been first boiled in water until they
be softened, and then strained.

But a more effectual strong medicine, which is to be used
with discretion and caution, lest it beget a contrary distemper:—
Take three or four ounces of the bark of oak, the outside being
scraped clean, and boil the same in spring water until half be
consumed; then strain it through a fine cloth, then add to that
quart another quart of red wine, and add thereunto one ounce of
cinnamon punned[1] to powder and half a pound of sugar. Boil all
these together until half be consumed, then put this liquor into a
stone-bottle, wherein it may be kept close so as it take no wind,
nor lose not its strength, and take evening and morning about four
or five spoonfuls; if you be in extremity, then it must be taken
the oftener, two or three times a day.

I found by my own experience burnt aquavitæ and papes-milk,[2]
well sodden with wheat flour, three or four eggs, and cinnamon; these
did me much good, but by reason of taking too liberally of burnt usquebaugh, here called aquavitæ, which was but twice, and not above
the half of a gill at either time, there was occasioned unto me, for two
or three days after, great pain and torment in parting with my urine.
To cure this I found new milk the best medicine I used.   This flux,
though it did not hold me above three days at first when I landed,
yet it brought a great weakness and indisposition upon me, the
rather the more by reason my body was sufficiently purged by
vomit at sea, which wrought with me more effectually than it ever
did formerly in my whole life.   During my stay in this kingdom
my body was always disposed and inclined to be laxative and
soluble, so as always every night it caused me to rise once about
three hour.   But all these formerly prescribed medicines did but a
little avail me when it seized upon me the second time, which was

[1] *Punned*, from *to pun*, to pound.
[2] *Papes-milk.* By this is probably meant white juice of poppies, whose narcotic qualities might be beneficial.

upon Friday last Jul. 18; and, as I conceived, it was occasioned by reason of drinking milk over-liberally at Ermerscorffie and at Mr. Hardye's at Parke; I purged exceedingly at Sir Adam Cocliffe's, more than two parts of a close stoolful of thin watery stuff, which came from me like a stream gushing; this continued with me two or three days, and although I used all the medicines I could learn, as claret wine well burnt with cinnamon, milk well boiled with rice, cinnamon and eggs, yet all these did nothing help to stay it; I did forbear all drink save claret wine, and was as curious in my diet as was possible.

These things by experience I found hurtful: fruit, gross or raw meat, milk, drink, especially Irish, cold, any violent exercise or motion; riding moderately is good, but when the body is weakened, I found nothing more hurtful unto me than going on foot from the ferry to Waterford, which did me much hurt, and weakened me exceedingly; winberries made me subject to fainting also, and are churlish things for the stomach.

The best things I found were these: usquebaugh with the yolk of an egg first and last, fast two hours after it; cinnamon water is also good and diacinamomum;[1] but I found cinnamon water did so distemper me in parting with my water as put me to much pain and torment. The best thing to drink is French barley boiled in spring water; to every pottle of water there being put one ounce of the powder of cinnamon, this an excellent drink; hereof you may drink sufficient, as much as you please; you may add some sugar to relish it, and the juice of almonds bruised. Sr. Marmaduke Lloyde[2] prescribed barley boiled in a bag as hot as may be to be placed in your close stool or under you when you go to stool, the fume hereof hath an excellent virtue; this was old Dr. Buttler's[3]

[1] *Diacinnamomum* is a medicine into which cinnamom largely enters, but the exact prescription would not much interest the reader, had we been able to discover it.

[2] Sir Marmaduke Lloyd, second Justice of Chester at this time, afterwards Chief-Justice of South Wales.

[3] Dr. William Butler, born at Ipswich 1535, died at Cambridge 1618, aged 82, and therefore well entitled to be called " Old Dr. Butler." He practised at Cambridge, but was occasionally consulted by King James when at Newmarket. His sagacity in judging of distempers was very great, and his method of cure sometimes extraordinary,

direction to him, and to ride as far and as fast as he possibly could
endure for a whole day. Sr. Urian Leigh[1] affirmed the fume of
sage burnt upon a chafing-dish of coals often renewed placed in the
close stool to have cured many.

Jul. 7.—We left Dromemoore and went to the NEWRIE, which
is sixteen miles. This is a most difficult way for a stranger to
find out. Herein we wandered, and being lost, fell amongst the
Irish towns. The Irish houses are the poorest cabins I have seen,
erected in the middle of the fields and grounds, which they farm
and rent. This is a wild country, not inhabited, planted, nor
enclosed, yet it would be good corn if it were husbanded. I gave
an Irishman to bring us into the way a groat, who led us like a
villain directly out of the way and so left us, so as by this devia-
tion it was three hour before we came to the Newrie. Much land
there is about this town belonging to Mr. Bagnall,[2] nothing well
planted. He hath a castle in this town, but is for most part
resident at Green Castle; a great part of this town is his, and it is
reported that he hath a £1000 or £1500 per annum in this
country. This is but a poor town, and is much Irish, and is
navigable for boats to come up unto with the tide. Here we
baited at a good inn, the sign of the Prince's Arms. Hence to

being both bold and singular in his practice. Fuller calls him the " Æsculapius of
our Age." " Compliments would prevail nothing with him, entreaties but little, surly
threatenings would do much, and a witty jeer do any thing. Neatness he neglected
into slovenliness, and accounted cuffs to be manacles; he may be said not to have made
himself ready for some seven years together." When called upon to attend Francis
Tresham, he put a piece of pure gold in his mouth, and upon taking it out pronounced
him poisoned.

[1] Sir Urian Legh of Adlington, near Macclesfield, Cheshire, knighted by the Earl
of Essex at the siege of Cadiz in 1592, and said to have been the hero of the ballad of
the Spanish Lady's Love. He died in 1628. See *Percy's Relics.*

[2] In Newry was a Cistercian monastery, which was conferred by Edw. VI. upon
Sir Nicholas Bagnal, and with adjoining property was styled *jurisdictio de viridi ligno,*
whence probably the name of Green Castle. His son was Sir Henry Bagnal, who was
for many years marshal of Queen Elizabeth's armies in Ireland, and for his services
received very extensive grants of lands. He was killed in an attack upon a fort at
Black Waller, 1598, and succeeded by his son Arthur, the person here mentioned, who
died in 1643.

Dundalke is eight mile; stony, craggy, hilly, and uneven, but a way it is nothing difficult to find. Before you come to Dundalke you may discern four or five towers or castles seated upon the sea side.

This town of DUNDALKE hath been a town of strength, and is still a walled town, and a company of fifty soldiers are here in garrison under the command of Sir Faithfull Fortescue.[1] This town is governed by two bailiffs, sheriffs, and aldermen; the greatest part of the inhabitants of the town are popishly affected, and although my Lord Deputy, at the last election of burgesses for the Parliament, commended unto them Sir Faithfull Fortescue and Sir Arthur Teringham,[2] yet they rejected both, and elected a couple of recusants. One of the present bailiffs is popish. Abundance of Irish, both gentlemen and others, dwell in this town, wherein they dare to take the boldness to go to mass openly. This town seated upon the sea so as barks may come within a convenient distance with the flood; much low, level, flat land hereabouts, which is often overflowed in the winter, and here is abundance of fowl, and a convenient seat. Here we lodged at one Mris. Veasie's house, a most mighty fat woman; she saith she is a Cheshire woman, near related in blood to the Breretons;[3] desired much to see me; so fat she is, as she is so unwieldy, she can scarce

[1] Sir Faithful Fortescue was a conspicuous character during the great rebellion. He was trusted and employed by Lord Strafford, came to England to solicit succours for Ireland, had a troop of horse raised for him, and was ordered to join the Parliamentary army as major to Sir William Waller. At the commencement of the battle of Edgehill he took over his whole troop and joined the royal army. After the murder of King Charles I, he accepted a regiment under Cromwell, which he brought over to Charles II, at Worcester. With the king he fled, and returned at the restoration, was made a gentleman of the privy chamber, and was always about his Majesty's person till his death.

[2] Sir Arthur Tyringham was of considerable influence in Ireland, and upon the breaking out of the rebellion in Ireland in 1641, was commissioned with Arthur, afterwards first Earl of Donegal, to command in chief within the county of Antrim.

[3] Sir William seems to have been ignorant of the exact connection between this fat landlady and his own family, and the county pedigrees do not throw any light upon the subject.

stand or go without crutches. This reported one of the best inns
in north of Ireland; ordinary 8*d.* and 6*d.*, only the knave tapster
over-reckoned us in drink.

Jul. 8.—We left Dundalke and came to TREDAUGH,[1] which is
accounted sixteen mile, but they are as long as twenty-two mile.
About five mile hence we saw Sir Faithfull Fortescue's house or
castle, wherein for most part he is resident, which he holds by a
long lease upon a small rent under my Lord Primate of Armath.
This is a dainty, pleasant, healthful, and commodious seat, and it
is worth unto him about   . During ten miles riding from
this town, much rich corn land, and the country well planted; the
other six miles towards Tredaugh, until you come near unto it,
not so rich land, nor so well husbanded.

This town, as it is the largest and best built town I have yet
seen in Ireland, so it is most commodiously seated upon a good
navigable river, called Boyne, whereinto flows the sea in so deep a
channel (though it be very narrow) as their ships may come to
their doors. This river is built on both sides, and there is on
either side a convenient quay; a stone wall built all along the
river, so as a ship may lie close unto this quay, and may unload
upon her. It is like the quay of Newcastle, and those channels I
have seen in Holland in their streets. This town commodiously
also situated for fish and fowl. It is governed by a mayor, sheriffs,
and twenty-four aldermen; most of these, as also the other inhabitants of the town, popishly affected, insomuch as those that have
been chosen mayors, who for the most part have been recusants,
have hired others to discharge that office. One man (it is said)
hath been hired by deputation to execute that place thirteen
times; the present mayor also is but a deputy, and the reason why
they make coy to execute that office is because they will avoid
being necessitated to go to church.

I observed in this city divers fair, neat, well-built houses, and
houses and shops well furnished, so as I did conceive this to be a rich

[1] Drogheda.

town; the inhabitants more civilized and better apparelled. But this is graced with nothing more than my Lord Primate's palace, which is seated near unto the East gate. This is a neat, handsome, and convenient house, built within this twenty years by Primate Hampton.[1] The building is four square of wood, rough-cast and not high; an handsome, plain, though long and narrow hall, two dining-rooms; one little neat gallery which leads into the chapel, which also pretty little plain and convenient chapel, whereinto there lead two ways, the one at the great door out of the hall or court, the other, which is more private, out of the gallery; there is a little pair of organs herein. Whilst Dr. Usher (my Lord Primate that now is) is here resident, he preacheth constantly every Lord's-day in the morning in the church. There is a sermon therein in the after-noon, and after the same is ended, one of my lord's chaplains repeats his sermon in his own chapel, whither not only all his own family resort, but also (the common door being open) those of the town that please may resort thereunto. In one of the dining-rooms is this conceit, the arms of this see and bishoprick, and Bishop Hampton's own arms or coat enquartered together, and underneath is this inscription or motto: " Fac tu similiter." Here is a pretty neat garden, and over against the window in the gallery end, upon a bank, these words, in fair great letters, are written: " O man, remember the last great day." The bank is bare, the proportion of the letters is framed and cut in grass. In this palace the Primate is most resident, when he is not at Dublin.

In this town are two churches; one placed on the one side the river, the other on the other, over which is a wooden bridge. In the great church my Lord Primate preacheth every Sabbath. In the body of the church, over against the pulpit, the communion table is placed lengthwise in the aisle; the body of the church is kept in good repair; the chancel, as no use is made of it, so it is wholly neglected and in no good repair; only herein is a fair monument

[1] Christopher Hampton, Primate from 1613 to 1624, when he was succeeded by the celebrated James Usher, who died in 1655.

for my Lord Moore,[1] his lady, Sir Edw. Moore[2] and Sir Tho.
Moore,[3] his sons, and their wives and children; amongst these is
one erected for the Lady Salisburie now living at Chester. On
the other side, opposite hereunto, is Sir Frauncis Roe's monument,
who died when mayor; he is pictured in his scarlet gown.

Jul. 9.—From Tredaugh we came to the SWORDES, which is
fourteen miles thence, and six from thence to Dublin. Here we
lodged at the sign of the Boot, a tavern, and were well used, and
found far better accommodation in so mean a village than could be
expected. The way from Tredaugh hither as dainty fine way as
I ever rid, and a most pleasant country, greatest part corn upon
the very sea-coast, almost Wirrall-like,[4] and very good and well-
eared corn; the barley now beginning to turn, and will be ripe
before the rye. Upon the left hand, about three mile from Tredaugh, my Lord N[5]　　　hath a pleasant seated house or castle,
the prospect whereof commands the sea, and a most plain, rich-
champaign corn country towards the land.

About two or three mile from Swordes my Lord Chief Baron[6]
hath a dainty, pleasant, high-built wood house, and much rich and
brave land about it, this placed on the right hand; his name is　　.
On the other hand, about half mile, Sir　　　hath a gallant pleasant seat, also　　　. Here I saw very fair large English kine;

[1] Sir Garnet Moore was created Baron Moore 1615, and Viscount Moore of Drogheda 1621; he died Nov. 9, 1627. His lady was Mary, daughter of Sir Henry Colley
of Castle Carbery in the county of Kildare.

[2] Sir Edward Moore, eldest son of the preceding, died in his father's lifetime; his
lady was Elizabeth, daughter of Walter Vaughan, of Golden Grove.

[3] Sir Thomas Moore, second son of Sir Ganet, died 1623, and was buried in St.
Patrick's, Dublin. His lady was Sarah, second daughter of Richard, first Earl of
Cork. She afterwards married Robert, Lord Digby. Upon this Sir Thomas the
manor of Roes, &c. was settled by the Sir Francis Roe mentioned below.

[4] Wirral, a hundred of Cheshire, north-west of Chester, between the river Dee and
Mersey.

[5] The only nobleman of Ireland at this time with this initial was Viscount Netter-
ville, whose handsome residence was at Dowth upon the banks of the Boyne.

[6] Sir Richard Bolton, Attorney-General of the Court of Wards, Lord Chief Baron
from 1625 to 1639.

I enquired the price, which about 2*l*. or 2*l*. 10*s*. or 3*l*. These worth in England double the price. Land here sold for about twenty years purchase, set some for 5*s*. or 6*s*. an acre, and meadowing for 2*l*. an acre, some for 1*l*. Some land about Dublin is set for 2*l*. 3*l*. and 4*l*. an acre.

We came to the city of DUBLIN, *July* 9, about 10 hour. This is the metropolis of the kingdom of Ireland, and is beyond all exception the fairest, richest, best built city I have met with in this journey (except Yorke and Newcastle). It is far beyond Edenborough; only, one street in Edenborough (the great long street) surpasseth any street here. Here is the Lord Deputy[1] resident in the castle, and the state and council of this kingdom. There is also an Archbishop of Dublin, which is the second in the kingdom. Archbishopricks in Ireland: 1. Armathe; 2. Dublin; 3. Casiell; 4. Tuam. Bishopricks in Ireland about eighteen, as they are now united.[2]

This city of Dublin so called, it is seated upon the river Liffie, which is not navigable above the bridge, nor far, nor flows not above one mile higher. The river is no good channel, but full of shelves and sands, and here is a very vile barred haven, over which few ships can pass that carry four hundred ton or thereabouts. The harbour here is very naked, plain, and the least shelter and protection from storms that I have found in any haven; the most ships ride by the Ringe's end, which is a point which runs into the sea, but it is so low, as it is very poor and bare shelter and little defence against the violence of the storms, so as the king's ship which lies here to scour the coasts (which is said to be the Ninth Whelpe, and the Bonaventure, a tall stout ship[3]) is constrained to remove for harbour, sometimes under the Head of Howard,[4] sometimes under the opposite shore.

[1] Earl of Strafford.

[2] There appear to have been nineteen Irish bishops at that time: Ardfert, Clogher, Clonard, Clonfert, Cork, Derry, Downe and Connor, Dromore, Elphin, Ferns, Kildare, Kilfenora, Killala, Killaloe, Kilmore, Limerick, Ossory, Raphoe, Waterford.

[3] See page 164.

[4] For Head of Howard, read " Hill of Howth."

As I came from Dublin to Hacquett's town, I saw the head of the Liffie, where she breaks out of the mountains; this is not above seven miles from Dublin, and yet fetcheth a course of forty mile before it come to Dublin.

There are about thirteen churches in this city: Christ church, a cathedral, where the lord deputy and state frequent; the chancel is only made use of, not the body of the church, wherein are very great strong pillars, though very short; the chancel is but plain and ordinarily kept; the body of the church a more stately building. St. Patricke's church is a cathedral, and prime church in this kingdom. It is denominated from St. Patricke, the tutelar saint and protector of this kingdom. It is in best repair, and most neatly whited and kept of any church I have seen in Scottland or Ireland, especially in the chancel, wherein it is curiously and very artificially arched and whited overhead. The body of the church is a strong, ancient structure, wherein are great and strong pillars, but this is not floored overhead. This structure affords two parish churches under one roof, in either of which there is a sermon every sabbath. In a corner, a small part of the middle aisle, there is a pretty, neat, convenient place framed, wherein there is a sermon every sabbath at 10 hour; and this, though it be very little and narrow, yet it is sufficiently enlarged to receive a great congregation, by reason of capacious galleries round about, wherein are abundance of seats placed one above another, with great advantage of room. There is also at one hour in the afternoon a sermon in the quire. In the higher end whereof was a very famous, sumptuous and glorious tomb of my Lord of Corke's:[1] this by the commandment of the Deputy is taken

---

[1] This monument originally stood where the communion table now is, and by the exertions of the Earl of Strafford, at the instigation of Laud, it was removed to the south side of the choir, where it now stands. The descendants of the Earl of Cork, and Lord Chancellor Weston, were grievously offended at the removal, and the latter especially is said to have revenged the supposed insult when Strafford was on his trial. The Earl of Cork had previously to this quarrel, given up many lay-impropriations at the suggestion of Laud; these, he now refused to surrender; so that the dispute was, in its results, most unhappy. Archbishop Bramhall, however, then Lord Strafford's chaplain, speaks warmly to the purity of his Lordship's intentions.

down, and is now to be erected in the side of the same quire; the marble whereof this was made was gotten within two miles of this city.

St. Warburr's[1] is a kind of a cathedral; herein preacheth judicious Dr. Hoile[2] about ten in morning, and three in afternoon; a most zealous preacher, and general scholar in all manner of learning, a mere cynic. St. Owen's[3] is the parish wherein my Lord Primate was born; and here in this church doth he preach every Lord's-day at eight hour, whilst he is in town. I heard him upon Sabbath last, the most excellent able man, and most abundantly holy, gracious man that I have heard. St. Bride's, where Mr. Jcrom preacheth.

Jul. 10.—This day I dined with my Lord Primate of Ireland, Dr. Usher, who is a tall, proper, comely man, about fifty-six years of age; a plain, familiar, courteous man, who spends the whole day at his study, except meal time. He seems to be a man of pregnant parts, who hath good intelligence; he is well read in antiquities. His entertainment good and plentiful, but nothing curious nor excessive. He is a most holy well-affected bishop, a good companion, a man of good discourse. Having some conference with him about the reading of the book which gives liberty for recreation upon the Lord's-day,[4] he used this expression: that

---

[1] St. Werburgh, daughter of Wulherus, king of Mercia. Part of her shrine now forms the bishop's throne in the cathedral of Chester. St. Werburgh's church was twice destroyed by fire. The beautiful spire, which was a great ornament to Dublin, was taken down, from a needless alarm, about the beginning of this century, instead of receiving an effectual, safe, and cheap repair.

[2] Joshua Hoyle, D D., born at Sawerley, Yorkshire, educated at Magdalen College, Oxford, removed to Dublin, became fellow of Trin. Coll. and Professor of Divinity. In 1641, the horrors of the rebellion drove him from Ireland, and he became vicar of Stepney; he sat in the Assembly of Divines, he witnessed against Laud, and in 1648 was appointed Master of University Coll. Oxford, in the chapel of which college he was buried, 1654. He was abused by W·¹ker, praised by Wood, and respected by Usher. See below, p. 144.

[3] St. Andoen's or St. Owen's; the present church occupies only a part of the western end of the former building, three-fourths at least being complete ruins. The steeple was blown down in 1668, but replaced immediately by a new one.

[4] *The Book of Sports*, first published by King James in 1618, and subsequently by King Charles, Oct. 18, 1633. The effect of the order was, doubtless, at the time, felt as a great boon by the people.—*Vid. Heylyn's Life of Laud*, p. 241.

there was no clause therein commanding the ministers to read the book, but if it were published in the church by the clerk or church-wardens, the king's command is performed; this was his sense and opinion.

Here was this day at dinner Doctor Richardson,[1] Bishop of [Ardagh] a Cheshire man born, an able man, and good scholar; he was born near Chester, and married Sir Hen. Bunburie's daughter, whom I went to visit after dinner; a tall, handsome, fat woman. This bishop is an intelligent man, and gave me good resolution and satisfaction in many things.

Hence I went to the Castle, wherein my Lord Deputy resides, within which are both the Houses of Parliament, whereof I took a view; much less and meaner than ours. The Lords' House is now furnished with about sixty or seventy armours for horse, which are my Lord Deputy's: this a room of no great state nor receipt. Herein there sat the first session about eighty lords, not so many the latter.

The Commons' House is but a mean and ordinary place; a plain, and no very convenient seat for the speaker, nor officers.[2] The Parliament men that sat in this house were about 248. There are about 30 or 32 shires, which send 60 or 64 knights for the shire, the rest are burgesses.

Herein this castle we saw the council-chamber, wherein stands a very long table, furnished with stools at both sides and ends. Here sometimes sit in council about 60 or 64 privy councillors. Here we saw the hall, a very plain room, and the dining-room, wherein is placed the cloth of estate over my Lord Deputy's head, when he is at meat. Beyond this is the chamber of presence, a room indeed of state; and next unto this is there a withdrawing chamber, and beyond that, a pretty, neat short gallery, which leads to the council chamber; this was lately built by my Lord Falkland, whilst he was here

---

[1] He was a grave man and good divine. Educated in the University of Dublin, born 1584, died 1658, aged 74. He was the author of " Choice Observations and Explanations upon the Old Testament," fol. 1655. His lady was Elizabeth, second daughter of Sir Henry Bunbury, by his first wife Anne, daughter of Geoffry Shakerly; they were married at Stanney in Cheshire, Aug. 10, 1612.

[2] In 1729 was commenced the magnificent buildings, which were enlarged from time to time for the accommodation of both houses of parliament, and which are now occupied by the bank of Ireland.

Deputy; the lower part of it is built arch-wise and very grace-fully, so as it is a great ornament to the castle, about which there are very high walls and of great strength, and a drawbridge which is pulled up every night.

The command which this castle hath over this city is from some of the leads and towers above on the top of the castle, whereupon there is ordinance planted; and one fair brass piece of ordinance is placed in the court before the gate. Parker committed a forfeiture here in taking out the stopple, for which he was seized upon, and I paid 6d. to redeem him. Here my Lord Deputy hath lately erected a gallant, stately stable as any I have seen in the king's dominions; it is a double stable, there being a strong wall in the middle, to either side whereof stand the horse's heads. Thirty horses may stand at ease on either side, the stalls being very large; these are exceeding high, at least five or six yards, and very near the same breadth; no planks made use of, but Holland bricks placed upon the edges, whereon the horses lie and you walk; these as easy to walk upon as to lie upon, and these are made of Holland earth, which is harder and more durable much than our clay: with these the streets are paved in Holland.

Jul. 11.—We went to Sir Thomas Rotheram[1] (who is a privy-councillor), who used us respectively, and accompanied me to the Castle, and showed me the courts of justice, which are conveniently framed and contrived, and these very capacious. The Star-Chamber, the Chancery, the King's Bench and Common Pleas,—these rooms as useful as ours in England, but here is not such a stately structure or hall to walk in as Westminster Hall. I saw also the church, which was erected by the Jesuits, and made use by them two years. There was a college also belonging unto them, both these erected in the back lane. The pulpit in this church was richly adorned with pictures, and so was the high altar, which was advanced with steps, and railed out like cathe-drals; upon either side thereof was there erected places for con-

[1] Sir Tho. Rotheram was descended from Tho. Rotheram, Abp. of York, who died of the plague in 1500, at the advanced age of 76. He was second son of George Rotherham of Somery, and lord of the manor of Luton in Bedfordshire.

fession : no fastened seats were in the middle or body hereof, nor
was there any chancel ; but that it might be more capacious, there
was a gallery erected on both sides, and at the lower end of this
church, which was built in my Lord Faulkland's[1] time, and whereof
they were disinvested, when my Lord Chancellor and my Lorde
of Corke executed by commission the Deputy's place.   This college
is now joined and annexed to the College of Dublin, called[2]   ,
and in this church there is a lecture every Tuesday.

We saw also St. Stephen's Hall, wherein are disposed about eighteen scholars, who are also members of the college, whereunto this
hall is annexed.   This sometimes was a cloister for the Capuchins,
who said mass, and preached in a pretty little chapel or chamber ;
this was likewise taken from them about that time, and now there is
prayers in it twice a day.   My Lord of Corke allowed 40*l.* per
annum to maintain this lecture in the Jesuit's church, but now
hath withdrawn this exhibition.   In this street, which is called
the Bridge-street, almost opposite to this hall, there died this day
an Irish merchant; and as we passed by, we heard either his wife
or sister roaring out as though she were violently distracted ; this
they say is very ordinary with the Irish, and is their custom.   I
went this day to view the College, which is called Trinity College,
and was erected by queen Elizabeth, and endowed with about
1400*l.* per annum.   There is a provost hereof, Dr. Chappell,[3] a
vice-provost, and six senior fellows, whose fellowships are worth 9*l.*
per annum, besides their diets : there are eight junior fellows,
whose fellowships are worth, besides their diet, 3*l.* per annum :
poor scholars about sixty, whose scholarships are only worth their
diets.   There are about sixty poor scholars, and about fifteen
fellow commoners.   In the chapel is a monument for Dr. Chal-
loner,[4] sometimes provost of this College, and father to my Lord

---

[1] Henry Cary, Viscount Falkland, was chief-governor of Ireland from Sept. 1622 to
May 1623, and again from 1625 to 1629.   From that time to 1633 the office was held
in commission by the Lord Chancellor, Viscount Ely, and Richard, Earl of Cork.

[2] Trinity College.

[3] Dr. Chappell was appointed Provost in 1634, consecrated Bishop of Cork and
Ross 1638.

[4] Dr. Luke Chaloner was one of four original fellows of this institution, and trea-

Primate's wife. Hereunto belongs a pretty little convenient garden. This house is seated in a good air, out of the city, and near the sea. They glory much in their library, whereof I took a full view, and there were showed unto me many manuscripts : one they highly esteem, which they call Friar Bacon's work; and say the same is not any where extant save with them; but he must have a stronger faith to believe it than mine, for it is new bound, a very fair manuscript without any blot or blemish; it treats of all manner of learnings; but that it is Friar Bacon's work doth not appear either in the frontispiece, title, or any part of the book, as also the subject seems unto me, and the style not to be Friar Bacon's work; but here it is so received and reported. This library is not large, well-contrived, nor well furnished with books. They say it is to be disposed of to some other uses, and a new library and schools to be erected.

Jul. 12.—I heard my Lord Primate at eight hour at St. Owen's church, which is his parish, wherein he was born, where he preacheth every sabbath whilst he is in Dublin. I never heard a more powerful and convincing sermon, and indeed he is a most holy and heavenly man, and as pregnant witted as any I have heard. He doth most industriously apply his study, which he hath placed at a good distance from his house, to prevent distraction and diversion by the access of any company to visit him, who are not admitted to disturb his studies. This his course and order is so public, as that few come to him at any time of the day, save at the hours of relaxation, which is from eleven to one, and so about supper time : the rest of the day, from five in morning until six in the evening, is spent ordinarily in his study. I dined with him also *Jul.* 13, and then he was much more free and familiar with me. I had much private conference with him, and after dinner he took me into his closet, where although there be not very many books, yet those that are, much used and employed. Herein he shewed me

surer of the fund for building it, but never Provost. On his death-bed he recommended his only daughter, Phœbe, to Usher for a wife. He died 1612.

the whole books of the Waldenses, which are very rare; they cost
him 22*l.* sterling; they are in octavo, about ten or twelve vol.
The language wherein they are printed is a miscellaneous language, twixt French and Spanish; these were sent him from a
counsellor in France, as also a copy of the plots and designs and
proceedings of the inquisitors in France. He shewed me his
Articles of Religion, printed 1563; but I left mine with him,
which was more ancient and orthodox than his. He did enforce
me to take away and read a packet of news (which came unto him
there) before himself had cast an eye upon it.

At ten hour this Lord's day I heard Dr. Hoile[1] preach at St.
Warburrs, and at three in afternoon in the same church. He is a
most holy man, full of zeal and grace, a general scholar, but not
sufficiently furnished with words to express that fulness of matter
which aboundeth in him; who is a mere cynic to the world, but
doubtless a gracious man in the sight of God. You may with
much ease and conveniency hear four sermons every Lord's day,
and, as I was informed, six sermons may be heard on one day.
This city of Dublin is extending his bounds and limits very far;
much additions of building lately, and some of those very fair,
stately and complete buildings; every commodity is grown very
dear. You must pay also for an horse hire 1*s.* 6*d.* a day: here I
met with an excellent, judicious and painful smith. Here are
divers commodities cried in Dublin as in London, which it doth
more resemble than any town I have seen in the king of England's
dominions.

Jul. 14.—Upon Tuesday, *Jul.* 14, I left Dublin and came to
HACQUETTS TOWN, about eleven hour at night. It is accounted
twenty-seven miles, but it is as long as thirty-seven. After you
pass four miles from Dublin, you travel through the mountains,
which are dry land, and some of them good pasture for cattle that
are young, and sheep, but these are not sufficiently stocked.
Towards evening we passed through troublesome and dangerous

---

[1] See above, page 139.

ways and woods, and had wandered all night, had we not hired an Irish guide, by whose direction we arrived at eleven hour at Hacquett's Town, where we lodged in a little, low, poor, thatched castle. Here Mr. Wattson, a Lanckashire man, hath a plantation. As we passed this way, I observed the head of the river Liffie, which comes under the bridge at Dublin, whence it is made navigable by the flood, which goeth a mile above the bridge, and little further; I passed also, about eighteen miles from Dublin, by the head of the Slane, which runs to Waxford, and is there navigable, and twenty miles above Waxford.

This town, called in Irish Haggerstowne, is built upon my Lord of Ormond's land, which he holds by lease for about fifty years; this is in the province of Leinster, and in the county of Catherloe.[1] It is lately made a market-town (a poor one); it is most inconveniently seated amongst the mountains, a barren dry soil, and not easily improved and made rich; a branch of the river of the Slane runs below this town, wherein are but a few straggling houses. Some land is here set by Mr. Wattson at 2s. and some at 3s. 4d. an acre, as to John Torkinton, and for thirty years. Here is good butter made as in England, and they say good cheese, but I tasted none. This is in the diocese of Loghlein, and so is Sir Morgan Kavenagh[2] his estate; the Bishop hereof was lately Dean of Limbreck,[3] Dr. . Here Mr. Wattson hath erected a dainty new church, and maintains a good minister, Mr. Roote's wife's brother. He allows him £40 pension per ann. and his house, and a competent provision of ground. He paid for the purchase of this lease above £500 fine, and he pays also an £100 rent. He hath already improved it unto more worth than £400 per annum, and hath much prejudiced his plantation by insisting upon overhard conditions and demands. Here we were very courteously and kindly entertained

[1] Carlow.

[2] This was probably Morgan Mac-Bryan Cavanagh, Chief of the Sept, called Sleight-Dermot, of Polomonty, in the county of Carlow, who died at Borrass, June 1636, and was buried at St. Molach.

[3] George Andrew was promoted from the deanery of Limerick to the bishoprick of Ferns and Leighlin in 1635; he died 1648.

U

all night by Mr. Needam, and   who married Mr. Wattson's
sister.

Jul. 15.—We went hence through Mr. Wattson's woods, wherein
is very little good timber, the most small, old and decayed, and
those trees which seem best are shaken and unsound at heart.
When we went out of his grounds, we entered upon Mr. Chambers'
land, and saw abundance of woods, more than many thousand
acres; and some of those parts through which we travelled, the
ground was so thronged and pestered with wood which was fallen
and lay upon the ground, as the ground was thereby made of no
use.   Out of this part of the wood the best hath been made use of
for pipe-staves, which were sold for £6 a 1000; upon every 1000
of these there is now a custom imposed of £3, which doth so much
deduct as there is no valuable advantage, the charge of hewing
being £1. 10s., besides conveying them down by water to Enner-
scoff, which is twelve miles, at which time there is required the
aid and endeavour of a hundred men to conduct and guide them
in this narrow, shallow and crooked river, which runs through
this wood.

Before we passed this wood and river, we passed by Minmoare,
a little Irish town, where a brother of Chambers dwelleth.   Two
miles hence is Carnue, the town wherein Mr. Chambers his castle
is erected, and which is a neat, rough-cast, and well contrived
convenient house.   Here calling to drink a cup of beer (the weather
being extreme hot), Mr. Chambers overruled us to stay all night,
where we had very free and courteous entertainment.   Two of his
daughters, now married, are with him, my Lord Brabseon's lady,
and Mr. Sandeforde's wife.   Here is now Mr. Odell, who doth
commend and magnify beyond all measure the park belonging to
this house, which is about seven miles in compass, and wherein are

---

[1] Calcot Chambre, of Denbigh in Wales, and of Carnew in the county of Wicklow.
He left a son and two daughters: Elizabeth, married to Francis Sandford; and Mary,
married in 1632 to Edward, Lord Brabazon, afterwards the second Earl of Meath, who
was drowned, 1675, between Holyhead and Beaumaris.   Upon this lady and her heirs
the Wicklow estates were settled.

both fallow and red deer good store. Here is good butter and cheese made, and they say fair English cattle are here bred, though the ground seem but barren and poor, and moorish hereabouts; but here he hath a brave, large scope of ground, and it is of the best sort that this county of Wickley yields. Not far hence, about a quarter of a mile, he hath erected an iron-work, which is called a   . Herein the sows[1] of iron which are brought from Bristow are melted into iron-bars. They stand in 5*l*. a ton, being laid down at the door, and are worth in bars xxlb. a ton.

Jul. 16.—We left Carnue about seven hour, and went thence into the county of Wexford to CLAGHAMAN, my Lord of Balta-moare's[2] town, where he hath a brave house, but of no great strength, nor built castle-wise. Here I saw lime burnt, wherewith they use to enrich their ground. This town is seated upon the bank of river Slane, which doth hence carry down to Ennerscoffe, and so to Wexford, all pipe-staves, boards and other timber which grows in the woods near adjoining. We passed through Sir Morgan Kavennah's woods, wherein (we were informed in the morning at Carnew) there were lurking about sixteen stout rebels well appointed, every of them with his pistols, skene, and darts; they have also four long pieces, but we saw none, only we had one lusty young fellow in jealousy[3] in the wood. Herein there hath been good store of good timber, though now there remains little timber useful save to burn, and such as cumbreth the ground, but they say he hath better timber in his more remote woods from the river. This is a commodity which will be much wanting in this kingdom, and is now very dear at Dublin. In this wood, there runs a little river which divides the counties of Wexford and Catherloe, over which when we had passed we went to Clen-

---

[1] We know not whether " sow" is a term now used amongst iron manufacturers, or whether the modern word " pig" is used as more delicate, or expressive of a different form or weight of rough metal.

[2] Cecilius Calvert, Lord Baltimore, to whom Charles I. granted the province of Maryland, with very extensive powers, in 1632.

[3] *Jalousie*, i. e. *lattice* or *grate*, from behind which any one may unperceived watch another.

moullen, the castle[1] and seat of Sir Morgan Cavenagh, who seems to be a very honest, fair dealing man, and his lady[2] a good woman, but both recusants. Here we were entertained with good beer, sack and claret, whereof he was no niggard. He demands a £1000 per annum and a £1000 rent for twenty town lands, and, as he saith, it is about 12,000 or 13,000 acres, but I cannot conceive it less than 20,000 acres; much hereof mountain wood, and the rest but poor land, all overgrown with ferron and brachon, and not to be improved, but with great charge and trouble.

Here he shewed me a convenient seat for an iron-work, which may be supplied with sufficient water and charcoal; for this respect I do believe he doth set a far higher valuation and price upon his lands, which he doth much overvalue and esteem. In this wood I observed and tasted of the dew which fell upon the oak leaves, which glistered and shined and tasted like honey; doubtless this kingdom is a most fruitful place for bees. This castle and seat of Sir Morgan Kavenah is an old, high, narrow and inconvenient building; the stairs leading up into the dining-room and chambers being narrow and steep, like a steeple stair; this also seated in a most solitary, melancholy place, woods on two sides, and plains on the other; these are moors and mountains, whereon they say there are wolves. This also is in the Dufferie,[3] which hath always been reputed a thievish place, but Sir Morgan, being demanded, said that the sixteen rebels before-named were most conversant about Ross and in the county of Kilkennie.

In the way to Ennescorffie, about two miles thence on the other side the Slane, I went to survey (over the river) the manor of the Ollort, in the county of Wexford, in the parish and diocese of Fernes and Loghlein, which is to be sold with these parcels following: Taencurrye, Taenknock, Rahennemonye, Bollincahine, and Sherewelch.

[1] Clonmullen Castle appears by the Ordnance survey of Ireland to be situated in the parish of Banagh, Co. Carlow.

[2] This lady was Eleanor, third daughter of Edmund, second Lord Mountgarret.

[3] The Dufferie appears to have been an ancient Irish district or division, but it, as well as Clonmullen Castle, appears to have entirely escaped the notice of all gazetteers, &c. The name is preserved in Duffry Hall, a seat of the Colcloughs, in the parish of Templeshanbo, Co. Wexford.

Hereunto belongs a court-leet, a court-baron, and one fair. It is mortgaged by one Mr. Darbie Cavenah, in Irish called Dormaunt MacDoullin. This land is now in mortgage to one Turner, an apothecary in Dublin, for £800, and may be redeemed whensoever the money is paid. This land adjoins to Sir James Caroll's new and stately house, which hath almost sunk him by the charge of building the same. It is called Ballyeskerne. This land lies upon the bank of the Slane, which is plentifully furnished with salmon and trouts; down this river abundance of timber is conveyed down to Waxford, so to be transported by sea. Upon this river bank many pleasant convenient seats for houses or towns may be found out. Here are coneys belonging hereunto. It will keep cattle, and good sheep and horses; these I saw, though by reason of the most extreme, violent drought, both that land and all this country is burnt up and no grass, so as you cannot look upon this land but with much disadvantage, yet it seems to be a good sweet-natured earth, but it hath been overtilled, and much wronged by the Irish husbandry. It is given in for 1,000 acres, but it is by those who know not how to guess at 1,000 acres; for doubtless there is no less than 1,000 acres of arable and pasture land, which may be made rich land by lime, which may be conveniently provided very cheap for 2d. a barrel, and may be conveyed by water at a small charge. Our host, Mr. Plummer (who lives in Ennerscoffie, and is a Scotchman; his wife, an Englishwoman) affirmed that the third part of the corn (for so the Irish tenants sow their landlord's grounds, and allow them the third sheaf, and take two sheaves for their pains) which grew last year upon that ground, was sold for £120. There is meadow land and bog, which being guttered, ditched and drained (which may be done with £20 or £30 charge) will be good and rich meadow; this is no less than 500 acres. Of commoning also, which yields ferron and gorse, and would be made good land with a small charge, there is about 800 acres. Here is woodland belonging hereunto, but how much I am uncertain. Little good timber I saw; some part of the wood may easily be cleared of the oullers[1] and underwood, and make good meadowing. Here is as

---

[1] Alder trees.

handsome an Irish hall upon this ground as ever I saw in this kingdom, and if Sir James Carroll will part with his house, it stands most conveniently to be occupied herewith; and it is generally believed that both house and lands may be purchased upon easy terms. This were a brave seat for a younger brother, but this will not be sold, for Mr. Darbye Cavenah himself came to me at Washford, and would have made a lease for 21 years or for 200 years, paying in the interim ten shillings an acre, which was a most senseless demand, and as much as the lands can be improved unto at the end of the 200 years; hereupon we brake off.

This kingdom is now divided into four provinces: 1. Linster, 2. Munster. 3. Ulster. 4. Connaught. Linster containeth these counties: 1. Eastmeath; 2. Westmeath; 3. Dublin; 4. Kildare; 5. Louth: these five called within the English pale; 6. Longford; 7. King's County; 8. Queene; 9. Kilkennie, one of the finest counties in Ireland; 10. Carloe; 11. Wexford; 12. Wickley. Munster divides itself into these shires or counties: 1. Waterford; 2. Tiperarie and Cross Teperarie; 3. Corke, greatest in Ireland; 4. Kerrie, furthest point of Ireland, southwest; 5. Limbreck, the richest land; 6. Toemond. Ulster: 1. Denegell, furthest north-west county; 2. Euneschelyn, or Fermanough; 3. Cavan; 4. Monohain; 5. Tyrone; 6. Londonderie; 7. Armath; 8. Downe Patrick; 9. Antrim, wherein stands Carick-Fergus. Connaught: 1. Gallaway; 2. Mayeo; 3. Rosscommon; 4. Letrim; 5. Sligoe.

We lodged on Thursday, *Jul.* 16, at ENNERSCORFFIE,[1] at one Andrew Plummers, a Scotchman, his wife an Englishwoman, where we paid 1*s.* ordinary for ourselves, and 6*d.* for our servants. Here is a neat little castle in good repair. This and the town and the lands hereabout belong unto Sir Henry Walloppe,[2] who hath a

---

[1] Enniscorthy.

[2] Sir Henry Wallop, of Farley Wallop in Hampshire, was knighted in the reign of Queen Elizabeth, was possessed of very extensive property in that county, in Shropshire, and other places; and had great political influence. He and his son sat together in several parliaments. From James I he received a grant of the tithes of

very brave command and royalty and revenue hereabout. This town is seated upon the fair river Slane, which ebbs and flows even to this town, the greatest part of all the wealthy inhabitants whereof (there cannot be many) are wood-merchants. Here our host informed us that Mr. Chambers had now at least, there landed and coming down the water, an hundred thousand pipe-staves, &c. which were worth at Wexford ten [shillings] an hundred: there his money to be received, out of which he cannot gain less than half in half.

July 17.—Here I bought of John Torkinton a little white mare; the price was 2*l.* 4*s.* He said if I returned her to Hacquetts Town when I had finished my journey, I should not abate above 3*d.* a day. I hired also a grissell gelding, for which I deposited 4*l.*2*s.*6*d.* and covenanted in this manner : that if I returned the horse within thirty days, I was to receive my money back again, allowing an abatement of 1*s.* a day for so many days as I had the horse ; only by this agreement I was to keep the horse ten days at least, so as if I returned him next day, I must abate 10*s.* of the 4*l.* 2*s.* 6*d.* This horse was one Mainwareing's,[1] steward to Sir Henry Walloppe : he descended out of Caringham house, and is uncle to Mr. Mainwareing that now is. This money was left with Mr. Andrew Plummer, who undertook the performance of conditions.

Here we parted with Mr. Needam, who appointed with me to

Enniscorthy, and confirmation of his lands in Ireland, in which was comprised the castle of Enniscorthy, of which he was governor. He is said to have been a very learned gentleman, and of exemplary morals, a judicious manager of his estates, and to have kept a very hospitable house, in all respects suitable to his fortune, one of the largest among the commoners of his time. He died Nov. 1642, aged 74.

[1] Roger Mainwaring, fourth son of Henry Mainwaring of Kermincham or Carincham, sheriff of Cheshire, 1575, was appointed in 1612, by Sir Henry Wallop, constable, governor, and keeper of Enniscorthy Castle, with all jurisdiction and privileges, and general receiver of all his rents, &c. with the yearly fee of 20*l.* English money. He died without issue. Carincham is now held by Mr. Uniacke, descended from an heiress of the Mainwarings ; but the name of Mainwaring was assumed, in 1809, by sign manual, by another descendant, in the female line, of the same heiress. Sir W. Brereton afterwards calls him cousin, but the pedigrees do not show this exact alliance. There were at an early period intermarriages which might have occasioned the use of a word which is sometimes applied in a very general way.

meet me on Tuesday morning next at Carick, where my Lord of Ormond lives. Hence I sent to Dublin by John Torkinton the two horses there hired, which were promised to be delivered there the day following, which I made use of, and was to pay for five days, for which I paid in Dublin twelve shillings beforehand.

We went hence towards Wexford, which is accounted eight mile, but they are very long miles. We crossed the water at Ennerscoffie on horseback, and at the Carick, a mile from Wexford, we passed over a narrow ferry: all the grass in the country is burnt up, and here they complain of drought, and affirm they never felt such extreme scorching hot weather in Ireland. Here are divers of the Roches, which have much land about Wexford, and who would willingly set or sell; their land lieth very convenient for a Cheshire man.

About a mile hence lies a farm called the Park, which is now leased unto one Mr. Hardye, an Englishman, who lives upon it, and hath an estate in it about thirteen years. The landlord is one Mr. William Synode of the Lough, a man that needs money. This land is almost an island, and the rent which Mr. Hardye pays is about 16l. per annum. He saith it contains about three hundred acres, others say two hundred acres, and that it will keep twenty or thirty milch kine, yield sufficient corn for a small family, affords abundance of rabbits, whereof here there are too many, so as they pester the ground, and here may be more fish and fowl provided than to keep a good family, for on three sides it is compassed with great loughs a mile or two broad, so as the flood being in it flows to the very bank sides; when the flood is out, the shore being mud is bare and dry; when the tide is out, the depth of the mud is half a yard or a yard; but I could not find the mud bare, and this was the reason given by Mr. Hardye: that so long as the wind blows west, it clears it of water, but now the wind being at east keeps the tide in; when the flood is in, it is said to be not above one yard deep of water (except at some extraordinary spring tides). I cannot believe but that this mud will much fertilize and enrich the ground: this I do believe is a place of much security to such cattle or goods as are therein kept, and they affirm that they have not lost any since they came thither, which is about eight years. Here is the best feeding for fowl that I ever saw. This grass which comes from the mud is good food for them, and there is good store of it, and here is a little grove of oaks, wherein is no good timber, but it so stands as it is most strong shelter to the fowl that feed or frequent under it.

Here is the most commodious and convenient seat for a c[oy] that ever I saw, but there is no more room whereupon to erect a c[oy] betwixt the water and an high bank of the wood than four or five rood in breadth, but sufficient in length, so as you must either make so much of the mud firm land, whereupon to build your c[oy], or else you must only make good one side with two pipes, or you must erect your work upon a point of land which lieth much eastward, and is in view of the town, and much more inconvenient, or you must carry away abundance of earth to make a pond, and pipes in some ground, as yet much too high at the north-west end of the wood. Here grow ollers[1] sufficient to plant a coy, and here is sufficient wood to cleave into stakes for all uses ; and, as I am informed, reed may be provided out of Sir Thomas Esmond's lands which is on the other side the water, and all necessaries may be supplied by water from the Slane. Mr. Hardye demands for his interest, which is for thirteen years, 55*l.* and will abate nothing.

And herein grow good cherries, and all wood here planted flourisheth well. Mr. Turner, father-in-law to Mr. William Synode, demanded an 100*l.* fine for a lease of eighty years in reversion after the determination of the thirteen years now in being : of the unreasonableness of which demand being convinced, he sent next day a messenger and letter to his son-in-law Mr. Synode, who desired to know what I would give. I would offer nothing, but Mr. Mainwareing offered 20*l.* per lease for eighty (years). Mr. Turner replied that 40*l.* would not be accepted, and an augmentation of the rent 4*l.* per annum from 16*l.* to 20*l.* Upon this we broke off.

---

[1] Alder trees.

We lodged at WEXFORD at the sign of the Windmill, at the house of Paul Bennett. This town is seated upon a brave spacious harbour, capacious of many thousand sail, but it is much prejudiced and damnified by a most vile barred haven, which notwithstanding is far better than formerly. Two narrow banks of sand run along on both sides the channel into the sea, betwixt the points whereof is the channel or passage. Trade much decayeth in this town, and it is very poor by reason of herring fishing here failing. They report here of an incredible multitude of herrings ordinarily taken in one night in this large and vast harbour by five or six men in one boat of ten ton burthen, sometimes to the value of 20*l*., sometimes 30*l*., sometimes 40*l*., sometimes more. This was informed me and affirmed by one that ordinarily fished here and took this proportion. Now of latter times, the herrings having forsaken this coast, this town is much impoverished and decayed. Their quays go to ruin, and are in no good repair; there belonged sometimes unto every great merchant's house seated on the shore either a quay, or a part interest in a quay, or a private way to the quay. Their haven was then furnished with five thousand sail of ships and small vessels for fishing, and is now naked.

Jul. 18.—This day I went to the court (the assizes being now here held for this county of Washford,[1] which began on Wednesday last, and ended this day) where is their shire hall. The judges that ride this circuit are Sir George Sherley, Lord Chief-Justice of Ireland, and Sir John Fillpott, one of the Judges in the Common Pleas, a little, black, temperate man. The one, viz. my Lord Chief-Justice, sits upon Isie-prices,[2] the other upon matters of misdemeanours and trials for life and death. Here I saw four justices of peace sit upon the bench with Sir John Philpott,[3] amongst which was one Devereux[4] and my cousin Mainwareing, uncle to

[1] The name of Wexford frequently so written.

[2] Nisi prius.

[3] Sir John Philpot, one of the justices of the Common Pleas from 1621 till his death in 1637.

[4] Nicholas Devereux, of a family of high respectability, was settled at Ballymagar, in the county of Wicklow.

Mr. Mainwareing[1] of Caringham that now is, a courteous, grave, civil gentleman, who came from the bench, and saluted me in the hall, and accompanied me to the tavern, and bestowed wine upon me. He is agent unto Sir Henry Wallopp, and is a justice of peace of this county, and was a burgess for the parliament. He told me there were three rebels condemned, as also he advised me rather to go by Balliehack and by the way of the Passage than by Ross, because of the rebels which frequent thereabouts; hereof, he said there were about six or eight, and these furnished with some pieces, pistols, darts, and skenes, and some of them most desperate spirits, and so cruel, that the inhabitants of the country dare scarce travel that way; these are proclaimed rebels, and such as are to be hanged, drawn and quartered, so soon as they are apprehended. So also are those to be dealt withal, who are now to be executed. One of them I saw in the streets returning towards the castle, and the women and some other following making lamentation, sometimes so violent as though they were distracted, sometimes as it were in a kind of tune singing; one of these ('twas said) was his wife. This is the Irish garb.[2] This town is governed by a mayor and two bayliffs or sheriffs, and ten or twelve aldermen.

Beyond the bar also, it hath a very safe harbour and shelter for ships to ride at anchor in, who want tide to bring them into the haven. Sir Adam Cotcliffe[3] told me that he had dined at Milford in Wales and supped in this town, which is about twenty-four hours' sail from Bristoll, and as much to Dublin. By reason of the assizes here, the inhabitants of the country resorted hither in greater numbers and better habits (Irish garments I mean) than I have yet seen. Some gentlewomen of good quality here I observed clothed in good handsome gowns, petticoats and hats, who wore Irish rugs, which have handsome, comely, large fringes, which go about their necks, and serve instead of bands. This ruggy fringe

---

[1] See before, page 151.   [2] Habit, practice, custom.

[3] Sir Adam Colclough, of Tintern Abbey in the county of Wicklow, was created a baronet in 1628; he married Alice, daughter of Sir Rob. Rich, Knt., master in Chancery in England. In his grandson, the title became extinct.

is joined to a garment which comes round about them, and reacheth to the very ground, and this is an handsome, comely vestment, much more comely as they are used than the rug short cloaks used by the women upon festival days in Abbleveile, Bullein, and the nearer parts of Picardie in Fraunce. The most of the women are bare-necked, and clean-skinned, and wear a crucifix, tied in a black necklace, hanging betwixt their breasts. It seems they are not ashamed of their religion, nor desire to conceal themselves; and indeed in this town are many papists.

Jul. 19.—The present mayor, Mr. Mark Cheveu, attended the judges to the church door, and so did the sheriff of the shire, both which left them there, and went to mass, which is here tolerated, and publicly resorted unto in two or three houses in this town, wherein are very few Protestants, as appeared by that slender congregation at church where the judges were. This morning I went unto and visited both the judges, and was respectively used by them; the mayor, a well-bred gentleman, an inns-of-court man, who is a counsellor, a gentleman that hath an estate in the country, and was knight of this shire for last parliament, invited me to dinner, as also to supper, with the judges. He is an Irishman, and his wife Irish, in a strange habit, a threadbare short coat with sleeves, made like my green coat of stuff, reaching to her middle; she knew not how to carve, look, entertain, or demean herself. Here was a kind of beer (which I durst not taste) called Charter beer, mighty thick, muddy stuff, the meat nothing well cooked nor ordered. Much discourse here, complaint and information given against the rebels, the captain whereof is called Simon Prendergrasse, whose brother also will be brought in trouble for relieving, &c. Three carriers were robbed betwixt Ross and this town on Friday last, and two other travellers, and one in his lodging, by three of these rebels well appointed, who said if they could have taken my Lord of Kildare,[1] who passed through them nakedly

[1] George, sixteenth Earl of Kildare, succeeded to the title and estates, when not quite nine years of age. He was a person of considerable trust and influence, and upon

attended, he should have procured their pardon. There was a letter sent and read this night at supper, advertising a gentleman in town that last night they came to his house with a purpose to take away his life, because he prosecuted against them, and informed that they had taken from him to the value of £200. The judge here said, if all the justices of peace did not wait upon them to Ross to guard them from these rebels, he would fine them deeply. The junior judge told me of a very wise demeanour of the now mayor of Ross, who being informed that three of these rebels lay asleep near the town, and being required to send out some ten or twelve with him to apprehend them, he answered that he would provide for the safety of his town, commanded the gates to be shut, the drum to be beat, and pieces, warning-pieces, to be discharged, whereby they awaked, and took notice thereof and escaped.

Jul. 20.—We left Washford, and the Lord provided a good guide for us, and directed us to a better course than we intended; for instead of going over the passage (which was this day so much troubled and so rough as my Lord of Kildare was in great danger there, and himself and servants constrained to cut the sail ropes and tacklings) we took up our lodging at Tinterden,[1] a dissolved abbey, where now Sir Adam Cocliffe lives, and where we were exceedingly kindly and courteously entertained. Now my disease began to increase upon me. This a very fair, large, stately house, and of great receipt. He keeps a good house, and hath a great estate here, and his lady is dainty, complete, well-bred woman. She is Sir Rob. Rich his daughter. The land on this side Washford about four or five mile and so to Balliehack is much better land than that which I saw in any other part of this county. This day we had more rain than upon any day since we came from

the breaking out of the rebellion in 1641, was made governor of the county of Kildare. He died about the year 1660.

[1] Tintern, or Kinneagh, an abbey founded by William, Earl of Pembroke, who placed in it Cistercians from Tintern Abbey in Monmouthshire. It has long been in possession of the family of the Colcloughs.

home. Here they say no rain fallen this two months, all extreme dry, but nothing so much burnt up as in the other side of this county.

Jul. 21.—We went hence about eight hour, and came to Ballihack, a poor little village on this side the passage over the river of Waterford, which here is the broadest passage said to be in Ireland, and a most rough, troubled passage, when the wind is any thing high. Here last day the boat, wherein my Lord of Kildare came over, was in danger to be run under water by carrying too much sail, and running foul upon the passage boat. Down this river come all the shipping for Waterford. Here we saw the 9th Whelp lying at anchor, to guard the fleet which now is ready to go hence to Bristoll fair. Sir Beverley Newcombe is captain of her, and is now at Waterford. They say there are about fifty sail to go to St. James fair at Bristoll. The Irish here use a very presumptuous proverb and speech touching this passage. They always say they must be at Bristoll fair,—they must have a wind to Bristoll fair; and indeed it is observed they never fail of a wind to Bristoll fair; yea though the fair be begun, and the wind still averse, yet still do they retain their confident presumption of a wind. It is most safe here to hire a boat to pass over in, not with horses, which is rowed over with four oars. I paid for the hire of it 2*s.* This is a full mile over. The passage boat which carries your horses will not carry at one time more than two or three horses. Here is far better coming into the boat and landing than at Port Patricke, but less and worse boats. On Munster side is good lodging and accommodation.

This day we passed over the land of a gentleman whose name is   . He died about seven days ago of a gangreen; his fingers and hands, toes and feet, rotted off, joint by joint. He was but a young man, of above 1000*l.* per annum, and married an old woman, a crabbed piece of flesh, who cheated him with a 1000*l.* she brought him, for which he was arrested within three days after his marriage.

We came to WATERFORD about three hour, and baited at the

King's Head, at Mr. Wardes, a good house, and a very complete gentlemanlike host. This town is reputed one of the richest towns in Ireland. It stands upon a river (called Watterford river) which maintaineth a sufficiently deep and safe channel even to the very quay, which indeed is not only the best and most convenient quay which I have found in Ireland, but it is as good a quay as I have known either in England, or observed in all my travels. A ship of three hundred may come close to these quays. This quay is made all along the river-side without the walls, and divers fair and convenient buttresses made about twenty yards long, which go towards the channel. I saw the river at a spring tide flow even with the top of this quay, and yet near unto the quay a ship of three hundred ton full loaden may float at a low water. Upon this river stand divers forts and castles which command it. At the mouth of the river is there a fort called Dunkannon, wherein lieth my Lord Esmond's company, consisting of fifty good expert soldiers. Here is also a company of fifty soldiers, which are under the command of Sir George Flowre,[1] an ancient knight. These are disposed of in the fort, which is placed without the gate towards Caricke, a pretty little hold, which stands on high and commands the town. There stands upon this river the Carick twelve miles hence, and Clanmell about eight mile thence; hither (as I have heard) the river flows. There is seated upon this river also Golden Bridge, and there is a passage by water from Cullen and Limbrecke. This is no barred, but a most bold haven, in the mouth whereof is placed an eminent tower, a sea mark, to be discerned at a great distance; yet this river runs so crooked as without a W.

[1] Sir Geo. Flower was an active officer employed against the rebels in Ireland in 1600, and commanding a body of troops of from 1200 to 2000 men. In 1601 he was made serjeant-major of his Majesty's forces, and performed many gallant, daring, and successful achievements, for which he received the honour of knighthood. In 1627, he was appointed governor and constable of the fort then newly erected at Waterford, and appointed one of the commissioners to execute martial law within the province of Munster. Soon after this he died. See *Lodge's Peerage of Ireland*, vol. v. p. 284. He appears, however, to have been alive, though " an ancient knight," in 1636.

or N.W. Hence went a great fleet to Bristoll fair, who staid long here waiting for a wind.

This city is governed by a mayor, bailiffs, and twelve aldermen. Herein are seven churches; there have been many more. One of these, Christ Church, a cathedral; St. Patrick's, Holy Ghost, St. Stephen's, St. John,—but none of these are in good repair, not the cathedral, nor indeed are there any churches almost to be found in good repair. Most of the inhabitants Irish, not above forty English, and not one of these Irish goes to church. This town trades much with England, Fraunce and Spaine, and that which gives much encouragement hereunto is the goodness of the haven. This town double-walled, and the walls maintained in good repair. Here we saw women in a most impudent manner treading cloathes with their feet; these were naked to the middle almost, for so high were their clothes tucked up about them. Here the women of better rank and quality wear long, high, laced caps, turned up round about; these are mighty high; of this sort I gave William Dale money to buy me one. Here is a good, handsome market-place, and a most convenient prison that I ever saw for the women apart, and this is a great distance from the men's prison. Herein dwells a judicious apothecary, who hath been bred at Antwerpe, and is a traveller; his name is (as I take it) Mr. Jarvis Billiard, by whose directions and good advice I found much good, and through God's mercy recovered from my sickness. After I had dined here, I went about four or five hour towards Caricke, where I stayed at a ferry about a mile from Watterford a whole hour for the boat, wherein we and our six horses were carried over together.

Hence to CARICKE is accounted nine miles, good large ones, but very fair way, and very ready to find. We came to Caricke about nine hour. We lodged at the sign of the Three Cups at Mr. Croummer's, where is a good neat woman. Here my disease increasing, I wanted good accommodation. Here is my Lord of Ormond's[1] house, daintily seated on the river bank, which flows

---

[1] James, twelfth Earl and first Duke of Ormond, whose talents and virtues are too well known and appreciated to require or admit of notice here.

even to the walls of his house, which I went to see, and found in the outer court three or four hay-stacks, not far from the stable-door; this court is paved. There are also two other courts; the one a quadrangle. The house was built at twice. If his land were improved and well planted, it would yield him a great revenue; for it is said he hath thirty-two manors and manor-houses, and eighteen abbeys. This town of Carick is seated upon the bank of a fine, pleasant, navigable river, but it is a most poor place, and the houses many quite ruinated, others much decayed; here is no trade at all. This hath been a town of strength and defence; it is walled about, and with as strong a wall, and that to walk upon, as is West Chester; the church in no good repair, nor any of the churches in this country, which argues their general disaffection unto religion. Here in this town is the poorest tavern I ever saw— a little, low, thatched Irish house, not to be compared unto Jane Kelsall's of the Green at Handforth. 'Twixt Water-ford and this town are many spacious sheep-pastures, and very fair large sheep as most in England, the greatest part of the land here-abouts is converted unto this use.

Jul. 22.—From this town I returned back to Waterford, fearing indeed lest the country disease should so far prevail upon me as to disable me to endure, whereas indeed immediately after my de-parture I did begin by degrees to recover, and was within a few days, and before my departure out of that kingdom, perfectly recovered, and my body rather inclined to be costive, but yet this did not continue with me above two days; and whereas I feared faintings by reason of sea-sickness, I thank God I was nothing subject thereunto, though I was never well at sea. Here, by promise, Mr. Needam of Hacquett's Town stood engaged to meet me, and sends in his stead Mr. Robert Cooke, an English gentle-man who lives about one or two miles from this town, upon a farm called Tibruchne (as I take it) which is my Lord of land; he is my Lord of Ormond's uncle; he pays £120 rent for this farm, and paid an £100 fine: his term in it is twenty years or thereabouts; the quantity of the ground hereunto belonging, as he valueth and esteems it to be, about 1000 acres English measure; but, upon my view and survey thereof, I could not judge it to be less than 1200 or 1400 acres. This is all good land, and a great part marsh land lying along the river in common and not enclosed, which, if it were but divided and enclosed, would yield more than the rent of the whole, and this would be a small charge to make only ditches; this is commodiously, sometimes and not over often, watered and enriched by this navigable great river, which runs all along this ground a mile or two.

Here I observed a very convenient seat . This was this day overflowed with the tide, by reason of a strong east wind concurring with this high St. James' flood; here abundance of fowl in winter. Here is a very fair, handsome English stone house new built, and also a castle, to both which there comes up at every tide in a deep lough or channel sufficient water to carry a boat, and when the tide is gone out this is dry; so as if a net be placed in the mouth of it (which is but narrow) you may be thereby furnished with salmon, flookes,[1] and other fish sufficient. There is now an Englishman tenant, who lives in the Castle, who keeps a dairy and rents thirty kine from him, who keeps them summer and winter; for every cow he is to pay 1*l.* 10*s.* per annum, and half of the calves, all which are to be reared. I tasted of their milk, butter and cheese, and it was excellent good; I never drunk so good butter-milk. Here the milk is so good, as they churn that in the evening which was milked in the morning, so as the butter-milk is much sweeter and wholesomer; they never yet sold any cheese, only butter at 4*d.* a pound. Here I saw abundance of cheeses. Here is a town hereunto belonging, inhabited by Irish, who have no longer estate than from year to year; they pay neither here nor elsewhere no rent in money, only plough the ground to the parts, and allow the landlord a third part; this is so slothfully and improvidently ordered, as the ground is much impaired, and yields much less than if well husbanded. But these

---

[1] *Flookes,* flounders.

unprofitable commodities may be removed at pleasure, and without any manner of inconvenience, exclamation, or exception. Mr. Robert Cooke, who now dwells here, affirmed that this farm would keep 120 kine, and their increase, sufficiently plentifully, both summer and winter. There is one now tenant upon another part hereof, who will take the whole one half of the farm, so much as is grazing ground for cattle, and will pay £90 per annum, and indeed Mr. Cooke is so honest a gentleman, as I cannot but believe his report. He saith it will also keep five or six hundred sheep, as good fair sheep as are Leicestershire or Northamptonshire, and sufficient good corn land may be reserved as will employ two ploughs; besides, the moor, which is a rich marsh like Saltney,[1] will keep abundance of young cattle, horses and colts, and in my judgment this marsh land cannot be less than 400 acres. Herein although the salt water this day overflowed in my view, yet owlers[2] grow and prosper well; hence you may go conveniently enough to Caricke to church, the church in this town being in decay. Mr. Cooke will part with his interest herein, and demands his £100 fine and the rent of £120 per annum; the reason why he will part with his interest is because he hath a kinsman of his name partner with him, who fails in the payment of his part of the rent, for which his cattle was distrained.

Jul. 23.—This day I rested at King's Head at Mr. Warde's, and prepared barley-water, cordials and perfumes, to take to sea, to preserve me from fainting, whereunto I was nothing subject (I thank God) at sea or land. Herein I made use of and spent most of the afternoon with Mr. Jarvis Billiard, the apothecary, who showed me the best Mercator[3] that ever I saw in my life; and

---

[1] Saltney Marsh was an extensive salt marsh, within the county of Flint, in the immediate neighbourhood of the city of Chester; it consisted of nearly 5000 acres, and under the powers of acts of parliament a new channel for the river Dee was cut through it, and a very large tract of land rescued from the encroachments of the sea. To accomplish this object a company of adventurers was formed and incorporated under the name of the River Dee Company.   [2] Alders.

[3] Gerard Mercator, a German, who died in 1594, invented a chart or projection of the earth, which after him was called a Mercator.

indeed, before my departure hence, I was freed from that indisposition.

24.—Next morning I went down to the passage, which was so thronged as I could not be furnished with convenient lodging; hard bed, without curtains, air or casements, a corn room. We lodged at Bell, 6d. ordinary, a most unquiet house at this time. The wind stood well for them (if they could have gotten out to sea) two or three days before, but it was so strong as they durst not adventure out of the river, for fear of being thrown upon some of the crooked points in this river.

25.—But upon St. James day, the wind was sufficiently calmed, and stood fair, and they in The Whelp discharged a piece of ordinance to summon us aboard very early, so I was constrained to go aboard without my breakfast. There I bought half a mutton, cost 3s. and eggs seven a penny, and three pullets at 3d. a piece, but wanted a stomach to make use of any save some eggs and pullets. About six hour I went aboard one of the king's ships, called the Ninth Whelp,[1] which is in the king's books 215 ton and tonnage

---

[1] The occasion of the building of this vessel, and the fate of some of its companions, we learn from the following extracts. Our traveller is not always very correct in his statements when measures of weight or distance are concerned, and his estimate of the tonnage of this vessel does not agree with that of the shipbuilder. The name *whelp* was probably given them facetiously in reference to their designation as barks.

" 1627. The 26th of February, attending the officers of the navy at Sir Sackville Crowe's house by Charing Cross, Sir John Penington came thither to acquaint them with a warrant from the Lord Duke (of Buckingham) directed to him and myself, for present bargaining with the yard keepers of the river for the building of ten small vessels, for the enterprise of Rochel, of some 120 tons a piece, with one deck and quarter only, to row as well as sail. The 28th day of the same month we concluded our bargains with the general yardkeepers, and drew covenants between us and delivered to them accordingly. In this business I was employed till the latter end of July that the ships set sail to Portsmouth. My son John was placed captain in the sixth Whelp, built by my kinsman Peter Pett. Having liberty from the Lord Duke to make choice for him amongst them all, I chose that pinnace before the rest, supposing she would have proved best, which fell out afterwards cleane contrary. The 4th September my son John took leave of me in the evening, and went on board his ship, whom I never saw after, being unfortunately cast away in the return from Rochel.

" 1628. In this interim I received certain intelligence of the great loss of my son John, his ship and all his company, who foundered in the sea about the Seames in a

in king's books. She carries sixteen pieces of ordinance, two brass sakers, six iron demiculverin drakes, four iron whole culverin drakes, and four iron demicannon drakes. They are called drakes. They are taper-bored in the chamber, and are tempered with extraordinary metal to carry that shot; these are narrower where the powder is put in, and wider where the shot is put in, and with this kind of ordinance his Majesty is much affected. This ship is manned with sixty men; the captain is Sir Beverley Newcomen;[1] lieutenant, John Newcomen; master, William Brooke; master's mate, William Purser, who hath lost an arm,—a temperate, well-governed, and well-affected man; master gunner, Joseph Dudley; boatswain, corruptly called boseon, John Green; purser, Thomas Morgan; serjeant, Nathaneell Gilson; and indeed the most of the better sort of the rest civilized and well-governed men, and divers of them I observed attentive and diligent at prayer. We had (through God's mercy) a quick, pleasant, and dainty passage, for within twenty-six hours after we parted with Ireland, the utmost point I mean of Irish shore, we were landed at MINEHEAD in Somersettshire. This is a most dainty steady vessel, so long as she carries sail, and a most swift sailer, able to give the advantage of a top-sail to any of the rest of this fleet, for whom we made many stays, and yet could not keep behind them, so as they did not put up all their sails as they otherwise might, but suited their course to the pace of this fleet, whom they waited upon to waft over from Waterford to Bristoll fair, and to guard them from the Turks, of

great storm about the beginning of November; not one man saved to bring the doleful news, nor no ship near them to deliver the certainty but a small pinnace belonging to the fleet that was within ken of her, and saw her shoot nine pieces of ordinance, hoping of succour."—*Journal of Phineas Pett*, MSS. in Brit. Mus. 9298.

"At the return of this fleet (from Rochel) two of the Whelps were cast away, and three ships more, and some five ships who had some of those great stones, that were brought to build Paul's, for ballast and for other uses within them, which could promise no good success, for I never heard of any thing that prospered which being once designed for the honour of God was alienated from that use."—*Howel's Letters*, sect. v. lett. 9.

[1] Sir Beverley Newcomen, Bart. of Kenagh in the county of Longford, probably grandson of Robert, on whom that honour was first conferred in 1623.

whom there was here a fear and rumour that they were very busy
upon the coast of Fraunce.   These are full of men, ordinance and
small shot.   This day we caused match to be made ready and prepared, and looked for them about Lundye next morning, but saw
none, only it was the captain's care to see all the sail before him;
for which end staying often, the vessel then (as also when she
wanted sail) tottered and rolled intolerably; this did make me
vomit extremely, and much more sea-sick than otherwise.

Here the captain's cabin was taken up by Alderman Joanes of
Dublin, and Dr.   [1] Dean of Christ Church in Dublin,
who came in her by sea from Dublin to Waterford, and so thence
for Bristoll; and the captain himself lodged in the master's cabin,
so as I could not be accommodated with any more convenient cabin
that the master gunner's cabin in the gun room, but I could not
endure under hatches, nor was I any longer in this cabin than
about four hours in the night, during which time I could not rest,
the ship tossed so exceedingly, so as I thought it had been tem-
pestuous, and yet was it very calm, fair and moon-shine night; and
sometimes the waves flashed into the ship at the loop-holes at
stern, so as I could not endure in bed longer than one watch, from
ten to two hour, and then I arose and went to the hatches, and
presently we discovered Lundye, which seems like a high rock in
the sea, and is an island: this is accustomed to be the pirates' harbour and shelter, but now we could not discover any.

The remarkable points, shores, sands, rocks and islands, in this
passage, are these: on Washford side, Dunkannon, which is a fort,
wherein my Lord Esmond's company is disposed; and a low point
whereon is placed the tower of Waterford, a white, eminent, conspicuous sea-mark: hence about four leagues are two islands called
the Saltes.   On Waterford side is Croydenhead, and the utmost
point is called Horselippes, so called from a shelf of sand.   Hence
to Lundye is about thirty leagues: this is an island which belongs
to a Devon gentleman, lying N. and S., and in length about three

---

[1] Randolph Barlow, Archbishop of Tuam 1629, held the deanery of Christ Church
in commendam.

mile, and in breadth about a mile; this is plentifully furnished with fowl and coneys, and good grass for cattle. Turks and men-of-war often commit spoil here, but, there being but one passage or entrance, ten men may repulse fifty. Though this seem an high rock, yet it is nothing so high as Elsey or the Bass. In the midst and fair way to this island are certain sharp rocks called the Smalls, very dangerous; and about six leagues to the N. lies St. David's point, and not far from thence is the poor city of St. David's, a village for a few fishermen: if there come any ships near to these rocks, there are strong tides which will hazard violently and forcibly to carry the ship upon them; these your expert mariners take care commonly to leave at a sufficient distance on the left hand, except the wind be north, then they haul close to the coast of Wales, Pembrokeshire, near to Millford Haven, a most capacious gallant haven, which is about twenty-five leagues from the tower of Waterford.

This island of Lundye lieth in the middle of the mouth of Severn, which is there about fifteen leagues broad betwixt the isle of Caldye in Pembrokeshire and Hartland Point in Devonshire; and this river runs all along to Bristoll about twenty-eight leagues, and thence to Gloucester. This Hartland Point is the westward point of the bay of Barnstable, and seventeen leagues hence on Devon side is a dry haven called Illfordcombe. Hence to Minehead in Sommersettshire, seven leagues: thence to Wattchett, two leagues; to Bridgwater, four leagues. On the coast of Wales, from Milford Haven to Tinbye,[1] which is in the isle of Caldye, is three leagues; thence to Caermarthen in Caermarthenshire; then to Burroe,[2] without which lieth a point called the Wormes-head; to the east lie Neith and Swanzie, Barrie and Sillie in Glamorganshire, all four dry creeks, whence comes much coals into Sommersettshire. From Sillie to the Holmes, about two leagues; to the north of these is Pennart Point, where alabaster is digged; this

[1] Tenby is on the main land, opposite to Caldy Island.
[2] Burry river, on the bank of which is Gower land, having Wormshead for its extremest western point.

about three miles from Cardiffe, which is thirty mile from Bristoll. Cardiffe stands in the mouth of river Tavye. Thence to Newport in Monmouthshire eight mile; this is placed in the mouth of the river Uske; upon the same river, three miles higher, stands Carlion, where King Arthur kept his court. Thence to Chepstow in Monmouthshire twelve miles; this stands in the mouth of the river Wye; all which rivers of Tavie, Uske, and Wye, are swallowed by the river Severn, and lose their name. From Chepstow to the Passage twixt Bristoll and Wales three mile; this passage is called Aust on English side, and Beateslay[1] on the Welsh side; it is two mile over. Here runs one of the strongest tides in the world, as Mr. William Purser, a judicious mariner and master's mate of the ninth Whelp, informed me.

In this passage I have omitted to take notice and tell you that about nineteen leagues from Bristoll in Severn, there are two islands, called the Holmes; in the one of them, which is to the north, grows good corn, and is lead ore gotten; which is in circumference about two miles; the other of these islands is called the Steepeholmes, an island of little value. Thence to Kingroade seven leagues, where now rides the ninth Whelpe at anchor, and which is about five mile from Bristoll. I must not forget how fortunately it pleased God to dispose touching my horses for the carriage over, whereof I had no warrant (and without a warrant none permitted to be transported), but meeting with Mr. Styles at Waterford, who had a warrant under my Lord Deputy's hand for transporting six horses, he was pleased to allow me under that warrant (which cost him 1l. 10s.), to transport a couple, paying proportionably unto him 10s.; and at my coming to passage, I found a barque fraught with cattle of Mr. Augustine's, a justice of peace, who was contented to allow my horses therein to be transported, for the carriage whereof I paid 2l. and 5s. for William Bayley, and 2s. or 3s. more; so my horses, beyond my expectation, came to me at Minehead, where I paid 2s. 4d. custom for them.

---

[1] Beachley.

But before I conclude this discourse of this sea-passage, I cannot but account well deserving to be committed to record all those names and terms which mariners use, which my memory is able to supply unto me. The fore part of the ship is called the fore-castle, wherein is placed the beak-head; the hinder part is called the stern, wherein is placed the rudder. This carries four masts: 1. the main-mast, which is placed almost in the middle of the ship; 2. the fore-mast, which is placed nearer to the forecastle; 3. the bow-sprit or sprit-sail, which stands sloping even over the beak-head, and which hangs so much aslope as I have sometimes observed to touch the water; 4. the mizen, which is placed in the stern, almost over the helm. Upon the mainmast and foremast there is also placed two other masts, that is, the maintop mast and topgallant, and the foretop mast and topgallant; and every of these hath a sail belonging to them called by the same name; as also it is to be observed that there belongs unto the mainsail and topsail, the main bonnet and top bonnet, which you may take off, or put on at pleasure, as occasion is offered; if the wind blow over stiff, you may take them off, lest they overset the ship, and in a short time also you may lace them on again. As the forepart of the ship is called the forecastle, and hinder part the stern, so the right side is called the starboard side, and the left side the larboard side. Terms of steerage: port, that is, put the helm to the starboard side, which turns the ship and makes her go clean contrary way; starboard, that is, to the right hand; larboard, that is, to the left hand. No near and bear up, that is, come no nearer the wind with the ship's head. Wear no more, that is, fall not off or aloof. Observe, that is the rudder which is without board, and is placed in the very end, which, being moved by the tiller and whipstaff, directs and turns the ship. Observe also, that the helm consists of rudder, tiller, and whipstaff, and except the ship move and make way, the rudder is of no use.

For wine, beer, and meat, you may have good accommodation. The captain keeps a good table, where is always fresh meat. Here is a good cook, who will make ready any thing desired. I gave

z

1*l*.10*s*. and Mr. Downes 10*s*., in toto 2*l*., which we gave to be disposed by the master and his mate and the gunner amongst the sailors; only I directed 10*s*. to be given the gunner for cabin, and 2*s*. to his man, and 2*s*. 6*d*. to cook, and 5*s*. to two of the captain's men; the residue was referred to their disposition. They have prayer twice a day performed by the chaplain, and oftentimes in the night, when the watch is set, some of the officers sing a psalm and pray.

Observe, touching the watch, this course is observed; the one half of the officers and sailors keep above hatches constantly, and during four hours they attend; then at the end of the four hours, another watch is set, and the residue of the officers and sailors succeed; and thus the whole time both of day and night is by them disposed in good order.

Jul. 26.—About 12 hour, upon 26 *Julii*, we left the ship and were carried ashore in the long boat, wherein we were more tossed, and in more apparent danger than in all the passage, the waves swelling and being mighty high and great upon and near the shore, so as we were glad to be landed upon any land, and were set ashore a mile from Minehead upon the sea coast, and near unto an house in Sommersettshire, which is said to be enchanted, wherein none dare lodge in the night, so as it is not inhabited. Here we found boys and others attending the orchard, which is well furnished with apples, which the fairies sufficiently guard in the night time.

This town of MINEHEAD is no market town, the greatest part of it said to be Mr. Lutterell's[1] land. It is a long, straggling-built village, whereinto there is great recourse of passengers for Ireland. We lodged at the sign of the Angel, and had 6*d*. ordinary. Hence I sent by boat, in a barque of 80 ton, Geo. Parker, Robin and Will., together with the cloak-bags, who went aboard about 11 hour at night, and landed at the King Road about 6 hour on Monday evening, who paid 1*s*. a-piece for their passage. Here is an high, strong pier, and a good, wide, open haven.

---

[1] Thomas Luttrell, of Dunster Castle, succeeded to the estates of his family in 1630, and died in 1647. Minehead was frequently represented in parliament by some member of this family.

27. Myself and cousin Downes departed from Minehead about 6 hour. Hence not far a fine, pleasant castle is seated of Mr. Lutterell's, who is an ancient gentleman, and of great revenue; they report he hath £2000 per annum, and £400 hereof is old rent of assise. In this country they ordinarily give eighteen or twenty (years) purchase for a lease for three lives. This gentleman hath two fair parks together. About four miles hence there is a little haven town, called Watchett. Thence to BRIDGWATER about fourteen miles; here we baited at one Mr. Peter Smethwick's house, a Cheshire man, and were well used. This town placed upon a navigable stream, deep and narrow like Bristoll: a pretty, sweet town, wherein is a fine market place, and a neat market house: these are the havens on Sommersettshire coast. On the other side of the land on Devonshire coast, Barnstable is the utmost haven; then Bidiford, both mayor towns; Appledoore, Melcombe,[2] haven towns.

. In this town of Bridgwater, which is also a corporate town, wherein are a mayor, recorder, sheriffs, and twenty-four aldermen. Here Mr. Harvie, a counsellor, is repairing a castle and beautifying it exceedingly, whereunto belongs large orchards and gardens, and pleasant walks upon the wall. By the way I observed a stately house of Mr. Angell Graye's at Stoye,[1] which house and town was purchased lately of the last Lord Audley, who was beheaded; a fine seat, and well watered with pleasant springs. Mr. Robert Brereton lived at Sandford, a mile hence, died without issue male, left two daughters and heirs. Sir Frauncis Rogers of Camugton is an eminent housekeeper as any in the country. Esquire Heale, of Wenborough in Devon, hath 7 or £8000 per annum. From Bridgwater to Woollavington four miles, thence to Marcke four mile, to Rodney-Stoake five mile. About half a mile hence is Orion's coy, which is placed very near a highway. This is a large, spacious coy pool, wood prospereth exceeding well; by

[1] Stowy.
[2] No such haven in Devonshire; Ilfracombe, or Combe Marlen, may be the place intended.

reason of the drought here was a great want of water, until it was
replenished and supplied with some late found out springs; earth
is herein laid to the cherry-tree roots to keep them alive, and this
seems but like mud.   There are five pipes in this coy as in mine;
the seatings within the coy are overgrown with wood; abundance
here is of tame fowl; drake, pellstarts and smeathes I saw, but no
ducks.   The coy-house is larger than mine, both higher and longer.
Herein I observed bees prosper very well, and took notice of the
hives, which were made of straw after the Dutch fashion; a little
hole square almost in the middle, through which the bees enter
into the hive; this not so wide as a crown-piece of silver.   He
advised me, if it were possible, to bring a spring into my coy, by
the means hereof they took good store of fowl last storm.   I
observed most part of the ground betwixt the pipes planted with
withens,[1] except one orchard of cherry-trees.   Here were three
dogs of different colours, none so little, nor seeming so nimble as
my coy-dogs.   Here much oats is used as in my coy; very few
ducks bred here this summer come to good.

Jul. 28.—Hence I went towards GLASSENBURYE ABBEY about
half seven.   This is eight miles hence distant, and here we hired a
guide per solid. and gave him 1*s.* 6*d.*   We lodged at George at
Mr. Stroude's, but could not be accommodated either with good
lodging or victuals.   Next morning we took a full view of the
town, which is a good, fair, large town, seated upon the lower part
of a hill, which is rich corn land; and on the other hand are very
large, capacious, fruitful marshes, and very spacious, dainty, fruitful
meadows as ever I saw, wherein, near the ditches, willows are
planted in good order, which prosper excellently, and yield a very
pleasing prospect.   In this town are still two churches constantly
upon the Lord's-day made use of; the one of them hath a very
stately, high, flat steeple, wherein I heard one bell of excellent
rich metal.   This is a neat little uniform church, and the pulpit is
placed towards the lower end of the church.   This is a market-

---

[1] Willow trees.

town, and is £400 old rent of assise, which now is the king's, but formerly belonged to the abbot of Glassenburye, who as I take it was one of the greatest abbots, and possessed greatest revenues of any abbot in this kingdom. Some here speak (but I believe hyperbolically) that he had as great revenues as the king of England. Mr. Stroude, mine host, reported unto me that he possessed in this county fifty manors and ten parks, the land of which parks, being now inclosed and improved, is more worth than £15,000 per annum, and this town was one of these fifty manors, which is also £400 old rent. It is said there was in this abbey, besides the lord abbot, one hundred and sixty monks. This was a most large, spacious structure; the walls which enclosed it were at least a thousand paces, an English mile about, and these were very neat, handsomely hewn freestone, and those towards the street, which are almost the whole length of the street from the gate (which leads to the holly thorn) to the market-house (which is a dainty one): this wall is as high a stately wall as I have seen, either at Glasgoaw or Winchester, or have met with in all my travels; this was then adorned with many rich and stately pictures cut in stone and placed in the wall, and within this wall are many corn fields and other large and vast grounds; so as indeed I am most certain that I have never met with so large a sumptuous, spacious cloister neither in England, Fraunce, nor in the king of Spayne's dominions.

Here was a most large, fair and stately church, called St. Marie's, all which is utterly demolished, save some small parcels of the walls at the sides and ends, which represent the dimensions and proportion of it, and as yet continue surviving monuments of that ruinating, large, and stately fabric. Here was a dainty chapel, called St. George's, under which there was a fair, capacious tomb, wherein they say Joseph of Arimathæa was interred; still it appears there was a fair tomb there. Here was a very fair, large hall, and under it they say was the abbot's wine-cellar, a mighty, vast, capacious cellar as I have seen, and a neat piece. If the beer-cellar were shaped and proportioned accordingly, it must needs be a most huge, vast, capacious room, but I saw it not. Here the last abbot, whose name they say was Whiteing, built a neat round kitchen (which still stands entire) wherein were four chimneys opposite unto one another, and in the middle of this structure there was a stone-ascending, tower-like building, almost like your lanthorns in college halls, but that it is all of stone, and higher, narrower at top, and wider shaped at the bottom, where it is also round; this edifice still stands, nothing demolished nor ruinated. Hereunto belonged a prison, and also authority to exercise all judicial power within themselves, even to hang and put to death all those that offended within their limits, and deserved death; and their limits and territories very large, including a great part of the country as well as the town.

Captain Brooke (for as I take it he is so called) lives in this abbey, in a neat, convenient stone house, and it is said he hath a lease thereof from the king for three lives, but a great part of the ground, which was formerly built upon, is now overgrown with ellers,[1] weeds, and the like; for all the cells and cloisters which belonged unto the monks are utterly demolished and ruinated. It is reported there groweth a walnut-tree within this abbey, which still blossoms about Christmas-day, but this I saw not. The holly thorn, which is so famous and so much visited and frequented on the day of Christ's nativity, grows about half a mile from the town, near unto the highway, upon the right hand as you go to Bridgwater; hereof I took a special view, brought away many branches and leaves, and left the first letters of my name thereon upon record; the tree and bark is much decayed (as I conceive) by this practise of those that visit it. Many of the boughs and branches are much broken off, and it is much blemished hereby, as being very naked; none almost resort thither without making bold with a branch; hereof no care is taken (as were fit), nor are there any who do regard and endeavour to preserve this tree, which is affirmed by so many persons of good credit to bud and blossom

[1] Elder-trees.

at or about Christmas day, and no blossoms to be found upon it after the twelve days, nor throughout the year, as I cannot but believe the truth hereof. A minister, a neighbour hereunto, who hath lived here many years, affirmed the truth hereof from his own observation and experience many years, who hath often been an eye-witness hereof, and who carrieth about with him some of the leaves hereof in his table-book. Divers branches have been taken from this tree, and engrafted; one there is at a tavern near the George, whereof they affirm also that it buddeth and blossometh upon Christmas-day: hereof also I bought away with me some branches. Here they report that although there be many grafts of the old thorn engrafted, yet all (save this) degenerate from this much-to-be-admired budding and blossoming at this time: this by the unanimous vote and consent of all with whom I conversed is affirmed (and I did not expostulate with a few) *nemine contra-dicente.* There is an oak in the New Forest, whereof the same is reported. And it is generally reported and here received that there grew a walnut-tree in one of the courts of this cloister or within the walls thereof, which blossomed or budded at the same time as did the thorn aforenamed.

Jul. 28.—Hence I went to WELLS, a city dainty, neat, pleasant, uniform, dry-seated town as most in England. Here is a fair spacious market-place, which is square almost, and in the middle of it a fair, stately market-house. On the one side of the street from this place to the palace is a neat, complete, uniform pile of building consisting of many houses. Herein stands the minster, which is a fine, little, neat and cleanly kept minster, little inferior and unlike to Durham or Canterburye. In the outside of that end wherein stands the great door, there is curiously carved in stone work the history of the creation. Our Lady's chapel in this minster is lately decked and adorned, and there is morning prayer said herein at six hour; this work done since Easter last. Therein are the monuments of these bishops: Beckington,[1] Lord Chancellor of England;

---

[1] Thomas de Beckington, bishop from 1443 to 1464. His tomb was built by himself on the south side of the presbytery. Beckington was never Lord Chancellor, that title

Wresley; Boubeth;[1] Harwell,[2] and March;[3] and there are six or seven more, whose names are not remembered. It is thought at the dissolution of Glassenburye abbey, some of the ancient monuments in that fair church were brought hither. Here is a pretty, neat chapter-house, with a pillar in the middle supporting the same. It is much less than Yorke or Salisburye, otherwise much resembling them, wherein there is represented (as is also in them) the history of the Bible, in painted glass window, which compasseth round about this structure. There are herein about fifty-two counterfeit marble pillars, proportioned to the number of the ecclesiastical persons belonging hereunto, which are fifty-two, which all, when they are summoned to a meeting in this chapter-house, sit every one betwixt two pillars, and do so furnish the whole house about. Hereunto belongs a dean and seven canons, called residents, and about forty-four prebends; the deanery hereof said to be about £700 or £800 per annum, the canons about £200 or £300 per annum. From this town to Glassenburye is seven miles; and indeed this is a sweet, neat town. Here we dined, and were well used. Hence we went to Bristoll, which is fifteen mile, and by the way we passed some poor lead works upon the moors, which belong either to the bishop of Bath and Wells, or to him of Bristoll; and for eight miles before you come to Bristoll, especially six or seven miles from Bristoll, there is most steep, hilly way and vile stony as any in England as I have met with in all my travels.

Towards evening we came to the rich city of BRISTOLL, where we found the town exceedingly thronged with Londoners, Irish, and others, who resorted to Bristoll fair, now at St. James' tide, so as we were constrained to make use of Mr. Warner's interest to provide us a lodging at an honest citizen's house, where we were

---

therefore refers to the next named, which was probably intended for Wolsey; but there is no monument to him, nor was he buried there. Amongst the bishops of Wells there is none with a name resembling Wresley.

[1] Nicholas Bubwith was bishop from 1408 to 1424.
[2] John Harewell, bishop from 1366 to 1386.
[3] William de Marchia, bishop from 1293 to 1302.

accommodated with a fair chamber, good linen, and victuals; herein we took four miles[1] for five persons, and we paid for lodging and all about 15s. I gave the maids 2s. The sign of this house was the   , and the master's name   . We paid here 1s. day and night for our horses for hay, whereof there is exceeding great want in Sommersettshire, so as where there was last year twenty load of hay, there is not now four load of hay. Mr. Warner, who bought our rape-seed, lives at the sign of   . He hath a rape-mill little differing from that I saw at Swammerdam in Holland, whereunto I must refer you, fol. 27.[2] Only herein they differ, that Mr. Warner makes use of two horses, one to turn the rape-mill, the other to turn the wheel which sets the press on work; the rape-seed cakes I observed laid up, which are sold into Holland at 2d. per dozen; a ship comes hither purposely every year to fetch them away. They employ this rape-oil to make of the old soap, whereof they make good store, and doubtless they make great advantage of it; this here is openly vended.

This city for wealth and riches may well deserve in my judgment to be reputed inferior to few except London. Yet Newcastle-upon-Tine was taxed towards the building of the late ships about £3,500, and this city about £2,400, Yorke not above £1,800; and as I take it, Wakefield, Hallifax, Leeds, and Bradford, were admitted to be joined with them in this taxation, and did ease them of £400 or £500.[3]

There are said to be about nineteen churches in this city: a cathedral or minster, which is one of the least and poorest I have seen in England; some call it Great St. Augustine's, others the Holy Trinity, but it is more probable to be called by the former name, seeing there is placed upon the same hill, and near the same, a little church called Little St. Augustine's. This minster is but a part of that structure and building which was formerly here erected; the only remarkable thing whereof I took notice herein was the proportion of a boy turning an hour glass with his heels

---

[1] Probably beds.   [2] Page 43.   [3] See p. 86.

A A

when the clock struck. In the higher end of the quire of the
minster the commandments are written in gold, and on the right
hand is Moses pictured bare-headed; on left hand Aaron in a cardinal's cap; herein is a monument for Sir John Young, and for
one of the Strangewaies, a knight; very fair organs in this minster
as I remember.

There are many fair, neat, curious churches in this city, indeed
I have not found so neat parish churches in England as generally
these are in Bristoll; the fairest and most renowned is Rettley's,[1]
or   church, so called after the founder's name, who was a
citizen of this town. Helyn reporteth this to be the fairest and
handsomest parish church in England. That which doth most
blemish and eclipse the glory of this rich town is the narrowness
of the streets. In divers parts of this city there are erected great
posts, about a yard high, headed with plates of brass; these placed
in the most eminent and most frequented parts of the city, as their
Exchange and such like, where their merchants meet, and these
are only used to count money upon, which argues this to be a
wealthy city; the like hereof I have not found. Here my cousin
Downes wanting an horse, I borrowed for him 5l. of Mr. Locke,
a rich merchant, which was to be paid to Mr. Edwards of Chester
after ten days. Here I bought of Mr. Warner a firkin of old soap,
which cost 16s. I bought also three dozen of stone bottles; two
containing quarts, the other pottles; the lesser cost 4s. dozen, the
greater 7s. 6d. per dozen: a dozen of these bottles of the lesser
were filled with wine; seven without thread are claret, three with
thread about the neck are Malligoe; two with white, with thread
about the handles; sack 1s. quart; claret 6d. These with the
soap, and one cloak bag wherein also was my portmanteau, green
stuff suit of clothes, and some other things, were delivered to Rich.
Reeves, a trowman of Shrewsburye, who was to receive 2s. 6d. for
carriage thereof thence to Shrewsburye: it was a great horseload;
and for carrying thereof thence to Chester I paid about 6s., and
herein I was beholding to Mr. Bennett of Chester, the draper, by

[1] St. Mary Redcliffe was originally founded by Symonne de Byrtone; and having
suffered extremely by lightning in 1446, was entirely repaired by William Canynge.

whose means it was procured carried. In Bristoll nineteen churches, and these for most part neatest and handsomest in England, except Gregorie's near Paules. In Bath five churches; in Gloucester twelve.

Jul. 30.—We went hence to BATH, and there lodged. Herein the small-pox had exceedingly raged. We were directed, and came, a fair, pleasant, easy way on top of the hill; we left the road upon the right hand about mid-way, and turned up the hill, and found upon the plain, about a mile or two from Bathe, a place where is a fair kept as in Ireland, and no house near save one. In this city are five churches, and one of them is as lightsome a pleasant church as any I have seen. In the side of the chancel is a little library lately erected; only one or two observable monuments, for Bishop Mountague,[1] whose arms also is curiously cut over the great door, which were also made at his charge, and are the most stately I find in this kingdom.

Jul. 31.—We went to Gloucester, which is about thirty mile, and lighting by the way, my mare chanced to eat some green corn, which did occasion her to shoot her belly, and scour intolerably, so as she lost her belly, her flesh, and became very weak and impotent. I found that rest did best conduce to settle her body.

Arriving at GLOUCESTER in the evening, which is a great, vast, old city, wherein are xi churches, and a great vast minster.[2] This town is commodiously seated in respect of the fair, navigable river Severne; rich meadowing adjoins thereunto, wherein the inhabitants suffered much last year in eating up the first spring of grass—this bad husbandry. Good store of fruit grows here about, apples, pears, cherries, plums, &c., even the hedge-rows in the fields and lanes. The minster here is a great vast structure, the pillars as strong as any I have seen, save in Paule's, but nothing neat nor lightsome. Herein are divers very observable monuments, and witnesses of the impostures and jugglings practised by the Romanists in times of superstition, thereby to delude those brute

[1] The first master of Sidney Coll. Camb. Consecrated bishop of Bath and Wells, April, 1608.

[2] The number of churches and religious establishments in this city gave occasion to the saying, " As sure as God's in Gloucester."

people, whose understandings and judgments were captivated with
the belief of those most gross, palpable, and absurd sleights and
practises which they used in the whispering place, and in the con-
veyance of the Holy Ghost, which appeared to descend from the
top of the church. These being the most notorious and apparently
delusive that I have found in this kingdom, I will a little enlarge
myself in the description thereof, being the more thereunto enabled
by two or three surveys I have taken thereof. This whispering
place (still, and most properly, so called) is seated over one corner
of the quire; and it is a vault or gallery about one yd. or one yd.
and dim. wide, and four or five yds. high; it is shaped after the
proportion of the half-moon, bending, turning or winding all one
way. It was contrived with as much art and exquisite skill as
there was delusion and abuse in the use of it; there being indeed
none so fit means, and so proper engines and instruments to delude
and cheat the vulgar as by the use of those arts and subtleties
which transcend their capacity and apprehensions; which arts
sometimes failing, these impostors being well versed in the magic
art, many of them made a supply of that by the help of the devil's
skill and endeavour, which their own art and learning could not
reach, and nothing is more ordinary in their practise than this in
all those false miracles which they work daily. This most properly
called the whispering place, because if you stand at the one end,
and place your mouth and voice close to the wall, though you
whisper and speak never so low that those who stand near unto
you do not hear one word which they understand, yet what words
you speak and pronounce are intelligibly conveyed to the other end
of the vault or gallery to those that place their ear to the side of
the wall, as you place your mouth; and I cannot compute the
length of this concavity to be less than about thirty or forty yards:
the use that was made hereof was for confession. Hitherunto the
people were ordinary brought to make confession; the penitentials
being placed at one end, and the priest at the other. In the middle
hereof there is a little chapel or oratory, wherein there was placed
some arch-priest, or superior grave father, who also might hear
distinctly every word spoken by the penitent, and who took special

notice thereof.   After the penitent hath made confession of his
sins to his confessor, he is by him pressed and persuaded to a more
free and full confession, urging and insisting that it may not be
safe for him to omit the acknowledgment of any more than he
desired should never be pardoned; adding further, that by how
much his sins were of more heinous nature, by so much he was
more necessarily obliged to a free and hearty confession and
humiliation for them.   By this means having extracted out of the
poor penitent the acknowledgment of some grievous sins, he
replied, to the torture of the poor penitent's conscience, "these great
sins are of so high a nature as that I cannot give absolution; I
must refer you to a superior," who is to be the same man that was
placed in the little chapel, and was privy to his whole confession:
hereby the silly penitentiary is so discouraged, as that when he is
brought before this more grave and reverend archpriest, he forbears
the confession of those sins, which hindered his former absolution;
whereunto being also further pressed by this severe and austere
confessor, (who, as he assumed unto himself the power and faculty
of pardoning sins, which belongs only to God, so also doth he
endeavour to appear endowed with Divine qualities, even to be able,
out of his own understandings, to discover and convince the sheepish
penitent of those sins which he did omit to confess unto him, and
had acknowledged to the former): then doth this tyrant (for so he
is to the conscience of this poor, seduced, pensive soul) in a most
majestical manner, as though he had also an All-seeing eye, and
could truly affirm, as sometimes Elisha said to his dissembling
servant Gehazi: "Went not my heart along with thee, when the
man turned again from his chariot to meet thee" (2 Kings v. 26),
so this impostor accuses of such other sins concealed as he did not
acknowledge, aggravating the same by the circumstances of time
and place, as though he had been an eye-witness, whereas indeed
he was only an invisible ear-witness of what was by himself confessed and acknowledged.   So exquisitely do they imitate their
superiors.   The pope assumes a Divine prerogative and Divine
honours unto himself; saints, angels, and images, are made par-

takers hereof by the worship which is given them, and those daily addresses which are made unto them; and to the end that these inferiors may be reverenced and esteemed to be more than human creatures by the seduced blind plebeians, they also endeavour to infuse into the people an opinion and belief that they are endowed with a more than natural knowledge in being privy unto those secret and private passages, whereof no mortal eye is witness.[1]

Another observable deceitful practise was the descension of the Holy Ghost, which was in this manner acted, most artificially acted. Over the higher end of the quire, in the false roof, there is still remaining a round hole, proportioned to a pigeon's nest in a dovecot, through which with wires it was so contrived as that the Holy Ghost, in the shape of a dove, seemed to descend with her wings spread directly straight down, even over the high altar, upon whose falling or lighting upon or near unto the altar, flames of fire ascended in token and sign of a gracious acceptance of the sacrifice of the mass then celebrated and solemnized. This fire also was natural and ordinary fire, as doth now most clearly appear, there being framed beyond the high altar a close concave place, about four or five yards long and a yard broad, wherein some of these cheating impostors, or others, privately lurking, being furnished with pitch, resin, and other combustible matter, which being kindled flamed on high, to the great admiration of the beholders, who were not suffered to approach, but kept off at a sufficient distance from being able to discern and discover the sleight and fallacy hereof, which is now most notorious and pal-

[1] This whispering place is a gallery which communicates from one side of the choir to the other, passing between the great east window of the choir and west window of the Lady chapel. This gallery is not closed on all sides, but has on the eastern side three perforations, one of which is a door leading to a small chapel over the entrance to the Lady chapel, which is doubtless the chamber which contained the listening "superior grave father" mentioned in the legend of our puritanical traveller. These marvellous legends are now worn out, and even the verger no longer entertains visitors with these lying wonders. The peculiarity of the gallery is doubtless an unpremeditated result of construction, and Rome has abominations enough to answer for without heaping upon her calumnies which have no substantial foundation.

pable, inasmuch as now, out of the aisle on the back and at the higher end of the quire, you may go into this hollow concave place, and there you may behold (as I did) the walls smoked even as a chimney; although, until this discovery was made, there was not known, acknowledged, or to be discerned, any such place or concavity, it being indeed not possible to be discerned, being a double wall at the higher end of the quire, reaching, as I remember, from one pillar to the other, there being an aisle (as is at Durham, Notre Dame in Paris, and divers churches in Holland) at the higher end, and on both sides this chancel. Herein are some ancient monuments extant: Osricus, King of the West Saxons; Robert Duke of Normandye, eldest son to William the Conquerer; Edward the Second; the last Abbot;[1] Bishop Goalesborrow;[2] two of Bishop Smithe's daughters.[3] Our Ladie's chapel is here neatly decked and adorned, and there is prayer said therein at six hour in the morning. On either side this chapel, about the middle of it, are two little chapels or oratories, one opposite to the other; in these they kneel, in the one with their faces towards Christ on the cross, which is there represented in the glass window; in the other with their faces towards our Lady holding Christ in her arms. Here are also to be found the tombs of Buttler, Earl of Ormond,[4] Humphrey Bohun, Earl of Hereford,[5] Bishop Eldred,[6] who was hence removed and made Archbishop of York.

August 1.—Being Saturday, we left Gloucester, and passing the fine river Severne, over which there is a fair bridge, the river but narrow, but securely navigable because the channel is so deep. Hence we directed our course into Herefordshire, towards HERE-

---

[1] The abbey was dissolved, and surrendered under the conventual seal in 1540, William Parker being the last abbot.

[2] Bp. Goldsborough occupied the see from 1598 to 1604.

[3] Miles Smith was bishop from 1612 to 1624.

[4] We cannot find any trace of a tomb of any Earl of Ormond.

[5] There is a monument ascribed to this person and his lady, but on doubtful authority.

[6] Abp. Aldred, who died 1069, was not buried at Gloucester, and as the tomb, supposed to have been his, is situated where Leland describes that of Abbot Serlo to have been, it is now generally assigned to him, who died 1104. The monument itself is of a later date than either of these personages.

FORD, which (as I take it) is hence distant about twenty miles. The country twixt these two old great cities is not champaign nor very pleasant, but enclosed, and the way something stony and uneven. This old city of Hereford is placed upon a pleasant river, seated low: this like unto Leicester, but the houses (though ancient as Leicester) better built and higher. Here we found good entertainment (and Mr. Arnold, being there with his wife, bestowed our dinner upon us), and as dainty, fine, pure, white bread as well relished as ever I did taste. Dr. Wren is bishop hereof, by whose command none are suffered to come to the Communion table, which is railed out, but when they receive or read the Gospel. Here is a fine monument for Bishop Bennett,[1] and by him lies Bishop Bruse and Bishop Stransberrie; here is a fine ancient monument of Charles Booth, a younger brother of Dunham house, who was bishop of this see eighteen years, and died 1635; this monument is in the north wall near the north porch, upon which there is inscribed: " Carolus Bothæus Episcopus Herefordensis, quum per 18 annos 5 menses et totidem dies, Ecclesiæ huic cum laude præfuisset, 5 die Maij, 1635, defunctus, sub hoc tumulo jacet sepultus." His arms are here quartered:[2] a boar's head with a rose in the middle. Here is a monument of Tho. Cantelupus Gallus,[3] and of Mr. Denton,[4] and a Bishop either of Westphalia,[5] Curla, or so called. Here we viewed the Bishop's house, a long

[1] Robert Bennett, Bp. from 1602 to 1617. Giles de Braos, or Bruse, from 1200 to 1215. John Stanbury, from 1453 to 1474. Charles Booth, from 1516 to 1536.

[2] The arms of Booth are three boars' heads, and so they appear on the tomb.

[3] Thos. de Cantelupe was bishop from 1275 to 1302. He died at Rome, whence his body was brought by his secretary and successor Rich. Swinfield, and buried at Hereford, where it is recorded to have performed many miracles. Pilgrimages were made to his tomb, and his name is registered amongst the popish saints.

[4] " Here lieth Alexander Denton of Hillesdon in the county of Buckingham, and Anne his wife," &c. &c. But Mr. Denton married a second wife, and was buried at Hillesdon, 1576.

[5] The supposed Bishop of Westphalia was doubtless Herbert Westfaling, who was bishop from 1585 to 1602, whose gravity was never seduced into a smile, and whose benevolence induced him to expend all his professional income in works of charity. The word *curla* evades explanation.

narrow hall, and but an ordinary house. Here is a pretty little Chapter-house, not so large as that of Wells. Hence we departed about four or five hour towards Ludlow, which is about fifteen or sixteen miles hence distant, and the way good untill you come almost to Ludlow. Here by the way we observed very good and rich land for wheat. We passed through Cottsall town,[1] which stands near about middle way twixt Hereford and Ludlow. This country of Herefordshire, famous (according to an ancient proverb) for three things, beginning all with a W, sci. Wheat, Water, and Wool, for which it is not inferior to any shire in England, for Cottsall wool is the finest in this kingdom; and as dainty springs, and brook, and rivers; and as pure white wheat (it is said) as are to be found in this kingdom. This Saturday late we came into LUDLOW, and rested there the day following. Here is the seat of the Council of the Marches of Wales, consisting of a President, (who is the Earl Bridgewater[2]), a Chief Justice, (which is Sir John Bridgman,[3]) and three other assistants, which are Sir Nicholas Overburye,[4] Sir Marmaduke Lloyde,[5] and Mr. Littleton;[6] always two of these are designed to this circuit of Chester, Flint, Denbigh. The Chief Justice here (Presidente absente) represents the President's person, and keeps the King's house, which is kept in the castle, which is a pretty little neat castle, standing high, kept in

[1] There is some mistake; the town he passed through was probably Leominster, which is about thirteen miles from Hereford, and eleven from Ludlow, and famous for its wool market. The Cotswold hills, which he means by Cottsall, are situated in the eastern part of Gloucestershire.

[2] John, first Earl of Bridgewater, second son and heir of the celebrated Lord Chancellor Egerton, appointed Lord President of Wales and the Marches 1633. His children being benighted in Heywood Forest, on their way to Ludlow to witness his entrance into his official residence, gave occasion to the masque of Comus.

[3] Sir John Bridgeman, serjeant at law, Chief-Justice of Chester from 1626 to 1638.

[4] Sir Nicholas Overbury, of Barton on the Hill, Gloucestershire, said, but probably erroneously, to have been made a justice of the Common Pleas, temp. Jas. I.

[5] Sir Edward Lyttelton, of Munstow, Salop., Chief-Justice of Common Pleas, 1639; Lord Keeper of the Great Seal, 1640; created Lord Lyttleton in 1641; died Aug. 1645, leaving no successor.

[6] Sir Marmaduke Lloyd, second Justice of Chester, 1622 to 1636, afterwards Chief-Justice of South Wales.

B B

good repair, within which also (as I take it) are the courts of
justice, to which belongs the principality of Wales. To this court
also belongs a secretary (which is the Lord Goreing,[1] which office
is said to be of the value of £3000); this office is executed by one
Mr. ——, his deputy there, an able man, and very fortunate. Her
is also an attorney, Mr. ——, an able gentleman, a great traveller.

August 2.—Here I was by the Judges invited to dinner, and
very kindly and respectively entertained. There is only one
church in this town, a large capacious church, wherein was only
one sermon; this town is seated on the side of an hill, and is built
from the bottom to the top, whereon the castle stands. The seat
hereof is more healthful and pleasant, than the land rich and
fruitful. Here we observed a smith's wife in a loose bodied gown,
gentlewoman-like, walking in the streets, whom the boys followed,
hooting, shouting, and jeering after her, who was in a mighty
perplexity and distraction, one pulling her by the arm, another by
the gown, another by her loose sleeve, whose pride and arrogance
was most justly rewarded with shame, reproach, and scorn.

August 3.—We departed hence early towards the famous town
of SHREWSBURYE, which is twenty long miles hence distant; much
barren, moorish land, and great high hills in the way betwixt
which you ride. About four, or five, or six miles hence you may
discern this town, which affords a very graceful and promising
prospect. The liberties of this town extend four or five miles.
This is a very fair, large, spacious town, famous for that trade of
stuff which is here maintained, and it is one of the richest towns
in these parts of England, Newcastle-upon-Tine excepted. It is
a very great town, governed by two bailiffs. Here is a very
stately market-house, a very great, vast brewhouse of Mr. Rowleyes,
the brewing vessels wherein are capable of 100 measures; a well-
ordered Free-school, and neatly contrived is the school-house,
which is divided into three rooms, in every whereof is there a
master; the first teacheth to read, who hath ten pound yearly;

---

[1] Sir Geo. Goring, created Lord Goring in 1630, and advanced to the title of Earl of
Norwich 1644, for his faithful and eminent services to King Charles I.

the second teacheth the grounds of the Latin tongue, and hath twenty pound per annum; the third, who is the most learned, teacheth the highest scholars, who are there qualified for, and thence sent unto, the University, who hath either a double stipend to the second, which is £40 per annum, or equal to both the other. This is a Free-school, and as well-ordered as any I have found in England, where, as with all care and industry it is endeavoured to train them up in learning, so it is a principal work of their care and endeavour to train them in the fear and knowledge of God. This town is seated upon the River Severne, which is hitherunto navigable, though with much strain, force, and pains, the vessels being hauled up by strength of men against the stream many miles. This town, as it is very rich, so it is very populous, and well governed and ordered: herein are six churches—parish churches. We took only a view of that church, of the parish whereof Mr. Stubbs is parson, who published (as I have heard) a false and unjust relation of the murder committed by a young man, Enoch ap Evans,[1] upon his mother. This church is of late gaudily painted, wherein you may find many idle, ridiculous, vain, and absurd pictures, representations, and stories, the like whereunto I never saw in England. Here we were well entertained at the Red Lion, where the hostess was Mr. Wallie's maid. Hence we went in the afternoon towards Whitt-Church, which is about fourteen or sixteen miles hence distant, and lodged this night at Sir Tho. Brereton's; whence I went next day to Chester, and so concluded this Summer's Progress.

[1] Enoch ap Evan, son of Edward ap Evan, of Shadwall, in the parish of Clunne, Shropshire, murdered his mother and brother, and cut off their heads; for which he was executed and gibbeted. His body was afterwards taken away privately and buried, at the instigation of his sisters. Mr. Peter Studley (not Stubbs) in a work called "The Looking-Glass of Schism," ascribed this horrid act to the influence of Puritanism and Nonconformity; in reply to this, Richard More, a magistrate of the county, wrote, but did not publish, "A True Relation of the Murders," &c. shewing that the unhappy man was insane. A second edition of "The Looking-Glass," with an "Answer to More," 1635, followed, which produced a publication of the "True Relation," with an Appendix, but not before the year 1641.

Coins current in Scotland.

In Copper.

Turners,   6

Placks,   3   To one penny English,

Baubyes,   2   or 12 Scottish.

Achesons, 1 and a plack

In Silver.

19s. or a Cardicue,	In English, 19d.	French money.
29s. Half a rijcks,	——— 29d.	
23s. Half a dog daeler,	——— 23d.	
36s. A Swedes daeler,	——— 3s.	Swedish money.
46s. A dog daeler,	——— 4s. wanting 2d.	Dane.
58s. A rijcks daeler,	——— 4s. 10d.	German.

Of these German there be sixty kinds current.

Only note their most common computation of moneys to be by marks rather than pounds, wherein their difference from the English is (as appears) that they call all their money twelve times as much as they do in England: viz. 1d. 12d , 1s. 12s., 1 mark is 12 marks, £1 is £12, and so in the rest.

SPEECH IN SCOTLAND.

We call here a clock, a knock; a watch, a munter; a dial, an orelege; a band, an ourlayer; for sleight, hough; a shop, a buith, or booth. In many words, as chest, shall, &c., here is not *h* pronounced; a cap, a mutch, if it be linen; a bonnet, if it be woollen or leather; a man's coat, a juipe, or joope. And generally they pronounce ow, oo, as towne, toone; and that which we spell in England with ou, but pronounce as if it were oo, as in the word enough, they call it enuigh, changing it into ui. Our a, that we in England pronounce as they do $\eta^{\tau a}$, i. e. as it were ae, they in Scotland pronounce as it were ao, and in some words ai; so that concerning their accent no few general prescripts will give any satisfaction, but only experience and use acquired by cohabitation among themselves. They have many words in the country that citizens understand not, but if all the properties of language were concurrent there, as well as significancy in pathetic speeches and innumerable proverbs and by-words, they might compare with any people in the world.

A JOURNAL SINCE MY COMING OUT OF CHESHIRE.

Junii 11. From Handford to Wakefield, 30 miles.—Lodged at the Bull, good usage.

12. Thence to Yorke, 22 miles.—At Mris. Keye's, excellent usage.

13. Thence to Allerstone, 22 miles.—With my sister Eggerton.

17. To Ellenthorpe, 26 miles.—With my uncle Aldeburgh.

19. To Newton, Mr. Hen. Blakestone, 26 miles.—Mr. Blakestone's in Bishopricke.

20. To Auckland, 7 miles.—My noble Lord of Durham's.

22. To Durham, 7; to Chester, 9; and to Newcastle, 3—19 miles.—At the Postmaster, Mr. Swan's, at the sign of the Swan, 8*d*. ordinary, mean entertainment.

24. To Morpeth, 12; to Anwicke, 16—26 miles.—At Postmaster's, good victuals and lodging, 6*d*. ord. supp., and 4*d*. breakfast.

25. To Bellford, 12; to Fennam, 5; to Holly Island over the sands, 2; to Barwick, 7—26 miles.—An excellent house at Crown, good lodging, 8*d*. ordinary, good victuals, and 6*d*. our men; this an honest inn.

26. To Aten, 4; Apthomas, 8; Dunglas, 2; Dunbarr, 6; Mussleborough, 16; Edenb., 4—40 miles.—Mr. Wallis his house in High Street over against the higher cross. We paid 18*d*. a night for lodging, and victuals out of a cook's shop kept in the same house.

29. To Lightgow, 12; to Failkirk, 6—18 miles.—At Mr. Flemming's house, good lodging, victuals 7 persons 6*s*. sterling, and hay 6*d*.

30. To Glasgoaw, 18 miles.—At Mr. David Weymes.

Julii 1. To Erwing, 18 miles.—Here we baited at Mr. James
          Blare's.

2. To Aire, 8 miles.—Lodged in Patrick Mackellen, good
   ordinary 8*d*., good lodging.

3. To Minibole, 6 miles, though we came by the Cave of
   Carick, which is 8 miles; thence to the Chapell, 32
   long miles, and stony, uneven way.—Here we lodged
   at one Hughe Boyde's, where we had ord. 6*d*. good
   meat; and 3*d*. a night for hay and grass, and 6*d*. peck
   provender; the best inn in Scottland.

4. To Port Patrick, 4 miles.—Here we dined with one Thom.
   Marchbanke. This day we went aboard about 3 hour,
   and anchored upon the coast of Ireland under the
   island Mague.

5. To Carick Fergus in Ireland.—Here we rested the Sabbath, and lodged in Mrs. Wharton's house, a Chester
   woman, most neat in her house; good victuals, good
   accommodation, 6*d*. ordinary, 3*d*. hay per horse, 6*d*.
   peck.

6. To Bellfast, 8 miles; to Lisley Garven, 7; to Dromemoore, 7—22 miles.—Here we lodged in Mr. Haven's
   house over against the bishop's house; here our ordinary was 8*d*. and more exacted upon.

7. To Newrie, 12 miles, where we baited at a good house, at
   the sign of the Prince's Arms; thence to Dundalke,
   8 mile; all this bad way to find, on stony hard way.
   Here we lodged at a fat widow's house, her name is
   Mris. Veasie, and this reputed and reported one of the
   best houses for entertainment in the north of Ireland.
   She is a Cheshire woman.

8. To Tredaugh, 16 miles, as long as 22 ordinary English
   miles; thence to Swordes, 14 miles—30 miles. Lodged
   at sign of the Boot, a tavern, and were very well used.

9. To Dublin, 6 miles. Lodged at my tenant, Raph Brian's,
   and were well used.

14. To Hacquett's Town, which is accounted to be 27 miles, but it is a moorish part of the country, and most tedious mile, at least 37 English. Here we were very courteously entertained at the Castle by Mr. Needham and Mr.   , Mr. Wattson's brother-in-law, and farmer.

15. To Carnue, where Mr. Chambers lives, about 8 miles. Here we were royally entertained by this good old housekeeper.

16. To Cle-haman, 4 miles; to Sir Morgan Kavenah's at Clenmullen, 3 miles; to Ennerscoffie, 8—15 miles. Here we lodged at a Scotchman's house, whose name was Plummer; a good inn, but 1s. ordinary—too dear.

17. To Waxford, 8 miles. Here we lodged at the sign of the Windmill, a Welshwoman hostess.

20. To Sir Adam Cockliffe's house, being an Abbey, 18 miles. Here we were kindly and neatly entertained.

21. To Ballihack, 5 miles; to the passage on the other side water, 2 miles; to Waterford, 5; to Caricke, 12—24 miles. Here we lodged at sign of Three Cups at Mr. Croumer's; good honest house, but not well furnished with victuals.

22. Returned to Waterford, 12 miles. Lodged at Mr. Warde's at King's Head; well used.

24. Went to the Passage, 5 miles; lodged at Bell, 6 ordinary, good house.

25. Went aboard the Whelpe.

A FURTHER INSTANCE OF GOD'S GOODNESS UNTO US IN RESTORING TO HEALTH, ETC.

At my being in London, May, 1636, my body was much indisposed by reason I enjoyed not the benefit of nature, sometimes not once in two days, yet was not my body costive and restringent, but soluble and laxative sufficient; this occasioned unto me a

constant pain in the bottom of my belly; this I conceived much
encreased by the use of apple tarts and apples; but that which
most encreased my distemper was this, that whilst my body was
thus indisposed, I went with Mr. White to Conningham in Essex,
which is about thirty miles, and returned back upon the 17 of
May, which was near sixty mile. Though we did ride very fairly
and orderly, yet was my body, thus indisposed as aforesaid, much
more distempered, my spirits and body both over-toiled, and my
blood much heated. Returning the same night about 10 hour, I
was only sensible of an extreme weariness and drowsiness; and
though I was hot when I went to bed, yet was I not sensible
thereof; but by reason of my late coming into the city, I took a
good quantity of mithridate and wood-sorrel. I slept well this
night; my body was feverously disposed the next day, Wednesday. I kept my chamber almost all day, save I went by water
to my brother Urian to Westminster, and to the Temple. This
day I took very much mithridate and wood-sorell, and that often,
abstaining from meat and drink until supper, save only I took a
little bread and butter and beer in the morning, and at supper I
did only eat a leg and wing of a chicken, and drunk not six
spoonfuls of beer; yet after this during 1 or 2 hour I was exceeding
feverously indisposed, sometimes suddenly cold and as suddenly
very hot, and much was I inclined to sweat; and when I went to
bed after 9 hour, I was most extreme violent hot, and burnt
mightily, insomuch as I feared a violent burning fever; but the
Lord, that all-healing Physician, who, as he had directed me to
the use of the means, so also gave a blessing and made it effectual,
so disposed my body to sweat, that I was no sooner warm in bed,
but I fell into a most natural, kindly, and gentle sweat, which kept
me waking until almost 1 hour, during which time, although I was
extreme hot outwardly, yet was I not any thing inwardly sick or
distempered, save only a little heated and dry, nor was my head
pained. From the 1 hour to the 5 I slept, and then waked, my
body very cool and dry and temperate, but not having sweated
sufficiently, nor my body so ordered with linen clothes to dry them

withal, as was fit; I placed myself upon my back, and so lay (that posture being most apt to sweat) a short space, and instantly began to sweat, and continued sweating until almost 10 hour, my body being duly and orderly rubbed with linen clothes warmed. Observe herein the goodness of His Providence, that nothing was taken purposely to provoke sweat, nor no constraint used, no addition of clothes more than ordinary; yet when this was concluded, my body was hereby restored unto the former temperature and health; whereunto this much conduced, that I had sparingly eaten four days together not above one meal a day, and drunk less; this I take to be a special cause that I was nothing inwardly disaffected and disturbed, save with some little wind in the bottom of the belly; to ease me whereof, and to help me ad evacuendum, Mr. Mathewes, the apothecary, 18 Maii, administered one glister, and his man, 19 May, administered a second; the first wrought once, the second twice; but these did not restore my body to its natural course, for I was constrained on Friday night circa mediam noctem, being 20 Maii, to take one of Dr. Buttler's pills, which gave me three stools, poor ones, not kindly nor natural; I found beer much to distemper me in my sickness, therefore I forbore it, and drunk barley water.

FINIS.

INDEX.

Bishops Auckland, 78, 79, 82, 189 ; Portraits at, 80.
Bishopsthorpe, 71, 72.
Blackadder, John, 97.
Blackiston, Sir W. 78, 82.
——— Mr. 78, 189.
Black Rock in Magu Island, 125.
Black Wall, or Swarte Wall, 5.
Blair, Sir James Hunter, 124.
Blare, Mr. James, 119, 120, 190.
Blosse, Sir Fr. Lynch, iv.
Boats at Haerlem, 52.
Bohemia, Queen of, 28, 33, 34 ; family, 28, 39, 58 ; Prince, drowned, 54.
Bohun, Earl of Hereford, Mon. 183.
Bois-le-duc, 95.
Bolton, Sir Rich., Lord Chief Baron, 136.
Bongrace, kind of head-dress, 103.
Bonaventure, ship, 137.
Booth, Sir George, v. 59, 87.
——— of the Dunham family. Bp. Hereford, tomb, 184.
Bowden Downs, 36.
Bowing at the altar, 81.
Box trees in form of soldiers, 38.
Boyne, river, 134.
Brabezon, Lady, 146.
Bradford, J., martyr, 80.
——— town, 177.
Bramhall, Archbishop, 138.
Bread turned to stone, 48.
Brereton, Mr. Robert, 171.
——— Sir Thomas, 187.
——— Urjan, v 192.
——— Sir William, v. 78, 79, 87, 100, 129, 133, 151 ; state of his health, 126, 129, 130, 131, 157, 160, 161, 163, 164, 191 ; his letters, vi.
Brewery at Shrewsbury, 186.
Brian, Ralph, 190.
Brick-making at Dort, 15.
Bridges, London, Berwick, Newcastle, Rochester, 85 ; in Scotland, 116.
Bridgeman, Sir John, 185.
Bridgewater, 167, 171, 174.
——— Earl of, 185.
Brill, 4, 5, 15.
Bristol, 85, 155, 158, 167, 168, 171, 176 ; churches, 177, 179 : fair, 158, 160, 165, 176 ; wind always fair for, 158.
Bromley, Hugh, 79.
Brooke, Captain, Glastonbury, 174.
Bruse, or Braos, Bp. of Hereford, Mon.184.
Bubwith, Nich., Bishop of Wells, 176.
Bucer, 80.

Buckworth, Theophilus, Bishop of Dromore, 129.
Buildings at Amsterdam, 66.
Bulches, bunches or humps, 35.
Bullinger, 80.
Bunbury, Sir Henry, 140.
Burghers, 10, 12.
Burgomasters, 8, 12, 13, 18, 21, 31, 46, 49.
Burrough bridge, 91.
Burry, river, 167.
Busses, Herring, 12.
Butler, Dr. William, 131, 193.

Caerleon, 168.
Caermarthen, 167.
Caghe, Caghe Meare, 48.
Calderwood, Mr., 101.
Caldy, island, 167.
Calvin, 80.
Camel, 36.
Campsie, Lord, 123.
Camugton, i. e Cannington, Somersetshire, 171.
Canal, Haerlem, 53.
Canne, Mr., Brownist minister at Amsterdam, 64.
Canon Row House, 74.
Cantelupe, Bishop of Hereford, tomb,184.
Canterbury Cathedral, 175.
Cantire, Mull of, 126.
Cardiff, 168.
Carick in Scotland, 113, 121, 190 ; rocks, 113 ; haunted caves, ib.
——— in Ireland, 152, 159, 160, 161, 191; castle,161 ; house of Lord Ormond, 160.
Carincham, Mainwarings of, 151.
Carlingwark, called Castle-Douglas, 123.
Carlisle, 89, 120, 123.
Carlow, 145, 147.
Carnew, 146, 147, 191.
Caroll, Sir James, 149, 150.
Carrickfergus, 126, 128, 129, 190.
Cassilis, Earl of, 118.
Catterick Bridge, 77, 78.
Cattle, wild, at Bishop's Auckland, 80.
——— price of, near Dublin, 137.
Cavanagh, Mr. Darby, 149, 150.
——— Sir Morgan, or Morgan Mac Bryan, 145, 147, 148, 191.
——— Lady, 148.
Caves at Carick and Cullen, 113, 121.
Chaloner, Dr. Luke, 142.
Chambers, or Chambre, Mr Calcot, of Hacquett's Town, 146, 151, 191.
Chapel, or Stranraer, 123, 190.
Chapell, Bp. of Cork and Ross, 142.

LONDON:
RICHARDS, PRINTER, 100, ST. MARTIN'S LANE.

ERRATA.

Page 4, last line but two, for *subsist,* read " subsisted."
— 33, line 20, for reference 2, read " 3."
— — line 27, after witches, insert reference " 2."
— — line 29, for 7, read " 28."
— 47, six from bottom, for 1814, read " 1612."
— 50, four lines from bottom, for *be,* read " the."
— 57, four lines from bottom, for *Books,* read " Brooks."
— 58, line 33, for *that,* read " wax."
— 91, line 23, for *Eyton,* read " Ryton."
—108, line 7 from bottom, for *steward,* read " Stewart."
—171, line 2 from bottom, for *Marlen,* read " Martin."

Chetham Society

FOR THE PUBLICATION OF

HISTORICAL AND LITERARY REMAINS

CONNECTED WITH THE PALATINE COUNTIES OF

LANCASTER & CHESTER.

Patrons.

The Right Honourable the EARL OF DERBY.
The Right Honourable the EARL OF BALCARRES.
The Right Honourable the EARL OF WILTON.
The Right Honourable the EARL OF BURLINGTON.
The Right Reverend the Lord BISHOP OF CHESTER.
The Right Reverend the Lord BISHOP OF ELY.
The Right Reverend the Lord BISHOP OF NORWICH.
The Right Reverend the Lord BISHOP OF CHICHESTER.
The Right Honourable the BARON DELAMERE.
The Right Honourable the BARON DE TABLEY.
The Right Honourable the BARON SKELMERSDALE.
The Right Honourable LORD STANLEY, M.P.
The Right Honourable SIR ROBERT PEEL, Bart, M.P.
The Right Honourable LORD FRANCIS EGERTON, M.P.
The Honourable RICHARD BOOTLE WILBRAHAM, M.P.
SIR PHILIP DE MALPAS GREY EGERTON, Bart., M.P.
GEORGE CORNWALL LEGH, Esq., M.P.
JOHN WILSON PATTEN, Esq., M.P.

Council.

EDWARD HOLME, Esq., M.D., *President.*

Rev. RICHARD PARKINSON, B.D., Canon of Manchester, *Vice-President.*

The Hon. and Very Rev. WILLIAM HERBERT, Dean of Manchester.
GEORGE ORMEROD, Esq., L.L.D., F.R.S, F.S.A., F.G.S.
SAM. HIBBERT WARE, Esq., M.D, F.R.S.E.
Rev. THOMAS CORSER, M.A.
Rev. GEORGE DUGARD, M.A.

Rev. C. G. HULTON, M.A.
Rev. J. PICCOPE, M.A.
Rev. F. R. RAINES, M.A., Milnrow Parsonage, near Rochdale.
JAMES CROSSLEY, Esq.
JAMES HEYWOOD, Esq., F.R.S.
WILLIAM LANGTON, Esq., *Treasurer.*

WILLIAM FLEMING, Esq., M.D , *Hon. Secretary.*

RULES OF THE CHETHAM SOCIETY.

1. That the Society shall be limited to three hundred and fifty members.

2. That the Society shall consist of members being subscribers of one pound annually, such subscription to be paid in advance, on or before the day of general meeting in each year. The first general meeting to be held on the 23rd day of March, 1843, and the general meeting in each year afterwards on the 1st day of March, unless it should fall on a Sunday, when some other day is to be named by the Council.

3. That the affairs of the Society be conducted by a Council, consisting of a permanent President and Vice-President, and twelve other members, including a Treasurer and Secretary, all of whom, with the exception of the President and Vice-President, shall be elected at the general meeting of the Society.

4. That any member may compound for his future subscriptions, by the payment of ten pounds.

5. That the accounts of the receipts and expenditure of the Society be audited annually, by three auditors, to be elected at the general meeting; and that any member who shall be one year in arrear of his subscription, shall no longer be considered as belonging to the Society.

6. That every member not in arrear of his annual subscription, be entitled to a copy of each of the works published by the Society.

7. That twenty copies of each work shall be allowed to the Editor of the same, in addition to the one to which he may be entitled as a member.

LIST OF MEMBERS.

Ackers, James, M.P., Heath House, Ludlow
Addley, H. M , Nelson-street, Liverpool
Ainsworth, W Harrison, Kensal Manor House, Harrow-road, London
Ainsworth, Ralph, M D., King street, Manchester
Ainsworth, Rev. Thomas, M A , Hartford Hall, Cheshire
Alexander, Edward N., F.S A , Halifax
Allen, Rev. John Taylor, M A., Stradbrooke Vicarage, Suffolk
Ambery, Charles, Market-street, Manchester
Armstrong, Thomas, Higher Broughton, Manchester
Ashton, John, Solicitor, Warrington
Atherton, Miss, Kersal Cell, near Manchester
Atherton, James, Swinton House, near Manchester
Atkinson, William, Weaste, near Manchester
Atkinson, F. R., Solicitor, Manchester

Balcarres, The Earl of, Haigh Hall, near Wigan
Baldwin, Rev. John, M.A , Dalton, near Ulverstone
Bannerman, Alexander, Didsbury
Bannerman, Henry, Burnage
Bannerman, John, Swinton
Bardsley, Samuel Argent, M D., Green Heys, near Manchester
Barker, John, Seedley Terrace, near Manchester
Barker, Thomas, Oldham
Barratt, James, Jun., Town Hall Buildings, Manchester
Barrow, Miss, Green Bank, near Manchester
Barrow, Rev. Andrew, President of Stonyhurst College, near Blackburn
Barrow, Peter, Surgeon, Manchester
Bartlemore, William, Castleton Hall, Rochdale
Barton, R. W., Springwood, near Manchester
Barton, John, Market street, Manchester
Barton, Thomas, Portland-street, Manchester
Barton, Samuel, Mosley-street, Manchester
Bayne, Rev. Thos. Vere, M A., Broughton, Manchester
Beamont, William, Warrington
Beard, Rev. John R , D.D., Stony Knolls, near Manchester
Beardoe, James, Manchester
Beever, James F. Solicitor, Manchester
Bellairs, Rev. Thomas H , M A., Stockport
Bentley, Rev. T R., M.A., Incumbent of St. Matthew's, Manchester
Birley, Hugh Hornby, Broom House, near Manchester

Birley, Hugh, Didsbury
Birley, Thos. H. York-place, Oxford road, chester
Birley, Richard, Upper Brook-street, Manchester
Bohn, H. G., York-st , Covent Garden, London
Booth, Benjamin W , Cooper-street, Manchester
Booth, John, Barton upon-Irwell
Booth, William, Dickenson street, Manchester
Boothman, Thomas, Ardwick-place, near Manch
Botfield, Beriah, M.P., Norton Hall, Nor tonshire
Bower, George, Solicitor, London
Brackenbury, James, Solicitor, Manchester
Bradbury, Charles, Crescent, Salford
Bradshaw, John, Weaste House, near Manches
Bright, Benjamin Heywood, Ham Green, Bristo
Brooke, Edward, Manchester
Brooke, James Brown, Ashton-under-Lyne
Brooks, Samuel, Manchester
Broome, William, Manchester
Brown, Robert, Winckley square, Preston
Buckley, Edmund, M P., Ardwick
Buckley, Rev. Thomas, M A , Old Trafford
Buckley, Nathaniel, F L S , Rochdale
Burlington, The Earl of, Holkar Hall

Calvert, Robert, Richmond Hill, Salford
Cardwell, Rev. Edward, D.D , Principal of St. A Hall and Camden Professor, Oxford
Cardwell, Edward, M.P., Regent's Park, London
Chadwick, Elias, M.A., Swinton Hall, near chester
Chesshyre, Mrs., Leaf-square, near Pendleton
Chester, The Bishop of
Chichester, The Bishop of
Chippindall, John, Chetham Hill, near Manches
Clare, Peter, Manchester
Clarke, George, Crumpsall
Clayton, Japheth, Spring Bank, Pendleton
Clifton, Rev. R. E. M A , Manchester
Consterdine, James, Manchester
Cook, Thomas, Gorse Field, Pendleton, near chester
Cooper, William
Corser, George
Corser, Rev. Thomas, M A., Stand, near Manche
Cottam, S. E. Brazenuose-street, Manchester
Coulthart, John Ross, Ashton-under-Lyne

Crook, Thomas A , Rochdale
Cross, William Assheton, Redscar, near Preston
Crossley, William, Broughton House, Higher Broughton
Crossley, George, Manchester
Crossley, James, Solicitor, Essex st , Manchester
Crossley, John, M A , Scaitcliffe House, Todmorden
Currer, Miss Richardson, Eshton Hall, near Skipton

Daniel, George, Brazennose street, Manchester
Darbishire, Samuel D. Solicitor, Manchester
Darwell, James, Ridgefield, Manchester
Darwell, Thomas, Jun.
Davies, John, M W S., Manchester
Dawes, Matthew, F G S , Westbrooke, near Bolton
Dearden, James, The Orchard, Rochdale
Dearden, Thomas Ferrand, Rochdale
Delamere, The Lord, Vale Royal, near Northwich
Derby, The Earl of, Knowsley
Dilke, C. W.(Athenæum Office),115,Sloane-st. London
Dinham, Thomas, Exchange-street, Manchester
Driver, Richard, Exmouth-terrace, Stretford-road
Dugard, Rev. George, M A , Birch, near Manchester
Dyson, T. J., Tower, London

Earle, Richard, Edenhurst, Heyton
Eccles, William, Wigan
Egerton, Lord Francis, M P., Worsley Hall
Egerton, Sir Philip de Malpas Grey, M P., Oulton Park, Tarporley
Ely, The Bishop of
Eyton, J. W. K. F.S A. L. & E , Elgin Villa, Leamington

Faulkner, George, Manchester
Fielden, Joseph, Witton, near Blackburn
Fenton, James, Jun , Rochdale
Fernley, John, Manchester
Farrington, J. Nowell, Worden, near Chorley
France, Thomas Robert Wilson, Rawcliffe House, Garstang
Fleming, Thomas, Broughton View, Pendleton
Fleming, William, M D , Ditto
Fletcher, John, Haulgh, near Bolton
Fletcher, Samuel, Broomfield, near Manchester
Fletcher, Samuel, Solicitor, Ardwick place, near Manchester
Flintoff, Thomas, Manchester
Ford, Henry, Solicitor, Manchester
Fraser, James W. Manchester

Gardner, Thomas, Worcester College, Oxford
Garner, J. G. 57, Upper Brook-street, Manchester
Garnett, William James, Quernmore Park, Lancaster
Germon, Rev. Nicholas, M A , High Master, Free Grammar School, Manchester
Gibb, William, Manchester
Gladstone, Robertson, Liverpool
Gladstone, Robert, Manchester
Goodlad, William, Manchester

Gordon, Hunter, Barrister, St. James's-square
Gould, John, Manchester
Grant, Daniel, Manchester
Grave, Joseph, Bond-street, Manchester
Gray, Benjamin, B A , Trinity Coll. Cambridge
Gray, James, Brown-street, Manchester
Greaves, John, Irlam Hall, near Manchester
Greenall, G. Walton Hall, near Warrington
Grundy, George, Chetham Fold, near Manchest

Hadfield, George, Solicitor, Manchester
Hailstone, Edward, F.S A., Horton Hall, Bi Yorkshire
Hardman, Henry, Bury, Lancashire
Hardy, William, Scott & Co , Manchester
Hargreaves, George J. Surgeon, York-street, Manchester
Harland, John, Guardian Office, Manchester
Harrison, William, Bootle lane, Liverpool
Harter, James Collier, Broughton Hall, nea chester
Harter, William, Hope Hall, near Manchester
Hately, Isaiah, Manchester
Hatton, James, Richmond House
Hawkins, Edward, F.A S , F.S A., F L S., Museum
Heelis, Stephen, Solicitor, Manchester
Henshaw, William, Marble-street, Manchester
Herbert, Hon. & Very Rev. Wm., Dean of Man
Heron, Rev George, M.A., Carrington, Cheshii
Heywood, Sir Benjamin, Bart., Claremont, ne chester
Heywood, James, F R S., Acresfield, near Mar
Heywood, John Pemberton, near Liverpool
Heywood, Thomas, F.S.A., Hope End, Ledbu fordshire
Heywood,Thomas,Surgeon,Pendleton, near Mar
Heyworth, Lawrence, Oakwood, near Stockport
Hibbert, Mrs., Crescent, Salford
Hickson, Charles, Manchester
Hinde, Rev. Thomas, M.A , Winwick, Warring
Hoare, G. M. The Lodge, Marden, Surrey
Hoare, P R , Kelsey Park, Beckenham, Kent
Holden, Thomas, Summerfield, Bolton
Holden, Thomas, Bookseller, Rochdale
Holme, Edward, M D , King-street, Manchester
Hoole, Holland, Salford
Hughes, William, Blind Asylum, Old Trafford
Hulme, Davenport, M D , Manchester
Hulme, Hamlet, Medlock Vale, Manchester
Hulton, Rev. A. H., M.A., Ashton-under Lyne
Hulton, Rev C. G., M A., Chetham College chester
Hulton, Hugh T.
Hulton, W. A. Preston
Hunter, Rev. Joseph, Torrington square, Londo

Jackson, H. B. 2, York-street, Manchester
Jackson, Joseph, Ardwick

Jacson, Charles R., Barton Lodge, Preston
James, Paul Moon, Summerville, near Manchester
James, Rev. J. G., M A., Habergham Eaves, near Burnley
Jemmett, William Thomas, Belmont House, Pendleton
Johnson, W. R. Burgess terrace, Hyde-road, Manchester
Johnson, Rev. W. W, M A, Manchester
Jones, Jos. Jun., Walshaw House, Oldham
Jones, W., Hanging Ditch, Manchester
Jordan, Joseph, Surgeon, Manchester

Kay, James, Turton Tower, Bolton
Kay, Samuel, Solicitor, Manchester
Kelsall, Strettle, Manchester
Kendrick, James, M.D., F.L S , Warrington
Kennedy, John, Ardwick House, Manchester
Ker, George Portland, Hulme place, Salford
Kershaw, James, Green Keys, Manchester
Kidd, Rev. W. J., M.A., Didsbury

Langton, George, 6, Bedford-row, London
Langton, William, Seedley, Manchester
Larden, G. F.,
Legh, G. Cornwall, M P., High Legh, Cheshire
Leeming, W. B., Marlborough-place, Salford
Leigh, Rev. Edward Trafford, M.A., Cheadle, Cheshire
Leigh, Henry, Moorfield Cottage, Worsley
Leresche, J. H., Advertiser and Chronicle Office, Manchester
Lloyd, William Horton, F.S.A., L.S , Park-square, London
Lloyd, Edward Jeremiah, Oldfield House, Altringham, Cheshire
Lomas, Edward, Leeds Railway Office
Lomax, Robert, Harwood, near Bolton
Love, Benjamin, Market street, near Manchester
Lowndes, William, Egremont, Liverpool
Loyd, Edward, Manchester
Lycett, W. E., Manchester
Lyon, Edmund, M.D., Manchester
Lyon, Thomas, Appleton Hall, Warrington

McClure, William, Peel Cottage, Eccles
McFarlane, John, Union Club, Manchester
McKenzie, John Whitefoord, 19, Scotland street, Edinburgh
McVicar, John, Masley-street, Manchester
Mann, Robert, Surgeon, Manchester
Mare, E. R. Le, Pendleton, Manchester
Markland, J. H , Bath
Markland, Thomas, Mab Field, near Manchester
Marsden, G. E , Solicitor, Princess-street
Marsden, William, 27, Cannon-street, Manchester
Marsh, John Fitchett, Warrington
Marshall, Miss, Ardwick, Manchester
Marshall, William, Penwortham Hall, Preston
Marshall, Frederick Earnshaw, Esq., Ditto

Marshall, John, Preston
Mason, Thomas, Copt House, near Ripon
Master, Rev. Robert M., M.A., Burnley
Maude, Daniel, Barrister, Salford
Millar, Thomas, Surgeon, Green Heys, Manches
Molyneux, Edward, Chetham Hill, Manchester
Molesworth, Rev. J. E. N., D.D., Rochdale
Monk, John, Barrister, Manchester
Moore, John, F.L.S , Cornbrook, near Mancheste
Mosley, Sir Oswald, Bart., Rolleston Hall, Staffor
Murray, James, Apsley Place, Manchester

Nield, William, Mayfield, Manchester
Nelson, George, Seedley, Manchester
Neville, James, Beardwood, near Blackburn
Newall, Mrs. Robert, Littleborough, near Rochd
Newall, W. N., Wellington Lodge, Littleborough
Newbery, Henry, Seedley, near Manchester
Nicholson, William, Thelwall Hall, Warrington
Norris, Edward, Mosley-street, Manchester
Norwich, The Bishop of

Ormerod, George, LL.D , F.R.S , F.G.S , Sedbury Gloucestershire
Ormerod, George Wareing, Solicitor, Mancheste
Ormerod, Henry Mere, Solicitor, Manchester
Owen, John, Solicitor, Manchester

Parkinson, Rev. Richard, B D , Canon of Manc
Patten, J. Wilson, M P., Bank Hall, Warringto
Pedley, Rev J. T., M A , Peakirk cum Glinton, M Deeping
Peel, Sir Robert, Bart.
Peel, George, Cheadle
Peel, Joseph, Singleton Brook
Peet, Thomas, Manchester
Pegge, John, Surgeon, Newton Heath, near chester
Percival, Stanley, Liverpool
Philips, Mark, M P , The Park, Manchester
Philippi, Edward Theod., Belfield Hall, near dale
Phillips, Shakspeare, Barlow Hall, near Manche
Piccope, Rev. John, M A , Manchester
Pickford, Thomas, Mayfield, Manchester
Pickford, Thomas E., Manchester
Pierpoint, Benjamin, Warrington
Pilkington, George, 25, New Cannon-street, chester
Pilling, Charles R., Caius College, Cambridge
Plant, George, Manchester
Pooley, Edward, Princes-street, Manchester
Pooley, John, Hulme, near Manchester
Porrett, Robert, Tower, London
Prescott, J. C., Summerville, near Manchester
Price, Bulkeley, Didsbury, near Manchester

Radford, Thomas, M.D., Higher Broughton, Manchester

Raffles, Rev. Thomas, D D , LL.D., Liverpool
Raines, Rev. F. R., M.A., Milnrow Parsonage, Rochdale
Reiss, Leopold, High Field, near Manchester
Rickards, Charles H. Walton's buildings, Manchester
Ridgway, John Withenshaw, Solicitor, Manchester
Ridgway, Mrs , Ridgemont
Robson, John, Surgeon, Warrington
Roby, John, M.R S.L., Rochdale
Royds, Albert Hudson, Rochdale

Samuels, John, Fountain street, Manchester
Sattersfield, Joshua, Manchester
Scholes, Thomas Seddon
Schuster, Leo, Weaste, near Manchester
Sever, Charles, Manchester
Sharp, John, Lancaster
Sharp, Robert C. Bramall Hall, Cheshire
Sharp, Thomas B. Manchester
Sharp, William, Lancaster
Sharp, William, 10, Staple Inn, London
Simms, George, Exchange-street, Manchester
Simms, Charles S. Market place, Manchester
Skaife, John, Union-street, Blackburn
Skelmersdale, The Lord, Lathom House
Smith, Junius, Strangeways Hall, Manchester
Smith, J. R. Old Compton street, London
Sowler, R. S. Barrister, Manchester
Sowler, Thomas, St. Ann's-square, Manchester
Spear, John, (Messrs Whitworth), Manchester
Standish, W. J. Duxbury Hall, Chorley
Stanley, The Lord, M.P., Knowsley
Sudlow, John, Jun., Manchester
Swain, Charles, Cheetwood, near Manchester
Swanwick, Josh. W., Hollins Vale, Bury, Lancashire

Tabley, The Lord De, Tabley, Cheshire
Tattershall, Rev. Thomas, D.D., Shaw-street, Liverpool
Taylor, Thomas Frederick, Wigan
Tayler, Rev John James, B.A., York-place, Oxford-road, Manchester
Teale, Josh. Surgeon, Salford

Thomson, James, Bookseller, Manchester
Thorley, George, St. James's square, Manchester
Thorpe, Robert, Manchester
Tobin, Rev. John, Liskeard, Cheshire
Townend, John, Polygon, Manchester
Townend, Thomas, Polygon, Manchester
Turnbull, W. B. D., Edinburgh
Turner, Samuel, Liverpool
Turner, Thomas, Mosley-street, Manchester

Vitri, Edward Denis De, M.D., Lancaster

Walker, John, Weaste, near Manchester
Walker, Samuel, Prospect Hill, Pendleton
Wanklyn, J. B., Crescent, Salford
Wanklyn, James H., Crumpsall
Warburton, R E. E., Arley Hall
Ware, Samuel Hibbert, M.D., F.R.S.E.
Wareing, Ralph, St. Ann's square, Manchester
Westhead, Joshua P., Manchester
Whitehead, James, Surgeon, 133, Oxford-road, chester
Whitelegg, Rev. William, M.A., Hulme, near chester
Whitmore, Edward, Jun , St. Ann's-street, Man
Whitmore, Henry, Bookseller, Market street, chester
Wilbraham, Hon. R. Bootle, M P., Blythe near Ormskirk
Wilson, William James, Mosley-street, Manche
Wilton, The Earl of, Eaton House
Winstanley, Thomas W., Solicitor, Manchester
Winter, Gilbert, Stocks, near Manchester
Worthington, Edward, Solicitor, Manchester
Wray, Rev. Cecil Daniel, M A., Canon of Man
Wright, Rev. Henry, M A , Mottram, St. Andre
Wroe, Thomas, Manchester

Yates, Joseph B., West Dingle, Liverpool
Yates, Richard, 15, Brown-street, Manchester

WORKS PROPOSED FOR PUBLICATION.

1. Selections from the Unpublished Correspondence of the Rev. John Whitaker, Author f the History of Manchester, and other Works.

2. Collection of the Tracts published during the Civil Wars, relating to the Battles, ieges, and Military Operations in Lancashire and Cheshire. (The Lancashire Tracts are in e Press.)

3. Pott's Discovery of Witches in the County of Lancaster, from the edition of 1613.

4. More's (George) Discourse concerning the Possession and Dispossession of Seven ersons in one Family in Lancashire, from a Manuscript formerly belonging to Thoresby, and hich gives a much fuller Account of that Transaction than the Printed Tract of 1600; with a ibliographical and Critical Review of the Tracts in the Darrel Controversy.

5. The Life of the Rev. Adam Martindale, Vicar of Rostherne, in Cheshire, from the MSS. the British Museum. (4239 Ascough's Catalogue.) (In the Press.)

6. A Selection of the most Curious Papers and Tracts relating to the Pretender's Stay in Manchester in 1745, in Print and Manuscript.

7. Proceedings of the Presbyterian Classes of Manchester and the Neighbourhood, from 646 to 1660, from an Unpublished Manuscript.

8. Catalogue of the Alchemical Library of John Webster, of Clitheroe, from a Manuscript the Rev. T. Corser's possession; with a fuller Life of him, and List of his Works, than has et appeared.

9. Dee's Compendious Rehearsal, and other Autobiographical Tracts, not included in the ecent Publication of the Camden Society edited by Mr. Halliwell, with his Collected corres- ondence. (In the Press.)

10. Correspondence between Samuel Hartlib (the Friend of Milton), and Dr. Worthington, f Jesus College, Cambridge (a native of Manchester), from 1655 to 1661, on various Literary ubjects.

11. Iter Lancastrense, by Dr. Richard James; an English Poem, written about 1620, ontaining a Metrical Account of the Principal Families and Mansions in Lancashire; from he unpublished MSS. in the Bodleian Library, Oxford.

12. "Antiquities concerning Cheshire," by Randall Minshull, written A.D. 1591, from a MS. in the Gough Collection.

13. Register of the Lancaster Priory, from a MS. (No. 3764) in the Harleian Collection.

14. Selections from the Visitations of Lancashire in 1533, 1567, and 1613, in the Herald's College, British Museum, Bodleian, and Caius College Libraries.

15. Selections from Dodsworth's MSS. in the Bodleian Library, Randal Holme's Collections for Lancashire and Cheshire (MSS. Harleian), and Warburton's Collections for Cheshire (MSS. Lansdown).

16. "Chester's Triumph in Honour of her Prince," from the Rare Tract of 1610, in 4to.

17. Annales Cestrienses, or Chronicle of St. Werburgh, from the MSS. in the British Museum.

18. A Reprint of Henry Bradshaw's Life and History of St. Werburgh, from the very rare 4to. of 1521, printed by Pynson.

19. The Letters and Correspondence of Sir William Brereton.

20. A Poem, by Laurence Bostock, on the subject of the Saxon and Norman Earls of Chester.

21. Bishop Gastrell's Notitia Cestriensis, on the subject of the Ecclesiastical Antiquities of the Diocese of Chester, from the Original MSS.

22. History of the Earldom of Chester, collected by Archbishop Parker, entitled De Successione Comitum Cestriæ a Lugone Lupo ad Johannem Scoticum, from the Original MSS. in Ben'et College Library, Cambridge.

23. Volume of Funeral Certificates of Lancashire and Cheshire.

24. Volume of Early Lancashire and Cheshire Wills.

ND - #0041 - 121124 - C0 - 229/152/12 - PB - 9781331247302 - Gloss Lamination